Theory and Educatio

Most empirical researchers avoid the use of theory in their studies, providing data but little or no social explanation. Theoreticians, on the other hand, rarely test their ideas with empirical projects. As this groundbreaking volume makes clear, however, neither data nor theory alone is adequate to the task of social explanation—rather they form and inform each other as the inquiry process unfolds. *Theory and Educational Research* bridges the age-old theory/research divide by demonstrating how researchers can use critical social theory to determine appropriate empirical research strategies, and extend the analytical, critical—and sometimes emancipatory —power of data gathering and interpretation.

Each chapter models a theoretically informed empiricism that places the data research yields in constant conversation with theoretical arsenals of powerful concepts. Personal reflections following each chapter chronicle the contributors' trajectories of struggle and triumph utilizing theory and its powers in research. In the end, this rich collection teaches education scholars how to deliberately engage with critical social theory in research to produce work that is simultaneously theoretically inspired, politically engaged, and empirically evocative.

Jean Anyon is Professor of Social and Educational Policy in the Urban Education Doctoral Program at the Graduate Center of the City University of New York.

Critical Youth Studies
Series Editor: Greg Dimitriadis

Theory and Educational Research

Toward Critical Social Explanation

Jean Anyon

with Michael J. Dumas,
Darla Linville, Kathleen Nolan,
Madeline Pérez, Eve Tuck,
and Jen Weiss

Routledge
Taylor & Francis Group

NEW YORK AND LONDON

First published 2009
by Routledge
711 Third Avenue, New York, NY 10017

Simultaneously published in the UK
by Routledge
2 Park Square, Milton Park, Abingdon, Oxon, OX14 4RN

Routledge is an imprint of the Taylor & Francis Group, an informa business

Transferred to Digital Printing 2011

© 2009 Taylor and Francis

Typeset in Minion by Keystroke, 28 High Street, Tettenhall, Wolverhampton

Library of Congress Cataloging in Publication Data
Anyon, Jean.
Theory and educational research: toward critical social explanation / Jean Anyon
with Michael J. Dumas ... [et al.].
p. cm. – (Critical youth studies)
Includes bibliographical references and index.
1. Educational sociology–Research. 2. Critical theory. I. Title.
LC191.A654 2008
306.4307'2–dc22
                        2008002337

ISBN10: 0–415–99041–6 (hbk)
ISBN10: 0–415–99042–4 (pbk)
ISBN10: 0–203–89414–6 (ebk)

ISBN13: 978–0–415–99041–7 (hbk)
ISBN13: 978–0–415–99042–4 (pbk)
ISBN13: 978–0–203–89414–9 (ebk)

Contents

Series Editor's Introduction

During the early part of the twenty-first century, we have witnessed nothing less than a full-scale assault on the "research imaginary" in a range of academic disciplines, including (perhaps especially) in education. The so-called "gold standard" in federally funded educational research—randomized control trials and experiments—has effectively marginalized thoughtful engagements with and between theory and research. This of course has been done in the name of "usefulness"—finding out "what works" in teaching and learning. While this tendency to draw sharp lines of distinction between social theory and empirical research has been around for quite some time now (see Jean Anyon's Introduction), never has it been more pronounced—and never has it been more inappropriate for understanding our contemporary circumstances.

All of which makes Jean Anyon and company's *Theory and Educational Research: Toward Critical Social Explanation* such an important intervention. Indeed, the volume is nothing short of a masterpiece—and I don't use that word lightly. Jean Anyon is (with Mike Apple) perhaps the most prominent neo-Marxist theorist and critic of education in the US today. From her earliest articles on social class and schooling to her recent work on new social movements, Anyon has shown by example what can happen when social theory is brought into authentic dialogue with empirical material. Data, to echo her introduction, are lifted off the ground. Data soar. Data sing. Such work inspires us to look at the world around us differently, to see our empirical projects as part of a rigorous and critical ongoing dialogue with others. Most importantly, such work is part of what she calls "critical social explanation"—or the complex moving back and forth between empirical particularities and broader, explanatory mechanisms and contexts.

In *Theory and Educational Research*, Anyon discusses the complexities of this moving between theory and research. In doing so, she underscores the dangers of pressing down exclusively on one or the other. On the one hand, the field of critical educational studies is marked by a tradition of theorizing, disconnected from ongoing empirical projects. Of course, this work has been enormously useful in key ways. Unpacking figures such as Marx, Freud, Derrida, and Foucault for educators has helped open up unexplored vistas for thought and reflection. This work has been vital. Yet, as these conversations become increasingly insular, they can serve as a kind of "crutch" for engaging with real-world problems that continually exceed our grasp. Such work can offer ready-made explanatory mechanisms that can make us intellectually and politically lazy—and ineffective. On the other hand, the field of educational studies more broadly is marked by an overwhelming tendency to conduct individual and individualized studies, focused on particular empirical problems or issues, outside of larger social and historical contexts. Such work has narrowed the aforementioned "research imaginary" in key ways. The social world here becomes a series of often-arbitrary problems to be solved, their relation to each other and other work a matter of narrow, technocratic rationality. Such work deadens the imagination and shrinks our vision of the world.

A rigorous engagement between theory and research, Anyon argues, can come only with intense reflection and hard, empirical work. In many respects, it emerges from the particularities of research projects themselves. In fact, the "meat" of this volume is the work of six of Jean's extraordinarily gifted current and former graduate students at The CUNY Graduate Center—Kathleen Nolan, Jen Weiss, Michael J. Dumas, Eve Tuck, Madeline Pérez, and Darla Linville. Each takes on a topic of keen relevance for the study of urban youth. Each deploys a particular set of theories to help them understand their data. We are thus privy here to top-notch ethnographic work—from a study of disciplining and policing practices in one urban high school to a study of teen sexuality in an after-school program. We also witness a range of theoretical actors "in motion"—from Bourdieu to de Certeau to Fraser to Deleuze and Guattari to Foucault to Butler and more. But perhaps most importantly, each of these authors offers intense personal reflection on their struggles with theory in their projects. This is not mere "navel gazing." Each shows how theory helped them to understand their data in different, more powerful and expansive ways. Their stories help contest the banal claim that theory is not useful, that it distracts us from research. Their stories underscore what wonderful things can happen when theory and research are brought together in mutually informing ways.

In showing how theory can be useful, *Theory and Educational Research* moves the reader beyond the often vexing and paralyzing question of how one "includes theory" in one's work. This is a particularly knotty question for graduate students who often see this as a daunting and distracting task. This volume shows how theory allows us to see our work in new and broader contexts, often allowing us to test, refine, and extend the theories themselves. Theoretically engaged empirical work allows a broader and more complex discussion between scholars—one that extends beyond the particularities of individual empirical projects. This is a struggle for anyone engaged in such work. Indeed, Anyon helpfully charts her own struggles with theory—in particular, how she has been challenged by the work of theorists such as Foucault. She provocatively asks what she might have seen differently had she brought a post-structural lens to her classic Marxist and political economic informed work. In doing so, she places herself side-by-side with her current and former students in this struggle—not above them.

CUNY Distinguished Professor Michelle Fine closes the book with a stunning epilogue that teases out the volume's key and common threads in characteristically eloquent and incisive ways. She underscores the methodological as well as political stakes involved in this bringing together of theory and research. Such work, she shows, allows us to see injustice and suffering across sites and part of larger patterns of oppression. Such work does not succumb to the reductive and reactionary notion that ethnographic work is not useful because it delves too deeply into particulars. Theory allows us to see these particulars as part of a larger, human struggle.

There is not much more I can say here that is not said more clearly and powerfully by the authors in this volume. With *Theory and Educational Research*, Jean Anyon has done the field a profound service. It is a critical resource for senior and junior scholars alike, as reactionary forces increasingly and incessantly assault our imaginations, professions, and vocations. Thank you, Jean.

Greg Dimitriadis
University at Buffalo, SUNY

Introduction

Critical Social Theory, Educational Research, and Intellectual Agency

JEAN ANYON[1]

In the early years of the twenty-first century, federal grant-funding agencies under George W. Bush defined education research so that empirically randomized controlled trials were the standard by which research was evaluated for government support. Qualitative studies received little attention, and the use of systematic theory to guide research was not valued. Such a position on what constitutes acceptable research often not only expresses conservative political attitudes but—in the case of theory—constitutes a formal acknowledgement of the long-standing avoidance by many in the US of theory as impractical. Data collection of any sort without theoretical guidance is what Foucault called "blind empiricism" (1977) and C. Wright Mills (1959) labeled "abstracted empiricism." Such research yields data, but very little social explanation.

Throughout US history, education policies, practices, and politics have been described and tested to yield empirical data, often with little attempt to place findings in a larger theoretical infrastructure that could provide them with increased explanatory, critical, or even liberatory power. Only a few US education researchers—Lareau, Lather, and Foley come to mind—bring theory and data into serious conversation.[2] While most "postmodern" scholars do work extensively with theory, they rarely if ever engage in empirical assessment of their ideas. The trend in education scholarship has been to separate theory and research.[3]

In this book we want to bridge the theory/research divide. We focus in particular on uses that critical social theory can have for educational research and explanation. We employ critical theory to direct us to appropriate empirical research strategies, and to extend the analytical, critical—and sometimes emancipatory—power of our data gathering and interpretation as we study urban schools, communities, and social change. Our project is a theoretically informed empiricism. And our point is to engage research and the data it yields in constant conversation with a theoretical arsenal of powerful concepts. Neither data nor theory alone are adequate to the task of social explanation. Our view is that they imbricate and instantiate one another, forming and informing each other as the inquiry process unfolds.

In the social sciences, "critical social theory" (following usage by the Frankfurt School) references systematic thought attempting an explicit analysis toward social justice, which distinguishes it from typical mainstream theory. The first critical social theorists were Marxists. Critique in the Marxian sense often entailed challenging belief systems and ideologies characterizing a society (e.g. "equality" or "meritocracy" in capitalism) by comparing them with the social reality of the society itself (e.g., individual and class inequality in capitalism). Marxist critical social theory, particularly for the Frankfurt School, also meant examining prevailing social relations in terms of the radical possibilities that inhered in capitalist democracies.

We employ the term "critical social theory" to include various types of scholarship that critique domination and subordination, promote emancipatory interests, and combine social and cultural analysis with interpretation, critique, and social explanation (see Calhoun, 1995). Within our purview are Critical Race Theory, Marxism, feminism, and postmodernism—authors as diverse as Michael Dawson, Jürgen Habermas, Pierre Bourdieu, Judith Butler, Michel Foucault, Gilles Deleuze and Félix Guattari, and political philosopher Nancy Fraser. Indeed, Fraser captures an additional, quite important sense in which we understand the label: A critical social theory, she argues, "frames its research program and its conceptual framework with an eye to the aims and activities of those oppositional social movements with which it has a partisan though not uncritical identification" (1985, 97).

Like many critical social scientists, we assume in our approach to social study an *analytics of exogeny* (to use sociologist Saskia Sassen's felicitous phrase). That is, we assume one cannot understand or explain *x* by merely describing *x*. One must look exogenously at *non-x*—particularly the context and social forces in which the object of study is embedded. Class size, curriculum, or student demographics; teacher experience, pedagogy, or skill; leadership, budgets, buildings, or library holdings are not all that makes a school what it is. And describing them does not constitute a satisfying explanation of what occurs there. Similarly, forms of mayoral or other control; state and federal rules and regulations; and policies funded or unfunded do not make a district. And describing how these work does not yield an adequate understanding of the problems, issues, or solutions that are possible.

One could manipulate and empirically test these and other characteristics endogenous to education systems, and still fail to assess fully how or why schools work, do not work, fail or succeed. Instead, one needs to situate schools and districts, policies and procedures, institutional forms and processes in the larger social contexts in which they occur, in which they operate and are operated upon. Trying to understand a school in East Los Angeles or South Bronx, New York, for example, without accounting for the context of poverty in which the schools exist is like trying to explain the flattened landscape after a hurricane without noting the velocity of the wind. One would miss explanatory principles that caused the hurricane's damage; and one would be in danger of ignoring the pitfalls and possibilities that inhere in preparations for the future.

We want to demonstrate in this book that critical social theory can be a powerful tool with which to make links between educational "inside" and "outside," between past, present, and future, and between research design and larger social meanings. Theory allows us to plan research that connects the ways in which social actors and conditions inside of school buildings, districts, and legislative offices are shaped and changed by what happens outside the classrooms, offices, and official chambers they inhabit. Conversely, theory can point us to the larger political and social meanings of what occurs in educational institutions and systems. As well, theory can embolden youth and community participants from whom theoretical engagement in general has been withheld.

We argue, then, that, without theory, our data on school experience or social phenomena do not go very far, and do not tell us very much that is not already obvious. Our data do not leave the ground on which they were found; our explanations do not soar, and they may fail to inspire.

Defining Theory

From the Latin and Greek, where theory referenced speculation and contemplation; from the modern tenet of theory as a model and a set of statements and rules of inference; and from our concern and experience with discursive and social systems that produce injustice, we derive our notion of theory as an architecture of ideas—a coherent structure of interrelated concepts—whose contemplation and application (1) help us to understand and explain discursive and social phenomena and (2) provides a model of the way that discourse and social systems work and can be worked upon. We assume that an extant theory may be valid if it has survived repeated application or use by others. But we believe that when existing theories are forced to negotiate with empirical data in our own research projects, they may require reconstruction or rejection if the data so warrant. Parenthetically, we note that a social scientist's interpretation of events may be idiosyncratic, while a theoretically enhanced explanation takes this interpretation and informs it with systematic sets of ideas tested by others.

It is clear from this that theory distinguishes good scholarship from even the best journalism. The most skilled investigative journalist is merely recording and reporting selected facts. The reporter makes no attempt to theorize with or beyond the facts. She may not be aware of, and rarely acknowledges, theoretical lenses that inform her choice of which events she enters into the narrative. But theory, whether covert or invited, carries a point of view. Hidden perspectives are not easily examined, and can channel our opinions unbeknownst to us. Most good scholarship, on the other hand, places facts in an explicitly recognized armature of concepts and ideas that gives them a generalizeable and explanatory power not otherwise accessed in allegedly raw data. We know, however, that even theoretically informed scholarship is not always politically progressive. Theory has been used to conserve an unequal social status quo as well as to challenge social inequities. In this book we employ theory in ways we believe will encourage our own and others' action against injustice.

And so we argue with Thomas Kuhn and the historians of science that no fact is theory-free. Every datum embodies and encodes—and is therefore understood through—theory laden explanations. One does not go into the field to "see"—one goes to "look" for various sorts of patterns and themes. Theory—acknowledged or not—dictates what kinds of patterns one finds. And *any explanation, no matter how small, involves a theory waiting to be explicated*. When we "understand" or try to explain an observed event or recorded interview, we are calling on theories, large or small.

An analogy captures how theory can extend and empower our research and our descriptions: A pebble on the beach is just a stone until it is studied, say, as an intricate instantiation of the theory of atomic structure. And the color of the stone is not merely a pretty sight; it exemplifies modern theories of energy and light.

Here is an analogy closer to the point of this book: An urban school may present as a collection of harried teachers and unmotivated students, until it is studied as an institutional repository of the effects of discriminatory macroeconomic, political, and racial policies and social forces (Anyon, 2005). This is a theoretical stance that informs our work.

The authors of the research in the following chapters were eager to call upon theory as they planned and executed their research. But as Jen Weiss demonstrates in her chapter, not any theory or bit of theorizing will do. Stephen J. Ball warned that

[t]heory can, and often does, function to provide comforting and apparently stable identities for beleaguered academics in an increasingly slippery world. Theory can serve to conjure up its own anterior norms and lay its dead hand upon the creativity of the mind. Too often in educational studies, theory becomes no more than a mantric reaffirmation of belief rather than a tool for exploration and for thinking otherwise.

(2006, 64)

We did not want to rely on theory—even critical theory—to do our thinking for us. Moreover, we believe that it does not suffice to "gesturally feature" an idea—to cite one's work as a "case" of this or that theorist's concept or notion, without full explication of the idea and extensive use of it (ibid., 21). Education scholarship is replete with terms such as resistance, hegemony, social capital, social structure, and Foucauldian "excavation," and "genealogy." These labels often appear egregiously in scholarly introductions and conclusions without informing the logic of the study or explicating its findings.

Rather, the authors in this book sought to constantly "knead the dough" of their data/theory mix, working it into a rich and heady brew (Miller, personal communication). For the goal is that theory should help us deepen our research process and raise the level of our studies' meanings, significantly extending and enriching the yield of our empirical work.

We claim sociologists C. Wright Mills and Michael Burawoy as forebears in a process of considering, applying, critiquing, and reconstructing theory until it explains what is apparent as well as that which lies beyond. These scholars argue that theory and data involve and invoke one another. For Mills, the point was to reveal that people's personal problems are in fact also matters of social structure, and that neither raw empiricism nor abstract theorizing can connect the two (Mills, 1959/2000). For Burawoy, the goal is to connect micro and macro arenas (and history) with theory that is successfully reworked during data gathering and analysis until the resulting theory explains a larger quantity of empirical content parsimoniously, or leads to "the discovery of new and surprising facts" (1998, 28; 1991).

Although Burawoy's strategy for creating new theory is productive, some of us have ventured *beyond* his prescription. As Kathleen Nolan demonstrates in her chapter, it is sometimes the case that a more satisfying assessment can be made by *combining extant theories* in novel ways. And we are not after theory for theory's sake. We expect social products. For example, taking an innovative step inspired in part by Linda Tuhiwai Smith's (1999) indigenous theory work, Eve Tuck demonstrates in her chapter how she encouraged and supported urban youth of color in *their* practice of "researching and theorizing back" to systems and policies of social injustice.

Using Theory

Theoretical labor is hard work. The conceptual vocabulary and grammar of ideas involved in a theory must be thoroughly mastered before they can be meaningfully translated onto data and analysis, or critiqued as a system of thought. And each time a different theory is encountered, or the next study undertaken, a new struggle begins. One wants to build a theoretical edifice that is sound and of good proportion. One wants the results and explanations to be right—and useful.

My own personal struggle with theory has been that the use of structural Marxism (in my early studies of social class and school knowledge) and then political economy (in, say, *Ghetto Schooling* or my most recent *Harvard Educational Review* article) produced important knowledge about the relation of education to the economic system, but these works provided little if any understanding of cultural meaning making or individual agency (1980; 1981; 1997; 2006). My theory was not capable of capturing these, and so I could not completely account for or explain what I saw. The contradiction I faced while preparing those pieces was that I did not want to excise culture and individual meaning making from the research I carried out, yet I was not able politically to give up the insights into an unequal system that I believed a class-based, macro perspective afforded me. I had no socially critical theory that I felt would successfully link macro and micro together.

What, for example, would those researches have revealed if I had documented informants' lay theories about the macro forces they encountered and had to negotiate? Might I—calling on Giddens (1976; 1981) or Sewell (1992)—have discovered in the five-school study the *reciprocity* of production and reproduction, showing, for example, the agency of teachers and students in co-creating and perhaps resisting the economic determinations of a school's social context? Might I in *Ghetto Schooling*—alerted by James C. Scott to the subtle advances achieved by disguised cultural critique—been able to penetrate the public transcripts of policy to understand how educators and families in Newark, NJ, pushed back and resisted the system that oppressed them? Or—in the language of Foucault—might I have perceived ways in which students and families refused to be normalized (victimized) by the gathering forces of ghettoization? Had I been able to weave these micro theoretical analyses into my exposition of macro structures, such researches could have produced richer data and fuller explanation of events than the reports I published. By portraying the instantiation of micro and macro processes in and with each other, I would have connected culture and political economy, and agency and structure; I would have provided a fuller picture of social production, reproduction, and the development of urban political economy. But I did not see the need for new theory at the time, and therefore did not look for the theoretical tools to attempt this larger agenda.

After teaching undergraduates for twenty years, I joined a doctoral program in urban education in 2001. I very soon noticed that most of my students knew very little theory—Marxist or otherwise. I myself had kept up with various theoretical developments in social science over the previous years, but had not read extensively outside the theoretical Left of Marx, Althusser, Bourdieu, David Harvey, Saskia Sassen, Fredric Jameson, and Chantal Mouffe, as well as scholars such as Habermas and Raymond Williams. To prepare for the theory courses I wanted to teach, I took on deep readings of the likes of Michel Foucault, Judith Butler, Arjun Appadurai, Saba Mahmood, Nancy Fraser, Michael Dawson, and James C. Scott. As I read, I realized that these theorists suggested ways to look inside systems and structures for the people and cultures that populate and create them. My 2005 book, *Radical Possibilities*, attempted a partial resolution of my conflict, as it reconstructed received social movement theory—which had focused on external resources and opportunities—to put personal and group sense making and agency center stage.

As I was wrapping up *Radical Possibilities*, I realized that three years of reading and teaching Michel Foucault was seriously challenging my conception of social *power*. Power, I began to see, does not only "descend" from the state or the corporate and political elites; it is, as Foucault alleged, the air we breathe. We produce power and are produced by it. Foucault's conceptual arsenal was clearly capable of undermining my structural Marxism. I have been searching for a vocabulary that will allow me to connect the two. Later in this Introduction I describe research consequences of this and other theoretical shifts my students and I have explored.

This synopsis of my personal relationship with theory is meant as testimony to the importance of thinking through how we think *with* theory, as we undertake the analytical labors of research and writing. The other authors of this book accompany their chapters with personal reflections on their own theoretical struggles and victories. We include personal reflections in this volume in order to provide guidance and reassurance to researchers new to the use of theory. Although theoretical labor is challenging, it can also be exhilarating for the researcher—not least of all because it deploys personal creativity and builds critical intellectual power.

Part of my job as professor and mentor is to prepare doctoral students to evaluate—and hopefully to value—theory and theoretical analysis. Such a task involves thinking about where theory enters the research process. How do we actually *use* theory—and how does theory use *us*—as we plan and execute our research? How does it improve our scholarly practice? In the following explication, I speak in my role of teacher. I describe attempts to help students see that theory enters the research process *everywhere*. Theory helps us understand, expand our understanding of, and critically judge what counts as relevant knowledge, appropriate units of analysis, research questions, methods, data and analysis, and explanation. It can also lead the way in efforts by researchers, participants, and others to render this society more just.

Students in our doctoral program who want to work with me take theory courses I offer. During these we work through the texts of Foucault, Bourdieu, Appadurai, Gramsci, Butler, Harvey, Richard Delgado and Derrick Bell, Saskia Sassen, James Scott, and Abu Lughod, among others. Why this list of critical theorists? Why not Stuart Hall, Lefebvre, Bhabha, Said, Deleuze, Soja, Sedgwick, or de Certeau? In fact, much of the list changes from year to year as my own interests change, and as I learn from the theoretical interests my students bring to class.

Typically a student will enter with undeveloped pre-theories—with theoretical leanings that can be nurtured and challenged. It is a matter of trying to assist them in seeing which theorists' work might fit their intellectual leanings, empirical questions, and research predilections. Many theories are possible; all are critiqued, and many are rejected as not aligned with students' interests or needs. We prune, graft, and replant students' political and experiential concerns with their theoretical and empirical predispositions.

I have found that reading theory invites more theory; reading one theorist invites comparison with others and expands the dialogue among theorists, and between personal interests and the many possible frameworks. The effort is to keep students' thinking focused on how the readings might inform and invest value in whatever empirical interests they want to pursue. Reading multiple theorists is a challenging task, but most students persevere. I sometimes liken the process of inundating oneself with many theories to the childhood pastime of making *rock candy*. Children overload a heated solution of water with sugar, and when it cools, the precipitate can be consumed and is delicious. So it is with theory: you read and think and read some more until, after a period of cogitation and planning, solid ideas precipitate and prove useful.

We choose theories because, in the end, we think they will produce the most explanation parsimoniously, because their adoption may lead to new and interesting data and explanations, and—importantly—because they may provide some purchase on progressive strategies for social change.

Occasionally a student will want to ignore theory, hoping that it will not be necessary. In conversations that ensue, I argue that without theoretically enriched work, their data lie rather uselessly on the ground, without breath or heartbeat. That in fact they can not gather empirical data with*out* theory, even if the theory remains unrecognized or covert—because the data they locate, or the explanations they give, are already laden with their own nascent theory coalesced from past reading and/or experience. A task is to make this proto-theory explicit. Once it is explicit, its powers can be unleashed. I promise them that *theory unleashed in one's mental labor yields an irresistible intellectual agency.*

Once they are conscious of the theories they already carry around with them, students can build on their unconscious work by reading and thinking that is consciously directed. They see that they are able to actively *theorize*—by expanding the coherence of their ideas and the breadth and depth of their interpretations and explanations. Once the student sees the increased intellectual agency that theory can provide, (s)he is usually willing to engage.

An important step in the preparation of doctoral students who are theoretically capable is to assist them in developing a conceptual dissertation *pre-proposal*. Thinking about theory and the background content that is relevant to the dissertation topic, they develop three or four literature critiques, each of which is prefaced by early formulations of research questions and a short essay that analyses the body of work. By keeping in mind the theorist(s) they are interested in, and relating that theory to the problem or issue they are concerned to study, they critique each body of past research by asking questions like the following: What is missing in the literature? Where are the theoretical and empirical silences? What does my experience, theory, or other reading tell me might be wrong or distorted in the literature? What impact could the literature have on my developing theoretical frame? What could I contribute?

Developing one's initial theoretical frame and this pre-proposal takes at least a semester, and is deeply difficult and intellectually labor-intensive. It amounts to nothing less than actually creating (theorizing) a personal universe of ideas and questions that are related, and that relate the theories one is reading to the material issues and problems one wants to study. Along the way, theories get jettisoned if there is no apparent fit between the student's interests, the field of study, and the theoretical content.

Students Develop Theories

As the students build their personal conceptual architecture, they think about methodology. They are already thinking, of course, about the empirical problem they are interested in and what their empirical questions suggest might be appropriate methods, units of analysis and data. But an adopted theory may also influence these choices.

Eve Tuck's chapter describes how a theory can assist a researcher in designing a study and devising data gathering strategies. Tuck was interested in Deleuze and Guattari's theory of the "rhizome" and "rhizomatics" (1987).

This theory challenges the traditional notion of social science in which knowledge stems from only one source, its one "root." Underground, a rhizomatic root does not grow upward, developing hierarchically, as most plants do. Rhizomatic growth precedes "horizontally through leaps where each germination marks a new root system and one cannot assign an origin or end-point" (Stivale 2005, 50). New growth can occur anywhere along the rhizome.

Tuck merged this theory with her interest in participatory action research, in which a research project can proceed without the hierarchy and binaries inherent in traditional models in which the scholar leads and research participants are led. With a group of urban teens who were her research partners, Tuck worked through Deleuze and Guattari's concepts until the group began to think with the ideas and were able to critique them. Out of this theorizing, research strategies emerged. They designed data gathering strategies that "spread horizontally" into techniques where data were captured in memoirs, "slam books," maps, and popular theatre enactments. For the youth researchers, as in rhizomatic theory, each thought (each germination) was a new beginning, and could lead in many directions.

I also discuss with students what their theories might suggest is an appropriate unit of analysis. A study motivated by political economy, as in this volume's chapter by Kathleen Nolan, might choose institutions and policies as sites where contradictions or oppression occur. On the other hand, a theoretical framework focusing on individuals, say James Scott's theoretical frame of private and public transcripts of resistance, as used by Jen Weiss in her chapter, would choose as units of analysis the behavior of individuals and groups that express disguised critique.

Part of melding theory and the research process necessitates asking what your theory suggests will count as data. If one is thinking of using a Gramscian analysis, one might create strategies that capture as data examples of contradictory consciousness. A Foucauldian analysis might count as data instances of technologies of power or "care of the self." Darla Linville's dissertation, informed in part by Foucault's work on normalization, thinks his work through Judith Butler's lens, and such a theoretical frame could lead her to count as data examples of Butler's "subversive repetition."

It is often the case that a theory initially becomes attractive for personal or political reasons. Jen Weiss had founded an organization for urban youth to write and perform spoken word poetry, and was keen on choosing theory that allowed her to theorize the creative activity of youth "from the bottom up," rather than, say, using what she considered "top down" theories of scholars like Foucault, Fraser, or Bourdieu. This desire led her to the work of de Certeau and James Scott, both of whose conceptual architecture was built close to the ground of individual activity. Madeline Pérez had been a community and parent organizer around school reform issues, and sought theories that might illuminate or encourage that process. As she worked with a group of urban parents, she realized that sharing with them theories based on Bourdieu's notion of social capital might offer the parents a way to strengthen and extend their knowledge of how to approach district and school officials. Michael J. Dumas, for whom racial politics had been pervasive during his years in public school, was initially attracted to Omi and Winant's theory of racial formation, and Stuart Hall's work on racial identity and Black culture.

As students prepare the full dissertation proposal, they craft both empirical questions and theory questions. Knowing what one wants to find out empirically does not suffice. If a goal of becoming "theory capable" is that one is able to use data and theory to interrogate each other, one needs to be explicit about what is being investigated in each area. One goes into the field, then, with empirical as well as theoretical questions, and their interaction may force both to change. Questions that test the theory's tenets— questions that ask how the data one is collecting may confirm or challenge the theory—are as instrumental as questions that support or challenge one's empirical findings.

For Jen Weiss, an intellectually tumultuous period of reading a variety of relevant theorists resulted in a pilot study through which she resolved which theoretical questions she wanted to pursue. For Michael J. Dumas, different and unexpected theoretical questions emerged over the first months of data gathering as he began to observe participant behavior and hear interview statements that he thought did not make sense given the theory he went into the field with, or that brought up philosophical or ethical issues he had not considered. As the experience of these students indicates, the process of coming to appropriate theory and theory questions is not complete when the dissertation proposal is done, but operates dialectically with field work, as the researcher reflects on interviews, archival and other data, or quantitative results in light of the theorists that have been read and contemplated. The researcher asks, are the theoretical constructs (still) useful or meaningful in explaining what I'm seeing? Does trying to make sense of my data challenge the theorists I'm using and require that I rethink that theory, or combine it with others?

The analytic aspects of a research study are thus also informed by theory. Whether one is considering the meaning of themes derived from data that is qualitative or quantitative, theory enters as a critical interpretive and explanatory tool. In her chapter, Kathleen Nolan demonstrates how theoretical concepts in the context of her research led to a new understanding of urban schooling. She studied an urban high school experiencing the implementation of a policy requiring "order maintenance policing" of students. Nolan wanted to place that policy and its consequences for youth in its larger political, economic, and cultural contexts. She read critical social theory about the roles of punishment and control in society, as a way to think about what others had identified as a school to prison "pipeline" in urban high schools. She read political economy to help her think about the relation of what she saw in the school to the job prospects the students would encounter. And then she thought about all this as it impacted educational "reproduction theory" as that has been framed in the literature. She had to check, as she went through the data gathering, if and how these theories might apply to what she was finding.

During field work she discovered that small confrontations between guards and students inside the high school often led to consequences *outside* the school—in the criminal justice system. But she also found that—contrary to the "pipeline" theory—relatively few students went to jail as a result of their contact with the courts for educational infractions. Rather, the way the students were controlled (in and out of school) was by the constant *threat* of incarceration. She realized she might need to rethink several of the theoretical expectations she went into the study with. Her readings in political economy had led her to expect the school to prison pipeline as a strategy of mass incarceration that "solves" the problem of mass un- and under-employment in urban neighborhoods. While there is truth to this argument, what she realized, as she thought about the "pipeline" and Garland's (2001) analysis in the context of educational reproduction theory, was that, as Garland argues, crime control responsibilities regarding low-income populations have now extended *beyond* the boundaries of the criminal justice system, into institutions of civil society. Nolan began to theorize urban schools as constituting an important site in this extension of population control.

She ultimately retheorized not only the "pipeline" notion (students sometimes ending up in prison because of educational indiscipline was only part of what the "pipeline" accomplishes) but the social reproduction function of urban schools as well (school for the urban poor is no longer a preparation for working class jobs so much as it functions as one of a number of civil sites of "soft" control over a population with few if any economic options). She put together theories from culture and punishment, political economy, and education as she observed, collected data, and developed her analyses and explanations.

Because the process of mutual interrogation of data and theory occurs as field work proceeds, I ask students when they are in the field to write each day about what they are seeing or hearing that confirms the theory they go in with, or that contradicts it. Data that seem to counter a theoretical precept may eventually lead to reconstruction of the theory, its combination or interaction with another, or its rejection as explanatorily insufficient. During field work, then, the continual "So what?" question needs to be asked about emerging *theoretical* themes as well as empirical ones.

In the writing up of theoretically informed empirical research, the dissertation sometimes emerges as an integrated set of answers to intersecting theoretical and empirical questions. In this case, the report may develop as answers to particular *empirical* queries as they impact the *theoretical* questions. Michael J. Dumas, for example, ordered the chapters reporting his research around his theoretical concerns. The findings in each chapter were presented as they bore on his questioning the theories of Habermas, Omi and Winant, Nancy Fraser, and Michael Dawson.

Other students find that the empirical patterns and themes do not tumble onto the page if they are encumbered by their theoretical meanings and consequences. Thus, even though the theoretical and empirical analysis has proceeded together, the student may find that (s)he has to write out the empirical findings first, and then in the next draft go back and attach the theoretical explications she has developed to these findings.

Sometimes as I watch my students grow in sophistication and skill, I feel that I have learned more from them than they from me. Undoubtedly, however, the process of "kneading" the theory/research/data mix in the years I have belonged to a doctoral faculty is an exciting process. It has catalyzed in me a new sense of intellectual agency that I find invigorating.

Theory and Our Research

At the heart of this book are chapters that present each author's empirical/theoretical quest. All are related to dissertation projects. As a prelude to this important work, I want to offer several examples of ways critical social theory has led us to challenge mainstream social science (and educational) scholarship and viewpoints in our discussions. The examples are about studying power, challenging prescriptive educational policy, crafting solutions to the problems of social injustice, studying resistance, and working with immigrant students.

A fairly typical social science view of power assumes that it resides in dominant social groups and persons. Powerful interest groups, political or business elites, or individual officials and politicians exert their influence through laws, regulatory mandates, access to the print and television media, and influence on the policies of institutions (among any number of examples of the study of social power in this vein are Wilson, 1997; Domhoff, 2005; and Dreier, Mollenkopf, and Swanstrom, 2005). Educators who study power this way often do so by assessing how these groups wield influence on education policies and opportunities (Mickelson, 1999; Lipman, 2003; Anyon, 2005; Apple, 2006). In this macro view of power's source, researchers may assess the effects of power by studying subordinated groups to see how they have been disenfranchised or otherwise denied opportunities by the system (e.g., Anyon, 1997). Research strategies typically used to study power conceived as emanating from the top include standard social science methods of institutional and policy analysis, social network analysis, and assessment of political, corporate or government legislation and policy.

Michel Foucault's notion of power, however, is among those that inspire a very different approach. Foucault's writings challenge the mainstream view that power comes from above and dominates those below. Although his notion of power changed over the course of his career, I would argue that a constant in his view was that, as "action upon action," power was coincidental with resistance; power is a relationship which, by its very definition, involves constant contestation and a measure of freedom. Without contestation and choice, there does not exist a situation of power, but one of domination— as in the slave/master dyad (Foucault, 1976, 1988, 1990; see also Simons, 2001; Faubion, 1994; and Paras, 2006).[4]

Foucault's descriptions of power open up an analysis of modern society that cuts across institutions and classes. In constitutional democracies, power resides not only in those at the economic or political pinnacle but in all of us. Power flowing from all points and persons opens the system to an exploration of ways in which we are all implicated in what occurs: Although power is everywhere, everyone has agency and is able to resist. Foucault mentions (but never codifies) a variety of ways people resist: for example, we may refuse received definitions of our subjectivity or "normalcy," reverse and thereby appropriate discursive messages and practices that would delimit us, push the limits of what is deemed acceptable, or enact aggressive technologies of care of the self.

Foucault's theory fosters analysis of a micro-physics of the circulation of power in daily activity and the consequences of this as we study how power (and the systems of knowledge that instantiate and legitimate it) produces people and is produced by them. We continually absorb, recreate, and resist the discourses and other forces that flow through and prod us. But studying power within this paradigm lets no one off the hook. A Foucauldian study of No Child Left Behind, for example, might not only assess the power nexus in and policies emanating from Washington DC but would seek to understand ways in which the law's discourses and other mandates are interpreted, enacted, and resisted on the ground. The consequences of the law (the way it works, say, to decrease educational equity) become not just a result of an imposition from above, as critics of the law typically argue, but a result of the actions (within discourses given and developed) of ourselves as well. Educators, officials, school boards, students, parents, and scholars acquiesce and/or resist in ways that produce the law's impact.

Darla Linville's chapter argues within a Foucauldian paradigm, suggesting that students negotiate received normalizing discourses of sexuality and gender by a complex of resistance and accommodation. Eve Tuck's chapter reports work her student research group accomplished by extending and revising Deleuze's notion of power as a centerless network of points (from which Foucault took and developed his own theory of power in the early 1970s). Both Linville and Tuck employ theoretical assessments that rewrite power not only as the exclusive production of elite policy-making groups, but also of students and other youth when their discourses speak and act back.

Political economy is of course another theoretical approach we discuss in my classes. This work also challenges a variety of received educational notions, but from a very different direction than Foucault. We read Saskia Sassen and David Harvey, who extend and rework traditional Marxist categories of production, accumulation, and imperialism. We apply a political-economy theoretic to mainstream education reform strategies in urban areas. Typical school reform approaches split large issues—say, low achievement of urban students—into pieces, focusing on one at a time—pedagogical improvements, class size reductions, increased funding, or structural administrative changes. But this fragmented approach has not produced even one large city in the US where the majority of students achieve at high levels.

The theoretical framework of Marx and his descendants, on the other hand, points to holistic, rather than piecemeal, solutions to educational problems like low achievement. Holistic theory provides schema for action and social change that address the entire nexus of relevant issues or problems. My own work—for example in *Ghetto Schooling* (1997)—theorized in this vein that education represents but one strand in the plethora of economic, political, and racial policies and social forces that impinge on low-income students and communities of color in urban areas. In *Radical Possibilities* (2005) I argued that the problems of schooling, jobs, segregation, police brutality, and incarceration are tangled together in the fabric of everyday living in poor neighborhoods, and form a knot of many tightly woven strands; only when the knot itself is undone do the threads come free. *I have retheorized urban school reform and educational policy, therefore, to include necessary reform of the public policies that cause the social problems that constrict educational possibility.* Issues of urban education and its improvement in this theoretical frame are not resolvable with positive outcomes for low-income students of color until, say, a low-income graduate of an urban high school has the resources to pay for a college degree, or has available a job with wages that are enough above the poverty line to support a decent life.

But—as *Radical Possibilities* points out—the vast majority of current graduates of even "successfully" reformed urban high schools have neither the resources to obtain the college diploma nor decent jobs awaiting them. Thus, school reform without economic reform is a partial and only partially helpful solution. What this approach to school reform entails, of course, is that we retheorize solutions to the problems of urban education as extending considerably beyond policies that we normally think of as "educational" (Anyon, 2006).

Without a theory that paints the whole picture, that fills in the spaces and lines forming the substance of the painting, only a fragmented image is produced. Sustainable school reform in cities requires that we have a complete view of education as one of several urban systems, and a holistic understanding of how the pieces fit together nationally as well as locally. I think it is fair to say that the chapters in our volume share this theoretical stance.

Our theoretical readings have also led us to challenge common educational formulations of student resistance. A long line of books and articles has been published on the topic of resistance (Bowles and Gintis, 1976; Willis, 1977; Apple, 1979; Anyon, 1980, 1981; Everhart, 1983; Giroux, 1983; McLaren, 1986; Foley, 1990; Solomon and Ogbu, 1992; Fordham, 1996; Dance, 2002; and Ginwright, Noguera, and Cammarota, 2006, among others). In all this work, resistance is assumed to be observed behavior that is defiant or contestatory. Yet an application of James Scott's (1992) theory of private and public transcripts unsettles this notion. A researcher using Scott's theory (as does Jen Weiss in this volume) would not be limited to the analysis of such behavior. Rather, the study would identify resistance that is part of an individual's or group's hidden transcript (their critique) and that is expressed obliquely and enigmatically in public displays of outward acquiescence. Such a study would analyze the "collective hidden transcripts" that are created by subordinated groups. The hidden strategies and codes that such groups develop would be understood as offering clues to how disguised rebellion might be made public and supported. For example, the ways that African slaves in the antebellum South turned the Christianity handed them—which glorified waiting submissively for heaven—into a creed advocating struggle for freedom here on earth, suggested clues that later, African American church ceremonies and rituals would be transformed once again during the civil rights struggle into means of revolt.

Scott's theory, then, yields a more subtle appreciation of resistance as a complex, sometimes invisible process. Weiss's chapter demonstrates that urban students who are not overtly contesting oppression and may appear docile and accepting of the system are not dupes or "bought off," but have complex and nuanced understanding of oppression, and myriad, varying ways of resisting it—even while appearing acquiescent.

Scott and Weiss argue further that an assessment of the ways subordinated groups organize and maintain the hidden transcripts (what Scott calls the "infrapolitics" of resistance) tells us something new about power relations in school and society. An understanding of the informal, disguised resistances might suggest ways to use these as building blocks of public political protest.

A final example here of a theorist whose work we consider fruitfully in my classes is anthropologist Arjun Appadurai. We use his 1996 book, *Modernity at Large*, to inform a critique of dominant approaches to immigrant education in the United States. Appadurai theorizes that the transnational flows of people, money, technology, media, and ideologies that characterize modern globalization do not homogenize populations or weaken local cultures, as many globalization critics argue, but rather provide diasporic immigrant communities with a bolder ethnicity—through what he claims are strengthened local "imaginaries" (ibid.). In immigrant communities across the globe, the media fill plans and hopes with once unimagined possibilities. Immigrant cultural strategizing of alternatives becomes a group effort, a "space of contestation" made possible by the various kinds of transnational flows. Diasporic public imaginaries are spaces of immigrant agency, strength, and possibility, Appadurai argues. In these immigrant communities,

> the imagination has become an organized field of social practices, a form of work (in the sense of both labor and culturally organized practice), and a form of negotiation between sites of agency (individuals) and globally defined fields of possibility ... [T]he imagination is now central to all forms of agency, and is itself a social fact, and is the key component of the new global order.
>
> (1996, 31)

The assessment of immigrant families implicit in this theory is that they are active agents of globalization—not only its victims or pawns. By contrast, the deficit view of immigrants in US schools as "English Language Learners" defines them merely by what they may not do well (speak English). Appadurai's theory suggests to educators rather that there are powerful global resources in the immigrant stores of knowledge and experience.

The "Funds of Knowledge" approach to research and teaching can be understood as a partial instantiation of Appadurai's theory. When Norma Gonzalez, Luis Moll, and Cathy Amanti take teacher candidates into the homes of immigrant families to learn about the skills and culture practiced there (2005), and then demonstrate how these strengths can become the basis for pedagogy, the deficit view of "ELLs" is transformed into a pedagogy of respect. Immigrant students are no longer defined by a temporary lack, but by the powers that they have.

Almost all the parents Madeline Pérez writes about in her chapter emigrated from Spanish-speaking cultures and have low-income jobs. Officials in large urban school districts pay little attention to such parents, and educators often assume they have no interest in or knowledge about improving the school system their children attend. Pérez challenges this point of view, assuming with Appadurai and the "funds of knowledge" theorists that immigrant and other low-income parents of color develop deep intuitive knowledge of the systems that oppress them, and actively imagine and strategize better lives. What they lack is access—and a systematic way to encode and thereby strengthen their thought and practice. When Pérez shares understandings based on Pierre Bourdieu's theory of cultural and social capital with the parents, it is to formalize, extend, and strengthen the perceptions they already have of the school system.

Doctoral students progressing through their studies have many theories to choose from; each theory has empirical, rhetorical, and sometimes social consequences. Authors of the chapters in this volume report different ways they used theory, and the consequences for their dissertation research. Their studies exhibit theory-work as a tool for rendering empirical research more valuable than it might otherwise be. They use theory as a research tool to enhance methodological prowess, or use it in analyses to produce greater generalizability and increased explanatory range, and often the critical empowerment of research participants. These students' work satisfies me that deep engagement with theory catalyzes intellectual agency and capacity. Chapter summaries are below.

The chapters in Part I of the volume focus most explicitly on the search for theoretically resonant and explanatory theory, while those in Part II are more concerned to utilize high theory in order to ratify and extend issues lived and felt by research participants. In Chapter 1, Kathleen Nolan reports on her institutional ethnography of a large comprehensive Bronx high school. As she listened and observed during the year a new disciplinary policy was brought in, she theorized that the urban high school was assuming new crime control responsibilities, and the implicit mission of the school was shifting to a culture of penal control. Within her theoretical framework, the implementation of criminal justice-oriented school discipline practices gained greater understanding as an important element in the penal management of an educationally and economically marginalized population. Her theorization challenges facile descriptions of unruly youth and common sense notions of "tough on crime" policies as natural, necessary, and neutral.

From within a landscape of pervasive and often punitive surveillance in public schools, Jen Weiss in Chapter 2 explores the use of theories of Michel de Certeau (2002) and James Scott (1992). They point her to student poetry as emergent, bottom up responses to the techniques and technology of school-based surveillance. She uses de Certeau's notion of "tactics," and "everyday practices hidden in plain view," along with Scott's method of analyzing subordinated groups' private discourse, to discover in student writing a form of resistance. Weiss was initially drawn to an analysis of public displays of defiance, such as when 1,500 Bronx students walked out of school to protest the use of surveillance devices in 2006. Weiss ultimately finds however that as powerful as such dramatic behavior seems, the most important sustained forms of resistance arose from a far less obvious source—student writing. Weiss focuses her research on the school's poetry club as a social site from which students generate a range of responses to increasing amounts of surveillance. She uses Scott's theory of subaltern groups' private critical practices as the privileged site for non-hegemonic, subversive discourse to reveal a new importance and meaning in student poetry.

In Chapter 3, Michael J. Dumas calls on Nancy Fraser's work on redistribution and recognition (1995, 2000). He argues that social actors concerned with education reform (whether as leaders, activists, or educators) theorize redistribution and recognition every day, as they attempt to make sense of the inequities in urban schools. In his historical ethnography of a Black community in Seattle, Dumas brings Nancy Fraser's formal theory into conversation with his observation and interview data, to explore how social actors in a specific context of racial politics grapple with education policy, do their own theorizing about this, and struggle with the limitations and possibilities. In this piece Dumas does not so much reconstruct Fraser's theory, but uses it to construct a bridge between observed political reflection and participants' social action.

Part II, in which authors are explicit in their concern to bring theory to participants as part of the research process, begins with Chapter 4 by Eve Tuck. She first used theory as a way to expand traditional notions of the research process. But her theory and her concern for youth lead her to organize and direct research so that her research participants can "theorize back," an approach aligned with the indigenous project of *researching* back described by Smith (1999). Tuck and a small group of youth action researchers engaged in a participatory action research project that depended on continual negotiation of/with Gilles Deleuze and Félix Guattari's (1987) theories of the rhizome, segmentarity and flow, and desire. Acknowledging that conversing with theory is rarely easy, and often somewhat awkward, the research took on a direct and urgent negotiation with Deleuze and Guattari's ideas because of Tuck's own indigenous status, and because her youth researchers, a collective of young women of color who, owing to their social locations, had historically been excluded from theoretical discourses. The group used Deleuze and Guattari's rhizomatic (hierarchical, non-linear) construct to design the project, collect data (through strategies like memoirs, mapping, and popular theatre), and interpret the results.

Madeline Pérez, in Chapter 5, reflects on her experience sharing theoretical constructs based on the theories of Pierre Bourdieu (1973, 1986) with a group of low income, immigrant Latina parents in Bronx, NY. Several of the mothers and their eighth grade children were concerned about negotiating the district's complex high school admissions policy, and Pérez thought knowledge of the theories of social and cultural capital might help them decide how to proceed. Pérez describes methods she used to relay to the group theory they had not had access to before. She reports that putting into socially legitimated, systematic conceptual form what they knew intuitively offered the parents tools for analysis and planning they had not utilized before.

Chapter 6 ends the substantive inquiry. Darla Linville interprets data from her research on lesbian, gay, bisexual, transgender, and queer (LGBTQ) youth in high school through the lens of Foucault (1978) and queer theorists Judith Butler (1990) and Mary Rasmussen (2006). These theories help her to challenge binary categorizations of gender and sexuality operating in schools. The theories also provide a framework for identity organizing by students. Linville reports interviews and journal data collected with a group of teens in a New York City after-school program. These teens talk about sexuality in their schools and the beliefs, languages and practices of students, teachers and school administrators regarding queer youth. Linville analyzes their responses through the lens of queer theory in order to move beyond the binary of seeing schools as either safe or unsafe places for LGBTQ youth, and LGBTQ youth as either "normal" or "deviant." Students' responses, and the emphases they place on different elements in the conversation, also speak back to the theory, contesting some of the priorities inherent in queer theory's past political applications.

The epilogue is written by Michelle Fine. Students who study with me generally take qualitative methods courses with Michelle, who is affiliated with the doctoral program in urban education. Several authors of this volume salute Michelle in their chapters for assisting them to devise inventive inquiry strategies. And since Michelle is also a lover of theory, we thought it appropriate to ask her to write a piece for the book reflecting on our work and practice.

Our overall approach to social study has been to assume that power inheres in the social contexts of schooling, particularly in central city and other segregated urbanized neighborhoods. We connect theory to research methodology, micro site to macro exigency, and the personal to the sociopolitical, and describe these connections by theorizing in terms that encourage generalization, explanation, and what might be called a "critical holism." This reworking of research data in ideational terms allows an array of issues and solutions to surface that might otherwise lie dormant in the mass of empirical facts.

We do our work knowing that schools and districts in urban communities typically do not function to the benefit of the majority of low-income students. In print, and in public conversations, officials agree that these students deserve a better chance—yet policies and practices continually deprive them of opportunities students in affluent districts routinely enjoy. However, cataloguing the differences between poor and affluent schools—in kinds of curriculum materials, numbers of students in classes, and even types of pedagogy—will not remediate the problem. The inequalities between these schools are symptoms of an underlying pathology. The racial, class, and political-economic biases that produce savage educational, health, and income inequities constitute the systemic sickness that must be addressed. While it is very important—indeed critical—to treat the problems that present in the everyday (to struggle for decency in educational funding, for example), it is clear to us that a deeper tonic is also needed: a set of policies and activities that treat the system, as well as the symptoms. We find that theory, as it nurtures our ability to see deeper, and to show connectivity and the whole in the parts, can be extremely useful in this endeavor.

Notes

1   I would like to thank my current and former students (the authors of other chapters in this book) for their constructive advice on prior versions of this Introduction. They are exacting critics—and I love them for it. I also thank Greg Dimitriadis for his sharp editorial skills and leadership, as well as Janet Miller, who gave the penultimate draft a crucial critical read.

2   Other education scholars who put theory and data in earnest conversation are Greg Dimitriadis, Ann Arnett Ferguson, Michelle Fine, Gloria Ladson-Billings, Janet Miller, Ricardo Stanton-Salazar, and Angela Valenzuela. In the UK, Paul Willis and Stephen Ball are exemplars. We do recognize, of course, that some education scholars (David Berliner and Gary Orfield among them) do very fine, extremely important empirical research that makes little if any explicit use of critical social theory.

3   One exception in the field of education is psychologically based research driven by theories like those of Piaget or Vygotsky.

4   I want to thank David Lee Carlson for mentoring me during my long bout with Michel Foucault (which continues).

References

Anyon, J. (1980). Social Class and the Hidden Curriculum of Work. *Journal of Education*, 162, 67–92.
Anyon, J. (1981). Social Class and School Knowledge. *Curriculum Inquiry*, 11: 1, 3–42.
Anyon, J. (1997). *Ghetto Schooling: A Political Economy of Urban Educational Reform*. New York: Teachers College Press.
Anyon, J. (2005). *Radical Possibilities: Public Policy, Urban Education, and a New Social Movement*. New York: Routledge.

Anyon, J. (2006). What Should Count as Educational Policy? Notes Toward a New Paradigm. *Harvard Educational Review*. 75th Anniversary Issue. March, 65–88.

Appadurai, A. (1996). *Modernity at Large: Cultural Dimensions of Globalization*. Minneapolis, MN: University of Minnesota Press.

Apple, M. W. (1979). *Ideology and Curriculum*. New York: Routledge.

Apple, M. W. (2001). *Educating the "Right" Way: Markets, Standards, God, and Inequality*. New York: Routledge.

Ball, S. (2006). *Education Policy and Social Class: The Selected Works of Stephen J. Ball*. London and New York: Taylor and Francis.

Bourdieu, P. (1973). Cultural Reproduction and Social Reproduction. In Richard Arum and Irenee Beattie, editors, *The Structure of Schooling: Readings in the Sociology of Education*. New York: McGraw Hill, 56–68.

Bourdieu, P. (1986). The Forms of Capital. In John G. Richardson, editor, *Handbook of Theory and Research for the Sociology of Education*. New York: Greenwood Press, 241–260.

Bowles, S., and Gintis, H. (1976). *Schooling in Capitalist America: Educational Reform and the Contradictions of Economic Life*. New York: Basic Books.

Burawoy, M. (1991). *Ethnography Unbound: Power and Resistance in the Modern Metropolis*. Berkeley, CA: University of California Press.

Burawoy, M. (1998). The Extended Case Method. *Sociological Theory*. 16:1, 4–33.

Butler, J. (1990). *Gender trouble: Feminism and the Subversion of Identity*. New York: Routledge and Kegan Paul.

Calhoun, C. (1995). *Critical Social Theory: Culture, History, and the Challenge of Difference*. London: Blackwell.

Dance, J. (2002). *Tough Fronts: The Impact of Street Culture on Schooling*. New York: Routledge.

de Certeau, M. (1984). *The Practice of Everyday Life*. Berkeley, CA: University of California Press.

Deleuze, G., and Guattari, F. (1987). *A Thousand Plateaus: Capitalism and Schizophrenia*. Minneapolis: University of Minnesota Press.

Domhoff, G. W. (2005). *Who Rules America? Power, Politics, and Social Change*. New York: McGraw-Hill.

Dreier, P., Mollenkopf, J., and Swanstrom, T. (2005). *Place Matters: Metropolitics for the Twenty-first Century*. Lawrence, KS: University of Kansas Press.

Edelman, M. (1985). *The Symbolic Uses of Politics*. Champagne, IL: University of Illinois Press.

Everhart, R. (1983). *Reading, Writing, and Resistance: Adolescence and Labor in a Junior High School*. New York: Routledge.

Faubion, J. D., editor. (1994). *Michel Foucault: Power*. New York: The New Press.

Foley, D. (1990). *Learning Capitalist Culture: Deep in the Heart of Texas*. Philadelphia, PA: University of Pennsylvania Press.

Fordham, S. (1996). *Blacked Out: Dilemmas of Race, Identity, and Success at Capital High*. Chicago: University of Chicago Press.

Foucault, M. (1976). *The History of Sexuality: An Introduction. Vol. I*. New York: Random House.

Foucault, M. (1977). *Language, Counter-memory, Practice: Selected Interviews and Essays*, edited by D. F. Bouchard. New York: Cornell University Press.

Foucault, M. (1978). *The History of Sexuality, Vol. I: An Introduction*. New York: Random House.

Foucault, M. (1988). *The History of Sexuality, Vol. 3: The Care of the Self*. New York: Vintage.

Foucault, M. (1990). *The History of Sexuality. Vol. 2: The Use of Pleasure*. New York: Vintage.

Fraser, N. (1985). What's Critical About Critical Theory? The Case of Habermas and Gender. *New German Critique*, 35, Special Issue on Jürgen Habermas (Spring–Summer), 97–131.

Fraser, N. (1995). From Redistribution to Recognition? Dilemmas of Justice in a "Post-socialist" Age. *New Left Review*, 212, 68–103.

Fraser, N. (2000). Rethinking Recognition. *New Left Review*, 3, 107–121.

Garland, D. (2001). *The Culture of Control: Crime and Social Order in Contemporary America*. Chicago: University of Chicago Press.

Giddens, A. (1976). *New Rules of Sociological Method: A Positive Critique of Interpretive Sociology*. London: Hutchinson.

Giddens, A. (1981). *A Contemporary Critique of Historical Materialism*. London: Macmillan.

Ginwright, S., Noguera, P., and Cammarota, J. (2006). *Beyond Resistance! Youth Activism and Community Change*. New York: Routledge.

Giroux, H. (1983). *Theory and Resistance in Education: A Pedagogy for the Opposition.* New York: Bergin and Garvey.

Gonzalez, N., Moll, L., and Amanti, C. (2005). *Funds of Knowledge: Theorizing Practices in Households, Communities, and Classrooms.* Maywah, NJ: Lawrence Erlbaum.

Lather, P. (1991). *Getting Smart: Feminist Research with/in the Postmodern.* New York: Routledge.

Lipman, P. (2003). *High Stakes Education: Inequality, Globalization, and Urban School Reform.* New York: Routledge.

McLaren, P. (1986). *Schooling as a Ritual Performance.* Lanham, MD: Rowman and Littlefield.

Mickelson, R. (1999). International Business Machinations: A Case Study of Corporate Involvement in Local Educational Reform. *Teachers College Record,* 100: 3 (Spring), 476–512.

Mills, C. W. (1959/2000). *The Sociological Imagination.* New York: Oxford University Press. Fortieth Anniversary Edition.

Paras, E. (2006). *Foucault 2.0: Beyond Power and Knowledge.* New York: Other Press.

Rasmussen, M. L. (2006). *Becoming Subjects: Sexualities and Secondary Schooling.* New York: Routledge.

Sassen, S. (2006). *Territory, Authority, Rights: From Medieval to Global Assemblages.* Princeton: Princeton University Press.

Scott, J. C. (1992). *Domination and the Arts of Resistance: Hidden Transcripts.* New Haven: Yale University Press.

Sewell, W., Jr. (1992). A Theory of Structure: Duality, Agency, and Transformation. *American Journal of Sociology,* 98, 1–29.

Simons, J. (2001). *Foucault and the Political.* London: Routledge.

Smith, L. T. (1999). *Decolonizing Methodologies: Research and Indigenous Peoples.* New York: Zed Books.

Smith, M. L. (2003). *Political Spectacle and the Fate of American Schools.* New York: RoutledgeFalmer.

Soloman, P., and Ogbu, J. (1992). *Black Resistance in High School: Forging a Separatist Culture.* Buffalo, NY: SUNY Press.

Stivale, C. (2005). *Gilles Deleuze: Key Concepts.* Montreal: McGill-Queens University Press.

Willis, P. (1977). *Learning to Labor.* New York: Columbia University Press.

Wilson, W. J. (1996). *When Work Disappears: The World of the New Urban Poor.* New York: Vintage.

PART I

Theory and Explanatory Analysis

CHAPTER 1

Critical Social Theory and the Study of Urban School Discipline

The Culture of Control in a Bronx High School

KATHLEEN NOLAN

> The cops in the school, it's like they run it. They are the school. But if you really look at it, the cops are supposed to be the *law*. Cops ain't supposed to be education. You know what I mean?—Student

In the mid-1990s, the issue of school discipline gained heightened public attention owing, in part, to an increase of violence among urban youth and a number of school shootings, primarily in white suburban high schools. In response, politicians and educational policy makers appropriated the "tough on crime" discourse associated with current criminal justice policies, and declared "zero tolerance" for offending students. Zero tolerance attaches swift and harsh consequences to student offenses. Suspension, expulsion, police intervention, and, at times, entrance into the criminal justice system for even minor, first-time offenses are typical responses (Skiba and Peterson, 1999).

Not surprisingly, new school discipline policies and practices rooted in a criminal justice logic play out differently in the lives of students along race and class lines—with low-income students of color disproportionately experiencing their punitive and exclusionary effects (American Bar Association, 2001; Brown, 2003, 2005). One factor in the creation of these disparities is the implementation of order-maintenance-style policing, along with zero tolerance, in large racially segregated urban schools (see Drum Major Report, 2005). Order maintenance policing, which was pioneered in New York City in the mid-1990s, is an aggressive neighborhood policing approach that involves the heavy monitoring of targeted areas and the cracking down on low-level violations of the law, the common use of "stop and frisks," summonses to criminal court, and arrests (Harcourt, 2001; New York State Office of the Attorney General, 1999). Under former Mayor Rudolph Giuliani, order maintenance policing was introduced to New York City. As city crime rates went down, order maintenance spread to cities throughout the US and elsewhere, and NYC served as a model.

In urban neighborhoods and schools around the country, zero tolerance and order maintenance policing approaches have gained public support as a commonsense solution to disorder and violence. In New York City, newspaper headlines such as "Mike [Bloomberg] Mops up the Dirty Dozen" highlighted the Mayor's supposed success in using criminal-justice-oriented disciplinary approaches to improve twelve of the city's most troubled schools. But how successful are these policies? And how are the new disciplinary approaches shaping the daily lives of students inside schools? How do they impact the school culture and the educative aims of the institution? What political or economic purposes might these policies serve at this historical moment, and why have they gained such widespread support?

This chapter describes a year-long ethnographic study of criminal-justice-oriented school discipline policies (i.e. practices and a logic appropriated from the criminal justice system) as they were experienced by students in a large, racially segregated urban public high school in New York City, which I call Urban Public High School (UPHS). In this school, as in a growing number of urban districts serving poor and working-class students of color, zero tolerance is augmented by a high-tech security apparatus, a heavy police presence, and order-maintenance-style policing. During a year of participant observation and in-depth interviewing at UPHS, I gained insight into the impact such discipline policies had on school culture and the educational mission of the school. I was interested in how students and others in the school community made sense of schooling and negotiated their environment in the context of the new disciplinary practices. Although my research examined several aspects of school culture and the cultural practices of students, for this chapter I analyze the interactions between students and school-based law enforcement officials that led to the use of criminal-procedural-level strategies, arrests, and/or the issuance of summonses to criminal court. The law enforcement team in the school was made up of police officers assigned to a special task force for school safety, officers from local precincts, and security agents who worked under the auspices of the New York City police department. "Criminal-procedural-level strategies" is the term officers and agents used when describing the approaches they would use during a police intervention. These approaches include, but are not limited to, handcuffing, frisking, and issuing summonses.

I discovered that students at UPHS were confronted by law enforcement officials on a daily basis for breaking *school rules*, not the law. And the behavior that was defined by the police as warranting a summons to criminal court or an arrest, more often than not, occurred *after* the student was confronted by an officer or security agent. In effect, the disciplinary practices helped to produce the behavior that was then criminalized. *critical social theories*

The purpose of this chapter is not so much to present the empirical data, but to explicate the usefulness of critical social theories in analyzing these data—specifically my findings on the study of school discipline. I demonstrate how I use critical theories of punishment to illuminate the institutional and macro-structural forces that shape contemporary urban school discipline. These forces are not immediately evident in the empirical data alone. For me, theory is an analytical tool providing insight into the relationship between urban school practice, institutions of the criminal justice system, and larger economic and social exigencies.

I argue that a theoretically informed analysis of disciplinary practices *theories of punishment* allows us to unravel the dominant ideological assumptions that legitimate current school discipline policies and present them as natural, necessary, and neutral. I call on theories of punishment to highlight how political, economic, and social forces shape criminal justice—and by extension, school discipline policies. The theories on punishment in society provide insight into how policies gain support within the mainstream culture. The work of David Garland (1990, 2001) in particular has been useful in developing an understanding of the ways in which—and the reasons that—urban schools with low-income students have taken on crime control responsibilities.

By using social theories of punishment to analyze what occurs in the school, I am also able to reconsider theories of social reproduction *via* schooling—as originally developed by Bowles and Gintis (1976), among others. When our understanding of the penal functions of low-income minority urban schools is illuminated, we can see that, while some schools (say, in middle-class suburbs) reproduce traditional social class hierarchies, schools in low income neighborhoods of color now assist in the production of a *criminalized* class.

In the following sections, I define critical social theory so as to highlight the specific ways in which I use the concept. I also discuss why such a theory is essential to the study of urban school discipline, and demonstrate how I use this conceptual armature to strengthen my analysis of the institution. I then present a small data set that illustrates how school discipline policies play out in the daily lives of students, and how institutional discourses serve to legitimize these policies. Finally, I illustrate ways in which my theory serves to reveal deeper social meanings embedded in these school data.

Urban Educational Research and the Usefulness of Critical Social Theory: The Case of School Discipline

With the exception of a relatively small body of literature (for example Anyon, 1997; Lipman, 2004; Willis, 1977) empirical studies of education have remained largely focused on examinations of the micro level (for example, the classroom or the individual student) removed from larger social, political, and economic contexts. The 2001 No Child Left Behind Act and the political rhetoric surrounding what counts as educational research have reinforced this tendency to micro-level analysis by privileging studies based on experimental and quasi-experimental designs or—in some cases—on micro-level *qualitative* approaches that narrow the investigatory lens, in the name of scientific rigor, to the point that what is examined is only that which can be observed directly or quantified—numbers, test scores, and slices of school life. Supporters of these paradigms insist that such research is more objective, value-free, and generalizable than, say, critical, theoretically informed ethnography.

However, the prevailing research paradigms, while they may have some strengths, are based on the underlying assumption that the classroom (or a school office or hallway) can be treated like a medical laboratory existing separately from the world outside its doors. Such endogenous educational analyses do not take into account, indeed they obscure, the complex set of external factors that get mediated through the micro-interactions inside schools.

Thus, that which is often not immediately observable—power relations and the socio-historical and economic forces that shape institutional life and the actions of individual agents, for example—goes unexamined. In the study of urban school discipline, for example, the potential exists within such narrow modes of research for students' misbehavior to be seen in purely psychological terms (Ferguson, 2000) and for social conditions that may be producing the behavior to be ignored. The reasons behind students' actions can be misunderstood, and the complex interplay of the causes of disruption and violence is likely to be oversimplified.

Theoretical sociologist Ben Agger (2006) defines critical social theory in a way that has been useful in my work. Agger writes that "critical social theory opposes the positivist notion that [social] science should describe natural laws of society, believing on the contrary that society is characterized by historicity" (4). The notion of historicity suggests that present conditions did not come about through universal or natural laws, and, although past and present patterns may appear to be intractable, they can in fact be changed through political and social efforts of oppressed groups. He goes on to say that another aspect of critical social theory is that it views the relationship between social structure (such as the regularities of economics, political systems, social institutions, culture) and human agency as dialectical; thus, individual knowledge of structure and its role in daily life can facilitate change in social conditions. Thus, in Agger's view critically theoretically informed research would have emancipatory potential, in part by critiquing ideology. Such research raises consciousness about oppression and points to possibilities for change.

Giroux (1997) similarly points to the value of historicizing empirical observations and interrogating ideologies, both of which can be accomplished through critical approaches. He describes current mainstream thinking that drives much research in terms of what he calls a "culture of positivism." He writes (13):

> Rather than comprehending the world holistically as a network of interconnections, the American people are taught to approach problems as if they existed in isolation, detached from the social and political forces that give them meaning. The central failing of this mode of thinking is that it creates a form of tunnel vision in which only a small segment of social reality is open to examination. More important, it leaves unquestioned those economic, political, and social structures that shape our daily lives. Divorced from history, these structures appear to have acquired their present character naturally, rather then having been constructed by historically specific interests.

Thus, the danger is that much educational research garnering support and legitimacy from policy-makers today works to reproduce inequality and obscure injustices. At the very most, such research might address student needs, for example by identifying a particularly useful learning strategy; but it does not address *the conditions* under which the strategy is needed or implemented, the historical processes that created those conditions, or the differential outcomes of implementation along race, class, or gender lines.

Many of the factors I would consider crucial to understanding urban school discipline deal explicitly with these exogenous conditions. For example, we live at a historical moment marked by severe social and economic stratification and drastically unequal opportunity structures (Anyon, 2005; Sassen, 2001; Wilson, 1996). Subsequently, the life courses for individuals along racial, ethnic, and class lines dramatically diverge. Unemployment and poverty plague many urban neighborhoods of color (Anyon, 2005). Public schools have become racially segregated at levels we have not seen since the late 1960s (Orfield and Lee, 2006); high school dropout rates are as high as 80 percent for some inner-city schools, and funding schemes in many states privilege suburban districts while penalizing the most needy urban schools.

At the same time, US rates of incarceration have skyrocketed, disproportionately imprisoning and impacting people of color and urban neighborhoods (Maurer and King, 2007). Imprisonment has become a regular, predictable, and often expected part of life for young black men living in urban neighborhoods as well as for an increasing number of Latinos and women of color (Garland, 2001; Western, 2006; see also Maurer and Chesney-Lind, 2002). Positive correlations have been identified between concentrated poverty, levels of educational attainment, and rates of incarceration (see Correctional Association of New York, 2002, 2005; Western, 2006). Finally, racist discourses that describe urban youth as a "new breed of super-predators" in our midst fuel public fears and encourage the most punitive criminal justice policies toward this group (Di Iulio, 2005). All of these developments and accompanying ideologies play into and shape what occurs in schools of low-income students of color.

While critical social theories have a variety of uses in education research, as delineated in other chapters of this volume, the theories I discuss here provide me the means with which to examine the relationship between the urban school, the criminal justice system, and macro-structural forces. Most specifically, my theoretical approach provides insight into the new role urban schools play in social reproduction: they manage poor and working-class youth of color as potential criminals. My theoretically informed lens also interrogates the rhetoric and the dominant cultural representations of urban youth, and the commonsense notions around crime and punishment now informing school discipline policy initiatives.

Examining the Data: The Policing of Misbehavior and the Creation of a Culture of Penal Control

The demographic context of UPHS is typical of many urban public high schools in racially segregated, low-income neighborhoods. It serves approximately three thousand students (with about another thousand students in the building attending one of six small schools there). The student population is predominantly black and Latino (99 percent non-white), and about 80 percent of the students qualify for free lunch, a common indicator of low socio-economic status. UPHS is considered a low-performing school by several frequently used measures. The vast majority of the incoming freshman read below grade level, and the dropout rate is approximately 60 percent. UPHS also has above-average levels of violence and disruption.

UPHS did not acquire its current characteristics in a vacuum. The social context of minority poverty in the city, and an institutional history of district-wide tracking and the discretionary powers of principals to bar students with disciplinary or criminal records from their schools, helped to create the existing conditions at UPHS. The school is located in a relatively stable working-class neighborhood of color many students come from nearby neighborhoods with higher rates of poverty and unemployment, giving weight to popular perceptions that UPHS is one of what the principal called the "dumping grounds" of the system (Nolan, 2007).

My analysis of interactions between students and law enforcement agents inside UPHS is informed by three sets of data—observations of interactions, the school occurrence reports (which provide official accounts of these interactions), and interviews with students and adults involved in the disciplinary process. What I found most striking in these data was the prevalence of incidents that began with an officer approaching a student who had not yet broken a rule or who had committed only a minor school infraction. The incident then would often evolve, through a series of exchanges and actions, into an "official police matter," and students would end up in handcuffs with a summons to criminal court. It also appeared that the meanings assigned to these interactions by representatives of the institution were central to the construction of the dominant cultural logic that legitimized this penal management of minor behavioral infractions.[1]

An examination of occurrence reports indicated a sharp increase in the use of court summonses since the onset of implementation of order-maintenance policing. Data from other schools show similar patterns (ibid.). At UPHS, at least 230 court summonses were issued to students during the 2006–2007 school year. Over half of all these court summonses were for Disorderly Conduct.

"Disorderly Conduct" is ambiguously defined. It is a common charge in neighborhood street-based order-maintenance policing, for behaviors that range from fist fighting to loud, disturbing, or menacing activities. Some researchers have critiqued the use of summonses for disorderly conduct (as well as other "quality of life" offenses), as they are often based on subjective views of an officer instead of set standards (McArdle and Erzen, 2001; Roberts, 1999). In this model of policing, thus, there is the potential that just about any behavior an officer finds objectionable can potentially be defined as "disorderly conduct."

In the school setting, what constitutes disorderly conduct becomes even more subjective. At UPHS, the majority of summonses for this offense occurred as a result of students refusing to show their school ID, which is considered the least serious type of school infraction.[2] Other summonses

whatever they consider disrespect

were given out as a result of different low-level offenses such as refusal to remove a hat or whatever the officer considered "disrespect." So in my research I asked: Why are students ending up before a judge in criminal court for committing minor school infractions? And how does the systematic policing of misbehavior impact the school culture?

What follows is an excerpt from my field notes describing an interaction between a student, school personnel, and law enforcement:

Late morning in mid-April, I walk down the dim basement hallway toward the Deans' office on my way back from Dunkin Donuts. I hear the commotion several seconds before I reach the room and take a long deep breath to prepare myself. It is one of those moments when the Deans' office has been transformed into a police precinct. As I walk into the room, I see the backs of three officers surrounding a chair where a student sits stiffly on the edge leaning back with his chin down. His legs are spread wide and planted firmly on the floor. His long thin arms disappear behind his back. He is wearing an oversized navy blue "hoodie" sweatshirt and jeans. His hair is pulled back from his thin face in simple, straight cornrows. I take a seat next to the door.

"I didn't do nothing," he says half demanding, half pleading. "Take them off me!" He twists his body in his seat and raises his cuffed wrists. He repeats his plea of innocence several times. The adults in the room—Assistant Principal Juarez, a couple of Deans, and several security agents and officers—appear to be growing uncomfortable. It's an ugly moment. Juarez bends down and whispers something in the young man's ear.

"What do you mean calm down?" the student retorts. He looks up towards Mr. Henry who stands a few feet away in the outer ring of adults surrounding his chair and appeals to the level-headed dean to intervene. "You've been arrested. I can't get involved. You know those teachers who got arrested [In another school a principal and a school aide were arrested for intervening on behalf of a student who had been confronted by police officers in a classroom]. This is the same kind of situation," Mr. Henry says with a mixture of sympathy and resolution in his voice.

The young man persists. "The whole thing's on tape." He repeats this several times. In the course of the situation, I realize he has been accused of taking a swing at a security agent. He claims that the agent grabbed him and he was only trying to release his arm.

One of the agents keeps making threatening remarks that seem only to exacerbate the situation by further frustrating the young man. The officers demand that the young man calm down before the cuffs come off. "I'll leave the cuffs on till 3:00," one of them threatens.

At one point, the officers stand the young man up, turn him toward a desk and conduct a body search. One of the deans glances at me. I wonder if the young man's humiliation is intensified by the presence of the lone spectator seated by the door watching all of this. Or perhaps in his anxious state he hasn't even noticed me.

The student is seated again. He is still finding it difficult to calm down while the cuffs are on and the imposing blue figures stand over him. He breathes deeply. "I'm not an angry person," he insists. He seems eager to explain himself. "I'm not always angry. I don't wake up all angry. I just don't like getting pushed up against the wall by a big male cop."

"Yeah, I pushed you. It's all on tape. You can report it!" one of the security agents says in a whatcha-gonna-do-about-it tone.

The young man says that he doesn't like getting pushed by a big white man. I get an uneasy feeling in my stomach, assuming that the officer will certainly not accept this as a reasonable explanation for the young man's non-compliance.

"Oh, so you don't like white people!"

"Let me rephrase myself." The young man realizes his mistake. "I have nothing against white people . . . I don't like cops." (Again, I assume he's not doing any better with explanations.)

"So why don't you like cops?" the officer asks in a surprisingly calm and curious manner.

"My neighborhood," the young man replies.

"But I don't work in your neighborhood."

The young man explains how he is tired of walking home to the projects and getting stopped all the time.

The tone of the dialogue has changed. The young man gets calmer. Everyone seems to be settling into waiting mode. *rationalizat*

Mr. Henry takes the seat next to me. Resting his elbows on his knees, he shakes his head. "He doesn't know how to be quiet . . . He shouldn't have been in the hallway." He attempts to makes sense of what is going on for me—and, I believe, for himself. I don't know what to say.

Several days later, I learn the young man's name is Jermaine.

Interactions like this one did not initially make sense to me. Here was a young man on his way to class (or perhaps not) who was approached by a security agent, perhaps ends up swinging at the agent, and winds up arrested, ᴗᴘᴇnding his afternoon in handcuffs in the local precinct house (where he was eventually brought) with a future trip to criminal court.

Only after I considered these kinds of incidents in conjunction with what I was reading in the occurrence reports and hearing during interviews did I begin to understand. Here is just a brief sample of the kinds of statements that I found in the occurrence reports. The first one describes the incident with Jermaine.

> (April 6, 2005) A male student was issued a summons by Officer Duncan of the School Safety Task Force for Disorderly Conduct. He refused to show his ID card and swung at SA Lopez. He received a principal's suspension.

> (March 21, 2005) A female student was issued a youth referral by Officer Jenkins of the 50 precinct for Disorderly Conduct. She was approached by Officer Jenkins and was disrespectful and used inappropriate language towards him. A suspension is pending.

> (November 5, 2004) A male student was issued a summons by Officer Stevens of the 50 precinct for Disorderly Conduct and insubordination. He refused to show ID and was cursing at staff members. Officer Stevens also arrested the student for an outstanding warrant.

lack of empathetic concern! or perspective-taking

dispasition

Data from interviews with students and adults were consistent with what I found in the occurrence reports. And in general, the only difference between students' narrations of these events and the adults' versions is that the students provided an explanation or a rationale for their non-compliance or anger, while the adults' versions, like the reports, placed the emphasis on the students' lack of respect for the officers—a disposition that, in their minds, warranted police action and penal consequences. When I asked Jermaine why students were non-compliant, he replied by saying:

> "So we could have our sense of respect, because they have their respect. They automatically have their respect the minute they say, 'give me your ID.' That's respect automatically. You look at the ID card, they have their respect. It automatically says, 'this card must be carried at all times. It must be shown upon request.' That's respect automatically. So where do our respect come in? We have no respect."

Other students made similar comments about the lack of respect law enforcement and school personnel show. In regard to getting approached by an officer in school, one student contended, "To me there's only like two choices. Like stay quiet and go home or stand up for what you feel is right and wind up in the precinct. And usually I stand up." Another common declaration students used to make sense of their non-compliance was: "I know my rights!" Many students insisted that police officers did not have the authority to request ID for "no good reason,"[3] and this is how they explained their non-compliance.

Dean Henry's explanation represents the perspective of many of the adults in the building. He stated, "These kids have to learn. They don't know how to talk to cops. Some of them have real issues with authority." Some deans and officers commonly expressed their views in a more punitive manner emphasizing how students "got what they deserved" when they were arrested because it was "stupid" not to cooperate with a police officer.

As students become entangled in confrontations with law enforcement agents, many, like Jermaine, perceive the treatment they receive as unfair and are therefore compelled to maintain a sense of respect by refusing to comply. But perhaps the more significant, or consequential, demand for respect is on the part of the adults involved. This is evident in the institutional discourses found in the occurrence reports and the everyday language of the disciplinary process. Note, for example, that the March 21 youth referral was given to a student who was approached by an officer and was "disrespectful." (A youth referral is issued to students under the age of sixteen. In these cases, students do not appear in criminal court; instead they are summoned to family court. A youth referral is roughly the juvenile equivalent of the "adult" summons.)

The demand for respect (not simply abidance of laws) was also revealed in the numerous times I observed deans and administrators warning students (as Juarez and Henry both do in the vignette above) that if they don't calm down or "shut up" when confronted by an officer, they'll end up with a summons. Then, when the students choose not to accommodate the law enforcement agents who entangle them in confrontations, the policing strategies to which they are subjected gain institutional legitimacy.

These findings are helpful in understanding the micro-world of the school. First, they provide a portrait of life inside a school with criminal-justice-oriented school discipline policies, and they illuminate the negative consequences of such school discipline policies. They also speak to how policies gain institutional legitimacy and begin to shift the culture of the school. The implicit mission becomes one of penal management, and the prevailing themes become control, contestation, and more control. Moreover, during my field work, I observed that the culture of control in the school *precluded* meaningful discussions of how to engage students academically or to prepare them for higher education or future employment.

This emphasis on control rather than education developed largely because student misbehavior was often viewed as *the* cause of school failure, and because "respect" through penal management was so often viewed as a precondition for academic engagement and success.[4]

These empirical findings may provide insight into the negative consequences of the over-policing of student misbehavior, but they do not, in themselves, explain the symbiosis of the urban public school and the criminal justice system that I argued above is developing; moreover, the findings leave unanswered questions of how the new arrangements serve a particular set of economic and social imperatives. Additionally, removed from a socially critical theoretical lens, student contestation cannot be understood as a moment of social critique.

The Shifting Function of Urban Public Schools: Linking Reproduction Theory to Social Theories of Punishment

In this section I focus on the role urban public schools play in the penal management of poor and working-class urban youth of color. I set the empirical findings above in a theoretical framework informed by scholarship in the sociology of punishment and critical education, and I use this framework to analyze the function of the school within the larger society; such a frame allows me to examine relationships between education and other social institutions. My empirical data demonstrates that new disciplinary policies facilitate a shift in the implicit mission of the school and of school culture toward penal management—to control by criminal justice system tactics.

How does the shift to penal management impact the role the school plays in the larger society? Theories of reproduction become useful here. Reproduction theory in education has been concerned to demonstrate how schools reflect social class hierarchies and as well serve to reproduce these in the economy and polity (Althusser, 1971; Anyon, 1980; Bowles and Gintis, 1976; Bourdieu and Passeron, 1977). Historian Michael Katz contended as early as 1967 that the function of the industrial urban public school of the 1900s was to produce a disciplined, low-wage labor force from the children of poor immigrants. Reproduction theorist Paul Willis (1977) introduced the notion of culture to reproduction theory: he described how the cultural practices of individuals (collective behaviors associated with one's cultural group), in tandem with economic structures, reproduce social and economic stratification. Willis demonstrated that working-class youth have a tacit understanding that schooling is not structured to benefit their group as a whole, and thus they become complicit in the reproduction of their own working-class status through a rejection of mental labor and a celebration

Reproduction theory

of masculinity through participation in violence, clothing choices, and other cultural practices.

Reproduction scholars provided an important framework for under-standing the relationship between schools and the larger society and schools and other institutions such as the labor market. But their theories were formulated and their research took place before the dramatic shifts in the political economy I described earlier. Their scholarship also focused primarily on the reproduction of a white labor force. So my theoretical research questions became: What is the significance of reproduction in the context of high unemployment, the mass incarceration of people of color in the US context, and in the case of UPHS and similar urban schools, school-based penal management? Indeed, is reproduction the most relevant framework for understanding the kinds and levels of racial stratification and economic and educational exclusion in today's political economy?

In order to answer these questions, I turned to theories of punishment. Many social theorists argue that myriad economic, political, ideological, and cultural forces influence the nature of punishment and social-penal control at any particular historical juncture (Christie, 1994; Foucault, 1977; Garland, 1985, 1991; Mennel, 1973; Rothman, 1971; Rushe and Kirchheimer, 1968; Tonry, 1999; Wacquant, 2001). For example, Foucault focuses on punishment as a political strategy of power, and Kircheimer's analysis points to the economic forces and the means of production as determinative. What these scholars accomplish is to analyze the historically specific forces *external* to the criminal justice system that shape its policies and practices. As I engage theories of punishment, I highlight the two main trends that constitute today's crime control project—mass imprisonment and order-maintenance policing.

In attempting to understand the dramatic rise in incarceration rates since the early 1980s and the punitive turn in crime policy, some scholars emphasize how in a post-industrial period marked by high unemployment and underemployment—particularly within African American residential areas (Anyon, 2005; Wilson, 1996)—prison and the criminal justice system have become a means for managing economically superfluous populations (Christie, 1994; Parenti, 1999; Wacquant, 2001, 2004). Empirical evidence exists to support these assertions. When thousands of jobs disappeared from the urban landscape between the 1950s and the 1970s and government-funded social service programs eroded in the early 1980s, the imprisonment rate in the Unites States began to skyrocket. Juvenile incarceration began to rise dramatically about a decade later (Zimring, 1998). Research by Western (2006) demonstrated a strong correlation between concentrated poverty and increased incarceration rates. His study also demonstrates how rates of incarceration increase in states where Republicans have been elected

rise of imprisonment

governor. These findings lend credence to political economic theories of punishment. Additionally, there is empirical evidence that indicates racial bias at every stage of the criminal justice process from policing to processing to sentencing (Coles, 1999).

The emergence of order maintenance policing has also been theorized as linked to emergent spatial arrangements in urban areas. For example, some scholars posit that the focus on low-level violations of the law (targeting vendors, homeless people, loiterers, and the like) has been employed in gentrifying urban neighborhoods like what Sassen (2001) calls "glamour zones"—such as New York City's SoHo in lower Manhattan. The purpose of order-maintenance policing in gentrifying zones is to sanitize these areas and provide a sense of safety to the growing middle and upper classes moving in (McArdle and Erzen, 2001; Parenti, 1999).

Little has been written about how urban schools might relate to these new trends in crime control, although Wacquant (2001) theorizes the segregated urban public school as a part of a prison–ghetto continuum. He writes, "Public schools in the hyperghetto have deteriorated to the point where they operate in the manner of institutions of confinement whose primary mission is not to educate but to ensure 'custody and control'—to borrow the motto of many departments of corrections. Like the prison system, their recruitment is severely skewed along ethno racial lines" (108). But Wacquant does not go beyond the most obvious description of schools as a place of confinement.

In theorizing the role of the urban public school as it implements criminal-justice-oriented discipline policies, I relied heavily on the work of Garland (1985, 1990, 2001). He offers a framework that theorizes how the myriad social forces, dominant cultural logic, and thinking within the field of criminology combine to produce today's policies. He situates his analysis on the cultural level, providing insight into the ways in which public sentiment, populist rhetoric, and emotive responses to growing social insecurity drive discipline policies aimed at urban youth of color.

The Culture of Control: Theorizing Urban School Discipline

Garland (1990) draws on a range of scholarly work in order to develop a complex theory of punishment—one that does not reduce punishment to "law and order" or narrowly view punishment as shaped only by economic forces. Garland's model conceptualizes punishment as rooted in economic interests and strategies of power, but also in "the configurations of value, meaning, and emotion which we call 'culture'" (249). He argues that the rationale for mass incarceration and "tough on crime" policies is not only an economic one; it also based on a "value rationale"—one that is expressive and moralistic. Criminal justice policies are supported through the dominant cultural logic and become thought of as "common sense." The increased use of punitive, tough on crime policies is justified on moral (rather than economic) grounds as control becomes a prevailing "cultural theme" (2001). The notion of disciplinary policies and practices being driven by a cultural logic became palpable in my empirical findings in the school. The institutional rationale for such practices was indeed moralistic and value-laden ("These kids have to learn . . ." and ". . . he got what he deserved").

The culture of control that Garland describes is informed by two distinct criminologies, or ways of understanding the nature of, reasons for, and responses to crime. While there has been an emphasis on putting "dangerous individuals" behind bars (at whatever cost), there has been, at the same time, a move toward "cost-effective" preventative strategies, such as order-maintenance policing, and a focus on low-level forms of repression. Garland's (2001) work helps explain how the contradictory strands of criminological thinking and practices grow out of distinct sets of political imperatives and divergent perspectives—populist conservatism and cost-conscious neo-liberalism. However, the divergent criminological/political perspectives work in unison to form the current societal crime control project in the United States, manage the "dangerous classes," and quell growing social and economic insecurities among the middle and upper classes. At the intersections of these criminologies is the theoretical space for examining urban school discipline and the institutional discourses supporting disciplinary practices.

Criminologies of Everyday Life

The first of the criminological strands Garland refers to as the new "criminologies of everyday life." In this framework, crime is viewed as normal; it is seen as an inevitable byproduct of economic arrangements. The policies emanate from the neo-liberal technocratic managerialism found among criminal justice administrators who view and approach crime in morally neutral terms and rely on a language of "cost benefit" and "fiscal responsibility." Their goal becomes prevention and situational control. That is, control is inscribed into the fabric of social life, and crime control tactics extend beyond the boundaries of the criminal justice system. Responsibility for crime prevention is thus shared with the private sector and the community. Block-watches, employers, business owners, property owners, transport managers, and school authorities are some of the social actors assuming new crime control responsibilities. A school that already has a disciplinary apparatus, like UPHS, would be a prime social institution for assuming crime-control responsibilities. "Preventative" measures in such a milieu seem to make good common sense. At UPHS, prevention manifested itself as the policing and criminalization of misbehavior and disrespect. Summonses to criminal court for "disorderly conduct" became the common-sense disciplinary catchall response.

Criminologies of everyday life do not pathologize the individual criminal (that is, construct the offender as criminally oriented or inherently prone to crime). Nevertheless, there is a shift away from a rehabilitative model to one focused on *creating social order through the integration of systems, or institutions, rather than of individuals into civil society*. When students are stopped regularly by the police in school for common misbehavior or when a dean must tell a student that there is nothing he or she can do to help a student because a disciplinary matter has become a criminal procedural matter, the integration of systems appears to be in effect. In a sense, the policing of misbehavior in the school can also be understood as an example of what Garland calls *responsibilization*: the hands of the criminal justice system extend beyond the boundaries of that institution into the school, and thus the school becomes "responsible" for the penal management of youth. Moreover, a confluence develops between the school, the precinct houses where students are brought, the streets where they experience the same policing strategies, the courts to which they are summoned, and even the prison. This confluence was reflected not just in disciplinary practices but also in the narratives of students when they were asked to make sense of school discipline. Students would often move fluidly between descriptions of school hallways and the streets as they described interactions with law enforcement officials.

Garland contends that "such an approach sits well with economic and social policies that exclude whole groups of people, so long as segregation makes the system work more smoothly" (183). The segregation that pre-exists in urban schools like UPHS, then, makes order maintenance in the school more feasible. Garland goes on to say, "It also has obvious affinities with "zero tolerance" policing policies that tend to be associated with low-level repression, discriminatory use of police powers, and the violation of the civil liberties of the poor and minorities" (ibid.). In schools where "unruly teens run wild" and students are expected to be disciplined, violations of civil liberties and discriminatory use of powers become less of a public concern.

Criminologies of the Dangerous Other

Garland's second framework shaping criminal justice policy that was helpful to my analysis of the new role of the urban school is what he titles "criminologies of the dangerous other." Garland writes that, unlike "everyday life" criminologies, those of the dangerous other grow out of a neo-conservative ideology and gain support through political rhetoric and media representations that demonize the poor and people of color. The focus is on excessive control with little concern for social costs or penal consequence. It is a model that speaks to people's fears and is not necessarily supported by the views of crime-control professionals.

Criminologies of the dangerous other are manifested in the conservative rhetoric summed up in Di Iulio's view that urban youth constitute a new breed of super-predators in urban neighborhoods—black and Latino youth (2005). This rhetoric and media representations of black and Latino urban youth as criminals (Dorfman and Shiraldi, 2001) have served as ideological justification for locking up even low-level offenders. In this ideological frame, the causes of social problems are located in whole social groups while the macro-structural forces that shape social problems are obfuscated.

Political and public discourse around urban school discipline, proclamations of "zero tolerance for minor infractions," and news headlines that herald trouble at "mayhem high" subtly, and not so subtly, call on this way of thinking about crime and punishment. While the goal of the disciplinary practices I observed were more aligned with a criminology of everyday life in that they were meant to be "preventative," the practices were justified through a logic consistent with a criminology of the dangerous other. *Indeed, I would argue that it would be nearly impossible to justify the criminalization of misbehavior if the youngsters subjected to the disciplinary practices were not already demonized.* Such punitive policies seemed fitting and were broadly accepted because, like incarceration, they were to contain, or get under control, a "violent and dangerous population."

The discourses I documented sometimes echoed such sentiments. Many of the teachers I interviewed would talk about "the culture these kids come from" or "the problems they had." While my research subjects clearly had many problems to deal with—poverty, frustrations with inaccessible curricula, hostile teachers, fragmented homes, and neighborhood violence to name a few—within a *critical* analysis the source of such problems would not be located solely in them. Indeed, these students had very little control over the conditions in which they lived. The deans, who expressed considerable sympathy for students and often resented what they considered an over-use of the criminal justice system, were less likely to locate the problem of school discipline solely in the students, but what emerged in interviews and conversations with these disciplinarians was a kind of discourse of responsibility. The blame may not have been placed on the student, but the onus for change (in behavior) was. I would argue this pattern occurred because the deans could not see beyond structure. Changing "the system" seemed insurmountable; changing the students held possibility.

The Urban Public School as Part of the Culture of Control

Urban public schools like UPHS are poised at the intersections of the criminologies of everyday life and the dangerous other. Such schools have been filled with the most vulnerable students—those who are academically under-prepared, economically marginalized, students placed in special education, and new immigrants. These schools are also highly segregated. Based on my empirical research and reading, I theorize that crime control responsibilities have moved beyond the boundaries of the criminal justice system and have seeped into everyday life interactions inside the educational institution, and schools like UPHS have become an integral part of the overall criminal justice project.

I theorize further that as this movement occurs, the reproductive functions of the school shift. Our traditional understanding of the social reproduction function of schools working-class students attend as preparing them for working-class jobs is called into question in the context of eroded academic missions and the policing of misbehavior in schools in the context of poverty, high unemployment, aggressive neighborhood policing, and mass imprisonment.

While urban schools, indeed all schools, still tend to sort and track students along race and class lines into various segments of the labor market, there is also a whole population of urban students who are what Anyon and I call "learning to do time" (Nolan and Anyon, 2004). These urban students are not being academically prepared for viable employment or higher education. Indeed, most are likely to leave high school before receiving a diploma. Given the dearth of jobs in inner-city areas that pay living wages (see Anyon, 2005 for a comprehensive analysis), it is not likely that these young people without diplomas will have the opportunity to enter viable careers.

Meanwhile, in their schools and neighborhoods, these young people become accustomed to having their movements policed and to becoming entangled in daily interactions with law enforcement officials. The prevailing culture in the school is one of control, and any potential for the development of engaging and effective curricula is undermined. In this sense, criminal-justice-oriented school discipline policies are intrinsically related to class and racial exclusions of low-income youth of color in a deeply stratified, post-industrial service economy.

Conclusion: Troubling Common Sense

Data from the New York City Department of Education and police department indicates that crime and violence are down in schools with a heavy police presence. But it is not clear that order-maintenance policing is responsible for the reduction in crime or even if there actually *is* a reduction in crime. The current disciplinary system depends largely on transferring students who get into serious trouble to suspension centers (special schools created as holding facilities for suspended students) where they may spend over a year. So, in essence, violence does not necessarily decrease; it is only moved. Additionally, according to my own research, almost every person in the school (adults and students) whom I interviewed attributed much of the reduction in violence to the new school administration and the team of deans who work very hard to use strategies such as meetings with parents, peer mediation, and counseling, to lower rates of violence and disruption (see note 3). Finally, as rates of violence appear to drop, the number of summonses remains high, suggesting that their use does not constitute a holistic or long-term approach to violence and disruption. If the issuance of summonses did indeed reduce violence and disruption, it would stand to reason that eventually fewer would be issued.

But the data from the Department of Education and the police department provide ideological justification for the policies; they become common sense. It is a "data-driven" system. The numbers tell us crime is down. The practices are supported by "scientific knowledge" produced within the criminal justice field; they are viewed as necessary and neutral. The disciplinary practices also gain credibility through dominant representations of black and Latino/a youth as criminals; their alienation from school and their entrance into the criminal justice system is viewed as solely their own doing and therefore justified.

However, the institutional policies overlook both the root causes of violence and disruption and the impact they have on daily life. Within the critical theoretical framework developed in this chapter, the ways in which economic imperatives and racist fears drive policy are brought to the forefront of the analysis, and root causes of violence and disruption are exposed. Student behaviors can then be analyzed in dialectical relationship with structural forces. Students' insistence on respect (as demonstrated through their non-compliance) can be seen as a response to the *institutional* insistence on respect, and the criminalization of misbehavior and *dis*respect.

Finally, I ask in whose interest are these current policies? If they do indeed work, for whom do they work? Rates of violence may have dropped some at UPHS, but dropout rates have not. My data show that student alienation from classroom life remains pervasive. And student frustrations with daily policing continue to grow. A critical approach to understanding school discipline calls for answers to these questions and for issues of social justice to be taken seriously. When school discipline is contextualized and interconnections between daily life in the school, the larger society, and the criminal justice system are theorized together, the school's complicity in the penal management of a marginalized group is illuminated. Additionally, it becomes clear that the official mantra, "crime is down," is, at best, only a small slice of the reality of urban schooling. A theoretically informed portrait of urban school disciplinary practices reveals the ways in which such practices support patterns of educational and economic exclusion.

Notes

1   During the course of my research, there were reductions in violence, but these reductions cannot be unequivocally linked to order maintenance. Virtually every student, administrator, and teacher I spoke with believed that the reduction in violence came about primarily through the efforts of a new school administration and the new team of deans (teachers who work as disciplinarians). Another common explanation for the reduction of violence was the removal of about a hundred over-age students who had few or no academic credits and histories of involvement in disciplinary cases.

2   Other court summonses were given out for a wide range of infractions, some that appeared to constitute a violation of the law or criminal act and others that did not. For a full analysis of various reasons students received summonses see Nolan, 2007 (unpublished dissertation manuscript).

3   Whether an officer has the right to demand ID from a student is a somewhat complicated matter. Within the school, representatives of the institution, including law enforcement agents, claim the right to demand to see ID as the ID card itself is considered official property of the school, not the card holder. Several administrators, deans, and officers explained this to me. The students, however, based their arguments on the commonly held belief that police officers do not have the right to demand ID from a civilian without reasonable cause that a crime is under way. Although students I spoke with did not always know the precise laws guiding police–civilian encounters and sometimes appeared to have an exaggerated sense of their rights, their arguments reflected the actual guidelines as written into the Terry laws for stop and frisk procedures (see New York State Office of the Attorney General, 1999).

4   I documented many instances when teachers and other school personnel critiqued educational policy and pedagogical practices as a source of pervasive disruption and student alienation, but there was no systematic effort to change policies or practices. In a sense, they were viewed as fixed and attention was shifted to how institutional agents could change students.

References

Advancement Project and the Civil Rights Project, Harvard University (2000, June). *Opportunities Suspended: The Devastating Consequences of Zero Tolerance and School Discipline Policies.* Washington DC: Author.

Agger, B. (2006). *Critical Social Theories: An Introduction.* Boulder: Paradigm Publishers.

Althusser, L. (1971). *Lenin and Philosophy,* New York: Monthly Press Review.

American Bar Association (2001, February). *ABA Zero Tolerance Report.* Washington DC: Author.

Anyon, J. (1980). Social Class and the Hidden Curriculum of Work. *Journal of Education,* 162, 67–92.

Anyon, J. (1997). *Ghetto Schooling: A Political Economy of Urban Educational Reform.* New York: Teachers College Press.

Anyon, J. (2005). *Radical Possibilities: Public Policy, Urban Education, and a New Social Movement.* New York: Routledge.

Apple, M. W. (2006). *Educating the "Right" Way: Markets, Standards, God, and Inequality.* New York and London: RoutledgeFalmer.

Bourdieu, P., and Passeron, J. C. (1977). *Reproduction in Society, Education, and Culture.* Beverly Hills: Sage Publications.

Bowles, S., and Gintis, H. (1976). *Schooling in Capitalist America: Educational Reform and the Contradictions of Economic Life.* New York: Basic Books

Brown, J. (2003, May). *Derailed: The Schoolhouse to Jailhouse Track.* Washington DC: Advancement Project.

Brown, J. (2005). *Education on Lockdown: The Schoolhouse to Jailhouse Track.* Washington DC: Advancement Project.

Christie, N. (1994). *Crime Control as Industry: Towards Gulags, Western Style.* New York: Routledge.

Coles, D. (1999). *No Equal Justice: Race and Class in the American Criminal Justice System.* New York: The New Press.

Correctional Association of New York (2002, March). *Rethinking Juvenile Detention in New York City: A Report by the Juvenile Justice Project of the Correctional Association of New York.* New York: Author.

Correctional Association of New York (2005). *Juvenile Detention in New York City.* New York: Author. Retrieved on August 26 2006 at: http://www.correctionalassociation.org/JJP/publications/detention_fact_2006.pdf.

Di Iulio, J. (2005). *How to Stop the Coming Crime Wave.* New York: Manhattan Institute.

Dorfman, L., and Shiraldi, V. (2001, April). *Off Balance: Youth, Race, and Crime in the News.* Washington DC: Building Blocks for Youth. On-line report: http://www.justicepolicy.org/downloads/OffBalancemediastudy.pdf.

Drum Major Institute for Public Policy. (2005). *A Look at the Impact Schools: A Drum Major Institute for Public Policy Data Brief.* New York: Author.

Ferguson, A. (2000). *Bad Boys: Public Schools and the Making of Black Masculinity.* Michigan: University of Michigan Press.

Foucault, M. (1977). *Discipline and Punish: The Birth of the Prison.* New York: Vintage Books.

Garland, D. (1985). *Punishment and Welfare: A History of Penal Strategies.* Brookfield, VT: Gower.

Garland, D. (1990). *Punishment and Modern Society.* Oxford: Oxford University Press.

Garland, D. (2001). *The Culture of Control: Crime and Social Order in Contemporary Society.* Chicago: University of Chicago Press.

Giroux, H. (1997). *Pedagogy and the Politics of Hope.* Boulder: Westview Press.

Harcourt, B. (2001). *Illusions of Order: The False Promise of Broken Windows Policing.* Cambridge, MA: Harvard University Press.

Katz, M. (1967). *The Irony of Urban School Reform.* Cambridge, MA: Harvard University Press.

Lipman, P. (2004). *High Stakes Education: Inequality, Globalization and Urban School Reform.* New York: RoutledgeFalmer.

McArdle, A., and Erzen, T. (2001). *Zero Tolerance: Quality of Life and the New Police Brutality in New York City.* New York: New York University Press.

Maurer, M., and Chesney-Lind, M., editors (2002). *Invisible Punishment: The Collateral Consequences of Mass Imprisonment.* New York: The New Press.

Maurer, M. and King, R. (2007, July). *Uneven Justice: State Rates of Incarceration by Race and Ethnicity.* Washington DC: The Sentencing Project.

Mennel, R. M. (1973). *Thorns and Thistles: Juvenile Delinquents in the United States, 1825–1940.* Hanover: The University Press of New England.

New York State Office of Attorney General (1999). *New York City Police Department's "Stop and Frisk" Practices: A Report to the People of the State of New York from the Office of the Attorney General.* Albany: Author.

Nolan, K., and Anyon, J. (2004). Learning to Do Time: Willis's Model of Cultural Reproduction in an Era of Post-industrialism, Globalization, and Mass Incarceration. In Dolby, N., and Dimitriadis, G. editors, *Learning to Labor in New Times.* New York: Routledge.

Nolan, K. (2007). *Disciplining Urban Youth: An Ethnographic Study of a Bronx High School.* Doctoral Dissertation, City University of New York, Graduate Center, 2007. *ProQuest Digital Dissertations* (AAT3245059).

Orfield, G., and Lee, C. (2006). *Racial Transformation and the Changing Nature of Segregation.* Cambridge, MA: The Civil Rights Project at Harvard University.

Parenti, C. (1999). *Lockdown America: Police and Prisons in the Age of Crisis.* New York: Verso.

Roberts, D. (1999). Race, Vagueness, and the Social Meaning of Order-maintenance Policing. *Journal of Criminal Law and Criminology,* 89, 775–788.

Rothman, D. (1971). *Discovery of the Asylum.* New York: Little Brown and Co.

Rushe, G., and Kirchheimer, O. (1968). *Punishment and Social Structure.* New York: Russell and Russell.

Sassen, S. (2001). *The Global City.* Princeton: Princeton University Press.

Scott, J. (1985). *Weapons of the Weak: Everyday Forms of Peasant Resistance.* New Haven: Yale University Press.

Skiba, R., and Peterson, R. (1999). The Dark Side of Zero Tolerance: Can Punishment Lead to Safe Schools? *Phi Delta Kappan,* 80, 372–382.

Tonry, M. (1999). Why are U.S. Incarceration Rates so High? *Crime and Delinquency,* 45: 4, 419–438.

Wacquant, L. (2001). Deadly Symbiosis: When Ghetto and Prison Meet and Mesh. *Punishment and Society,* 3: 1, 95–134.

Wacquant, L. (2004). The Penalization of Poverty and the Rise of Neo-liberalism. *European Journal on Criminal Policy and Research,* special issue on Criminal Justice and Social Policy, 9: 4, 401–412.

Western, B. (2006). *Punishment and Inequality in America.* New York: Russell Sage Foundation.

Willis, P. (1977). *Learning to Labor: Why Working Class Kids get Working Class Jobs.* New York: Columbia University Press.

Wilson, W. J. (1996). *When Work Disappears: The World of the New Urban Poor.* New York: Vintage Books.

Zimring, F. (1998). *American Youth Violence.* New York: Oxford University Press.

Personal Reflection

A Theoretical Journey

For me, stepping into the world of social theory was a little like my first visit to an African market about fifteen years ago—a veritable overload of thoughts and sensations. From the standpoint of the entrance, the directions in which you can take appear limitless. Your eyes catch hold of strange, colorful objects of all shapes and sizes, stuffed into rows of stalls that branch off into endless intricate mazes. A dizzying cacophony of languages and unknown sounds and smells have an intoxicating effect. You take several moments to scope out your field of vision. You spot ordinary things—earrings and fabric—whose uses are immediately evident. Other objects, a vegetable, for example, you only recognize as a vegetable; you have no sense of how it is to be prepared, or with what else it might be served, or what spices bring out its flavor. Finally, you choose a path, by instinct more than a sense of purpose or any confidence of what might be around the next corner. You come across beautiful sculptures and masks. You sense, even know, they hold symbolic significance and histories and perhaps practical functions, but while you recognize their beauty and the type of wood from which they're carved, the meanings of these objects remain obscure.

You're drawn to a set of smooth dark wood noble faces, and want to spend time examining them—deciphering the relationships between each little carving—but there is a woman with an inviting smile calling to you from some distance, wanting to sell you her wares. She calls in a musical language that resonates in your gut, but the meaning of her utterances eludes you. In the other direction, a small child with impish eyes also beckons—sitting in front of large woven baskets—and you think perhaps you have something to learn about this strange world from that child, and you become filled with indecision as to which way to turn.

Several years after my return from Africa, and still long before entering graduate school, I found myself at the entrance to the marketplace of social theory as I tried to make sense of my experience as a high school teacher in the South Bronx. I knew what I could see with my eyes—broken desks, worn out old textbooks, and a host of academically under-prepared students who did not always adhere to the behavioral norms of the institution but whom I found very endearing nonetheless (perhaps because their nonconformity somehow seemed reasonable, even admirable, given the circumstances). Then, there was the surrounding depressed neighborhood, the youth prison across the street, and the military recruitment center on the adjacent corner. These kinds of things and the grit of dense urban life—experiences of the senses—made up the observable reality.

A friend gave me a copy of Paul Willis's *Learning to Labor*, Althusser's essay on the ideological and repressive State Apparatuses, and a little book I would later hide at the bottom of the stack, called *Foucault for Beginners*. I read these books, pondering the meaning of such phrases as "partial penetration of the conditions of existence of members of the working class," making conjectures about their meaning much like one might guess at the symbolism and ritual use of a wooden mask by considering the feeling it evoked. I was told by my friend that these books contained theories that might help me see what was of great interest to me, but remained invisible—the relationships *between* the dilapidated school, the youth jail, the recruitment station, and even the McDonald's down the road, and the relationship between the students' behaviors and the school policies and external forces that shaped their lives.

My frustration with the material conditions of the school environment, my indignation at the injustice I saw, and the intellectual questions that arose while I taught in the Bronx led me to graduate school—the image of the youth prison, which I had been able to see from my classroom window, remaining prominent in my mind.

The first phase of graduate school is like stepping deeper into the African market and coming to the realization that you are lost—a momentary panic. Then, you accept your confusion and begin to explore further. I read everything that seemed related to my interest in the education of poor and working-class youngsters in the Bronx who attended school in the shadow of a prison. I read studies in political economy; I grappled with multiple perspectives on the economic, political and spatial transformations that had occurred in US cities in the last several decades. (*What warrants my attention—the social isolation of the hyper-ghetto [Wacquant]) or the new spatial arrangements created by continued immigration, gentrification, and uneven local development [Sassen]? And how central are theories of spatial transformations to my study?)*

I read competing theories about how we arrived at our current state of mass incarceration. *(Should it be understood, in the Foucauldian sense, as a strategy of power or as a by-product of a shift in the means of production and an attempt to manage surplus labor as the Marxists would suggest? Or, perhaps it should be seen as a cultural phenomenon.)* I sorted through a hodgepodge of new terms and estimated their usefulness in relation to my experiential knowledge. *("Ideological hegemony," "discursive formations," "carceral archipelago," "cultural reproduction,"—and there were dozens of others.)* And I read cultural studies of youth, theories of oppositional behavior and resistance, critical race theory, and historical analyses of urban schools. *(What is the difference between performativity and cultural practices, and what exactly is culture, anyway? Is oppositional behavior really resistance? Should I do a historical study, or is my goal to historicize my empirical data [and how does one do that]? How do race and class interact? Do I have too many theories? [The answer was unequivocally, yes!])*

While my graduate school experience certainly broadened my exposure to social theory and, at times, overwhelmed me, the mentorship I received there eventually provided me with the tools to take a more disciplined approach to theory. Even in the context of my confusion, however, I began to conceptualize a project and develop research questions. Through this process, I found myself returning to the same theories over and over and leaving others behind. The ones that became most prominent initially resonated with me more deeply than some others, but it was difficult still to articulate why this was so. At some point, I thought that I must just choose a lens that makes sense to me.

During the second phase of graduate school, I entered the field. I had decided to examine ethnographically school disciplinary practices that had been appropriated from the criminal justice system. I wanted to understand how students made sense of and negotiated those practices. Despite the unease I felt with theorizing at this phase, I entered the field (which for me was a high school not unlike the one at which I had taught, and related spaces outside the school, such as the street and the courthouse) with an understanding of the ways in which various theorists across a number of disciplines conceptualized schooling, punishment, the impacts of social and economic forces, and the cultural practices of subordinated youth.

Entering the "field" was in many ways a parallel experience to delving into social theory. And like the many paths of the African market, everything seemed connected, of great interest, and important! Quickly I lost sight of the boundaries of my study. Then one of my professors, referring to the field experience, said to me, "At some point, you'll find a thread. *Look for the thread.*"

That turned out to be crucial advice and as applicable to my theorization as it was to my empirical observations—not surprisingly, given how integrally linked these processes are. Soon, the theories that became most useful were the ones that seemed to be speaking to the patterns of daily life I was observing, and just as the tangential observations fell to the periphery, so did many of the theories that I had read about prior to entering the field.

There was, however, another set of dilemmas having to do with theory. That is, the data and the theory often seemed to belong together, but they also contradicted each other. And theory had to somehow relate to the theorizing my informants were doing as they went about their everyday practice. So I learned that a systematic empirical inquiry demands a systematic interrogation of *theory*, the search for yet more relevant theories, and the revision of old theories as the researcher places "her" theory in conversation with both the empirical reality she observes and the myriad theories produced by informants in the field. (Contending with these latter theories is often most confounding but essential to understanding the experiences of the very people whose lives are most impacted by the policies under scrutiny.)

During my analysis, I sought out some theories I hadn't previously read, such as Scott's notion of everyday acts of resistance to explain students' oppositional behavior, or Seaman's notion of alienation to help explain how institutional forces produced a sense of meaninglessness and "normlessness." But I also found myself constantly thinking about a few of the broad sets of theory I had already studied, including theories of punishment, and in particular the work of David Garland. Garland's theory of punishment became one of my overarching theoretical frameworks, and it worked well for a few reasons.

First, Garland acknowledges the role of the political economy in shaping crime control policies and the relationship between institutions of the criminal justice system and those of civil society, but he also brings his analysis to the cultural level as he emphasizes the ways in which public sentiments and discourses around crime and safety influence policy. This was appealing to a novice ethnographer who was in the process of examining the institutional practices and culture of the school and the cultural worlds of students. Secondly, Garland identifies schools as one of the many civil institutions that have assumed crime control responsibilities, but he does not explain the ways in which this might happen. I, therefore, perceived a need to extend his theory into the realm of the urban school. I could do this first by conducting systematic ethnographic research to learn about the ways law enforcement operated inside the school, the ways in which disciplinary practices worked to entangle students with the criminal justice system, and how institutional discourses legitimized such practices.

In order to understand *why* urban schools might take up this function, I also needed to place the social theories of punishment with which I was working in conversation with critical educational theory about social reproduction. That is, if schools had indeed acquired a punitive, criminal justice function, were they still primarily institutions that helped to reproduce social and economic structures? While it seemed evident that many students in public schools were being prepared for some segment of the labor market, many others, including the vast majority of those in my study, would not finish high school; nor would they land in factory jobs that paid living wages as Willis (1977) imagined for his lads. For my young men and women, fruitful legal employment of any kind seemed elusive, and all the while they were becoming entangled with the criminal justice system. Thus, the institution did not simply help to reproduce their class subordination, but facilitated the *production of them as a criminalized class.*

This particular theoretical perspective—which ties together theories of political economy, societal punishment, and schooling—allowed me to extend the explanatory power of my empirical data and make some inferences about the experiences of individuals struggling within failing urban schools and a precarious labor market, while simultaneously being confronted with increasing levels of penal management.

As I look back, I find the journey of engaging social theory to be cyclical, in that you visit theory, enter the field, revisit theory and rethink the field. And, like a trip through an African market, it is fraught with a number of wrong turns and alluring but perhaps ultimately useless options. For me, the journey began in a school while conversing with my students and colleagues and feeling the emotional weight of reality. Then, in grad school, there was a period of increasing confusion during which time certain theories eventually resonated with me, but perhaps on a solely emotional level rather than an intellectual one. It was only after re-entering a school and the lives of students equipped with enough discipline and know-how to carry out a systematic study that I begin to develop a more cohesive theoretical perspective (one that continued to resonate on an emotional level but which I ultimately became comfortable explaining intellectually). In essence, I found the thread . . . for now.

CHAPTER 2

Theorizing Student Poetry as Resistance to School-based Surveillance

Not Any Theory Will Do

JEN WEISS

> . . . Now when I walk into school listen
> to what security has to say
> "Good morning ladies and gentlemen,
> Please take all metal objects out of
> Your pockets, this should be done before
> You get up to the door, make sure you take
> Your belts off, cause if the detector goes off,
> To the back you go, don't tell me, 'o mister I ain't know'.
> Cause frankly, I don't care, whether you had a bobby pin in your hair,
> or a cell phone stashed in your underwear, that's on you see?
> Cause I guarantee, there's no way through security, so just
> Please obey the rules, and you'll have a wonderful day at school" . . .
> from a poem by Ben Torres, student at Bronx High School

More and more, public schools are becoming part of the network of post-9/11, state-sponsored surveillance—spaces in which students experience firsthand what it is to be monitored, feared, contained, and harassed—in the name of safety and security. Across the country, urban and suburban public schools are choosing to respond to issues related to violence and school safety by deploying an array of surveilling techniques and technologies. These include surveillance cameras, metal detectors, scanning wands, security and police personnel, and ID tracking systems. As has been documented in a series of recent reports, however, these measures do not necessarily produce a safer school environment. Students refer to an increase in the number of violent incidences, attest to harassment they experience at the hands of police and school safety agents, and describe a feeling of danger and disillusion (see Nolan, Chapter 1).

These policies are not only unsound, they are unjust: They are applied most frequently in racially segregated urban schools and surrounding poor communities. The disparate versions of surveillance policy occurring even within one district (New York City) signals a particularly racialized response to security (Mukherjee and Karpatkin Fellow, 2007; Sullivan, 2007; Balmer, 2006; Mediratta, 2006; Eskanazi, Eddins, and Beam, 2006; DMI, 2005; Noguera, 1995).

According to research performed by the New York Civil Liberties Union (2007), few opportunities exist for students or parents to raise their voices in protest against these policies. The risk in speaking against these policies from inside the schools is great, and there are no mechanisms in place for students to file complaints or hold school safety agents accountable for inappropriate or abusive behavior. Because the voices of youth—in this case urban youth of color—occupy a marginalized position, we lack exposure to their ideas, insights, and voices. This ignorance contributes to an increasing fear of them. Such fear has come to inform the discourse and policies around school safety and security (Nolan, 2007; Ginwright *et al.*, 2005; Males, 1996).

This chapter explores school-based surveillance by privileging the voices of those most directly targeted—low-income high school students of color. While the school itself offers an obvious site for ethnographic examinations of surveillance, I chose to focus my research on the students themselves; I found them to be the ideal subjects of such inquiry. In addition to testifying eloquently about their own experiences, the youth with whom I worked and learned for over eight months of research were also insightful and articulate about strategic and conceptual issues surrounding surveillance. They were as adept at recognizing an undercover cop, for instance, as they were at determining whether a video camera was being monitored by personnel or mounted only for show. Perhaps most significant was their capacity to understand the personal and structural implications of surveillance policy and practice. They responded not merely to the personal violence of feeling so heavily watched or of being harassed daily by security guards, but to the social violence that structural inequality and injustice represent.

In an effort to advance the voices and responses of urban students, this chapter addresses two issues. First, I use the writing of students as data not only for considering the consequences of surveillance-oriented policy on students, but also to bring to light the ways in which youth contend with and resist such policies. Taken with other data collected in the field, student poetry can and does provide vital information for understanding what is happening in schools today. In order to consider student writing as data, this chapter contends, secondly, that the theories of philosophers Michel de Certeau and James C. Scott, and of poet Adrienne Rich, help the urban educational researcher theorize student poetry as emergent, bottom up responses to the social conditions they experience. These theories do not interpret the poems themselves, but they help explain and interpret the significant role that writing and the space of an after-school poetry club play in the context of pervasive school surveillance.

Prior to my work with youth, I read surveillance and social control scholarship and a wide range of interdisciplinary theories including, among others, structuralists Michel Foucault and Pierre Bourdieu, Gilles Deleuze, John Devine, and David Garland. While I found their theories powerful and useful for understanding the larger context of discipline and social control in public schools, I discovered that it was difficult to apply their theories to the personal agency I was witnessing among the students themselves. Sociologist Michael Burawoy (1990) suggests that locating oneself within a particular theoretical tradition is an attractive research strategy precisely because of the power behind such a tradition. But, he continues, participant observers often find they must *reconstruct* theory because they become committed to those they study. This responsiveness to the participant is "often at odds with strong prior commitments to a particular theory" (27). Though my immersion in such a range of interdisciplinary theory shaped my thinking, I found that my commitment to the students' voices and their strategies for resistance required a particular kind of theoretical nuance, openness, and generosity that both de Certeau and Scott offer a researcher interested in working with emergent, bottom up signs of resistance.

Background

The data included here are from a larger study involving 20 youth participants—an admixture of boys and girls of color between the ages of 15 and 23, from New York City. Half of them come from an after-school poetry organization, Urban Word NYC[1]; the other half come from a large comprehensive high school in the Bronx[2] (referred to pseudonymously as Baldwin High School). Each of the participants is a self-identified writer or rapper and is someone who tends to fall in the "middle range." By middle range I mean the student is fairly successful, but not necessarily upper-tracked. In terms of schooling, the middle-range student tends to know how to avoid trouble, works fairly hard in classes, and is often neglected by the strong spotlight of punishment or surveillance.

I conducted one-on-one interviews with all of the participants, and focus groups with some of them. In addition to interviews and focus groups, I met students in their various schools—which gave me exposure to close to five different security protocols. I went with my participants on small outings, which gave me some sense of what it was like to be watched by security in stores, in subways, on the street, and/or in public squares.

I think of the students in the center of the surveillance-spotlight as "the usual suspects," and those at the periphery as "the Advanced Placement students." In locating my research participants, I borrowed from queer theorist Eve Kosofsky Sedgwick's usage of the "middle ranges of agency" as the place to look for "effectual creativity and change" (2003, 13). My decision to work with "middle-range" students stems from a desire to capture not only the ways that surveillance in schools affects the most vulnerable and marginalized students (i.e. those who skip class, wander the hallways, bring in contraband items, are more likely to be "pushed out" of school—those who tend to acquire the moniker of "trouble" students) but also its impact on students who are "doing right" according to the system. I believe that conducting research with middle-range students who hang in the balance (and often *just beyond* the grasp of punitive policy) helps inform our understanding of the factors that contribute to increasing dropout rates, push-out practices, and the criminalization of youth. It also helps us identify avenues, Sedgwick rightly points out, of "effectual creativity and change."

Below I relate my research with twelve students from Baldwin High soon after their daily school experience shifted from one in which they seemed to enjoy relative freedoms to one in which they were met daily with permanent metal detectors, armed police, and security guards. The installation of security machines meant that they were no longer able to carry cell phones or MP3 players to or from school; in place of their open campus lunch policy, students were now kept inside for what was unfortunately named "captive" lunch. In response, students bravely protested the installment of metal detectors, an increase of New York City Police and School Safety Agents on school premises, and a new rule prohibiting students from leaving campus for lunch, by choosing to walk out of school.

Organized by a small group of frustrated students on a youth website (Sconex.com) and unofficially supported by one local community-based organization (Sistas and Brothas United[3]), 1,500 students walked out of Baldwin in September 2005. Between first and third periods, students left the school building, marched three miles under police escort and called a meeting with their Region's Superintendent and other Department of Education officials, demanding that "metal detectors and security cameras be removed, that they be allowed to have lunch outside the school, and that an earlier ban on cell phones be lifted" (Santos, 2005).

In terms of its size and visibility, the student-organized walkout was the only protest of its kind in New York City. Covered extensively by local and national news media, the student-organized walkout was what first alerted me to Baldwin High School as the potential site of my research on how students were responding to school and community surveillance policies. When I began studying this subject, I thought I would be researching the seeds and outcomes of a large social protest against the metal detectors. But within days of beginning my research with students, I learned that the walkout represented disappointment for most students.

Jessica's sentiment is echoed throughout my interviews: "It could have been so much more and then it wasn't. I know a lot of [students] feel like they didn't really achieve anything. We still have metal detectors or we still have cops harassing us or embarrassing us in the morning." Although it was what initially drew me to my research site, the significance of the walkout for understanding how urban youth resist and respond to surveillance was not the walkout itself but its ripple effects. I came to realize that it merely represented the tip of an iceberg in terms of resistance. Its greatest achievement, in the minds of students, was that it "showed to a lot of officials that youth do have a voice" (Rafael). This helped inform where I would look next.

My time at Baldwin coincided with the formation of an after-school poetry and hip hop club, which was organized by a small group of students in the weeks after the walkout against metal detectors failed to initiate any change. Interestingly, they turned to poetry and hip hop as a vehicle to express their frustrations and anger at school policy (among other topics teens write about) because, as Ben put it in an interview with me, "there's no unity at the school." At the same time, the choice to convene a poetry and hip hop club was no less a response than was the protest. And, in my own view, the club proved a much more radicalizing choice. As Adrienne Rich points out, poetry, in its "rejection of conventional expectations," is "inherently subversive to dominant and oppressive structures" (2001, 116).

Student Writing as Research Strategy and Data

Many of the youth writers who participated in my research had not been writers for long, but used writing as a tool to express what was going on in their schools. Rhina, for instance, wrote her first poem ever after the metal detectors went into the school. John hung out in the poetry club after school, but rarely wrote a word down on paper. For him it was enough to be around writers his age. Others, like David or Lolo, had been rapping for "as long as [they could] remember."

Before the installation of metal detectors at Baldwin, students held lunchtime rapping competitions, or "ciphers," outside the building. Ciphers are closed circular formations where rappers and emcees, mostly boys, huddle up and compete against each other. Students generally refer to these ciphers as "battles," and the rapper with the most skill at rhyming, story-telling, and slyly insulting his opponent wins. Students I worked with said that some of the best lines of poetry came out of these ciphers. When someone busted out an amazing line everyone just turned around and walked away (and, presumably, went to class) signaling that the line was so hot it couldn't be topped. Once the metal detectors were installed, more rules were enforced, and security guards became more visibly present. The ciphers stopped altogether.

From the very beginning of my research, students alerted me to the power of these ciphers and I relate it because it illustrates the connection students made between the installation of metal detectors (and other surveillance practices implemented in their school) and lack of student voice. The more I spent time with my participants and their writing, the more I found that their raps and rhymes offered them another language, a language of *distance*, an outlet for being *heard* and a method for *analyzing experience*. Poet Adrienne Rich states that "we go to poetry because we believe it has something to do with us. We also go to poetry to receive the experience of the *not me*, enter a field of vision we could not otherwise apprehend" (1993, p. 85). I found this to be true of the students. Pervasive surveillance can suffocate and silence students. Responding to it through writing and spoken word became a way of coping that fell outside of the line of sight of authority. One of the newest to writing, Rhina, explained that even though "no one wants to be here [at the school], this year has really made me to speak out . . . When I started writing, I became more into it. My writing became more angry . . . Especially with the metal detectors, I started speaking back to that and I got more angry about it . . . I think that's more of my specialty with writing."

Regardless of how long each youth had been writing, or what form their efforts took, writing performed many functions in their lives. Below I explicate how writing was a *particular kind of response* to the highly monitored spaces of school (from school security metal detectors and scanners at the entrance and in the hallways, video surveillance cameras in the stairwells, to the constant presence of authority figures and peers in an overcrowded setting) chosen because students lack outlets for verbal protest and feel so heavily watched. The students involved in my research used writing, initially, as protest. Their poetry constituted data on a form of resistance to what they were experiencing in school; the writings constituted data offering me additional and significant insight into how students were experiencing the surveillance at school.

In attempting to explain, the poems also provided data on the extenuating circumstances at play in the school building, clues to the subtext of a complicated and chaotic school environment. The poems are a treasure trove for collecting "on the ground" qualitative accounts of what is going on in educational institutions and help fill the gaps overlooked by the traditional research methods. Finally, on a methodological level, student poems served as jumping off points from which in-depth interviews would follow.

Coping with Surveillance

A Baldwin student's average school day means regular encounters with the technology and authority we associate with surveillance. One student's experience at the metal detectors helps make clear the power of surveillance to discipline and silence students:

> One time I forgot to take off my belt, I was more worried about being late for this class . . . And I beeped and this cop is like "oh, hey, everybody, look at this stupid kid, you know, dumb enough to have her belt on. Everyone laugh at her" kinda thing. I even started crying. I was so embarrassed . . . So it's kind of like trying to make everyone feel like crap so you won't even dare talk back.

Jessica's testimony makes clearer a fundamental feature of surveillance: namely, that the power of surveillance *is* its ability to disrupt and silence dissent (Schlosberg, 2006). Further, harassment between security guard and student is not just a one-to-one relationship, but multi-dimensional. It occurs in the context of one's peers and authority figures, and in a school space that depends *ideally* on an established sense of trust and order to function well. In its ability to separate and target individuals, surveillance renders collective opposition difficult. Not only do situations like Jessica's happen before an audience of one's peers, the threat of these situations and the ongoing pervasiveness of them also help to create a silencing effect that lasts beyond any one incident.

And being surveilled is different from being merely observed or kept a close eye on because of its pervasiveness and the consequences associated with getting caught. "It's like stalking, almost" one student told me. School-based surveillance is, as Rafael tells it, "constant, often. Like if they were to observe me, they would observe the hair, or how my nose is always runny . . . But if they were surveilling me, they'd find out my habits. I like drawing. I write with a graffiti handstyle or I take the train home. Stuff they're not supposed to know out of observation."

Thus, trying to distance themselves from the power of surveillance to discipline and control, profile and patrol, is rooted not only in students' desire to resist its invasiveness but also in their effort to protect themselves from its sting. As the student poems in this chapter show, writing about the realities associated with school policies may be one of the most effective ways of maintaining some distance from the pain of policy effects.

As an African American teenager, David's experience with being heavily watched precedes the installation of metal detectors at his school. He is frequently given the message to turn around and leave as he enters a department store; and he is commonly stalked by security as he walks down the aisle of a drug store. In one story he told me, a jewelry clerk asked to see his money before he would show him an item he was looking at as a gift for his mother. One can feel his sense of powerlessness as he reflects upon these incidents:

> In those type of circumstances, I feel like I should've asked them like "what are you doing, why are you watching me," just because, like I said, I hate it—being watched like that. It's only because it's not worth my effort most of the time [that I don't say anything]. I can say it, but it'll go in one ear, out the other. They'll say "OK, OK, [but] I'm still watching you". It wouldn't change anything.

So when David began to encounter school security, he brought a similar attitude to school every day. As I would come to learn, his way of coping with such intense scrutiny was represented two ways; one, as avoidance, and two, as writing.

In *The Practice of Everyday Life*, de Certeau (1984) argues that the practices of those in subordinate positions are often considered passive or docile, and therefore overlooked as displays of tactical resistance. He argues that these practices come to represent the "dispersed, tactical, and makeshift creativity of groups or individuals" caught in what Foucault (1979) might call the net or grid of "discipline." For de Certeau, the "'miniscule' technical procedures [helped redistribute] a discursive space in order to make it the means of a generalized 'discipline' (surveillance)." This opened up a "new and different set of problems to be investigated" (xiv). Even though Foucault's "micro-physics of power" revealed how "from the wings as it were, silent technologies determine or short-circuit institutional stage directions," de Certeau was concerned to study the "popular procedures (also 'miniscule' and quotidian) [that] manipulate the mechanisms of discipline and *conform to them only in order to evade them*" (xiv). If we are worried about the magnitude of disciplinary power, de Certeau suggests, then we need to study the ways in which people resist being reduced to well-disciplined subjects.

de Certeau's attentiveness to the ways of operating which are "hidden in plain view" and his notion of "tactics" helped me elaborate and expand upon the shapes and forms student resistance could take. For de Certeau, a "tactic insinuates itself into the other's place without taking it over; a tactic is always on the watch for opportunities that must be seized." Using de Certeau's theoretical and methodological framework which "values the singularity of close attention to the specific located object," I uncovered a range of tactical responses undertaken by students.

One of the ways I observed that students dealt with security guards in their school was through what I called tactical avoidance. Tactical avoidance involved attempts at *evading* surveillance without eschewing the institution and its communities altogether. As Jessica's aforementioned quote reveals, increased surveillance and zero tolerance measures set up an environment of humiliation, harassment, and consequences for students. Tactical avoidance highlights an ability to cope under these conditions and resist consequences. An example of what I mean by tactical avoidance can be heard from David: "instead of taking the short way, I take the long way just so I can avoid security guards. I do that a lot. Let's say I'm walking with my friends in the hallways and we see security. Just so we can avoid their harassment, we'll go another way." The notion of "going another way" was echoed throughout interviews and came up also when students spoke about entering a corner deli or clothing store.

A slightly altered version of tactical avoidance is expressed by Jason: "When I go to a place that I don't know, first thing when I walk in is I look at the dude, I try to establish a sense that I'm just here to buy stuff." What I want to highlight with this concept is that if urban students are learning to navigate the entrances and hallways of their schools through tactical avoidance and evasion owing to the fear of being caught, what does this tell us about how they are navigating their classrooms? It may tell us that the aim of education in heavily surveilled schools becomes one in which students do best when they *conceal* rather than *reveal* who they are, what they know, and how they might get there. While concealing oneself may be conducive for coping with and resisting surveillance, it is certainly counterproductive for knowledge creation and academic learning.

Writing as Protest

Being under the constant gaze of video cameras, metal detectors, scanning machines, and security guards who have the authority to humiliate and penalize students for any infraction, in an environment which portends to be safer yet allows for newer and more sophisticated ways for fellow students to bring in contraband items, reminds us of the limited options for collective resistance and outright protest students have in these spaces. While tactical avoidance represents one point on a spectrum of possible responses to surveillance, it may be one that comes at considerable cost.

In *Domination and the Arts of Resistance,* James C. Scott (1990) maintains that conformity can be tactical and manipulative and thus "an art form in which one can take some pride at having successfully misrepresented oneself" (33), he cautions that "evasion . . . is purchased at the considerable cost of contributing to the production of a public transcript that apparently ratifies the social ideology of the dominant" (ibid.). Tactical avoidance evidences an awareness of one's lack of power in a given setting and suggests that resistance to being heavily watched means *not resisting any one thing* at all; it means *not* locating a target, and relies on the quickness of an individual response; not a collective one. Because the threat of being singled out by authority for doing something wrong is so real, tactical avoidance represents a form of individualized, often isolated resistance: a "to each his own" kind of attitude that does not lend itself to unified or collective protest. Nor does it offer an individual any greater insight into what, other than who they are avoiding, is keeping them down (i.e. the system, the policies, etc.). Now I turn to a different kind of response—one that I believe locates a target without running the risk of a confrontation with authority.

Fifteen students, most of them juniors and seniors at Baldwin, met in Room 306 on Tuesdays after school. They sat in desks formed in a U-shape. David volunteered to read his piece. He stood in front of the room—a silver Tupac Shakur chain dangled around his neck, his puffy North Face down jacket swallowed his graceful frame, his black Yankees cap covered his dark, attentive eyes. I sat and listened while he rapped from memory a piece he wrote called "Miseducation":

> Yo I have a dream
> That one day when I go to class
> I won't be asked for a pass by a fucked up staff
> They be spittin' madd game; got no comprehension
> What the hell you gonna gain by giving me detention?
> Got their views all twisted; rules is incorrect
> By locking us inside the building, who you trinna protect?
> For your safety-hats out of sight, keys away
> Shit—I'm in Macy and I see a fight everyday !
> Damn!—Were you successful 'cause I think you failed
> Everyday I'm trinna wrestle ma way outta this jail
> How I walk into the building—I'm already depressed
> 'Cause when I look at all the children—half of them is undressed
> Yo how you trinna protect us—with metal detectors—and when we
>   say you wrong you say "Don't try to correct us"
> Damn—We got the right—You messin' up our year
> Everyday I wake up and I dread to come over here

Treatin' us like animals—imprisoned creatures
And yo—I'm really gettin' tired of this same old pizza
Damn that can't be healthy—yo there gotta be more
Yeah I know the school ain't wealthy but come on—we ain't poor!
Yo the status of our school is gradually decreasin'
All the things we once removed is constantly repeatin'
I'm trinna get to my class—I gotta walk through a crowd
And all the lessons is bad—because the halls is too loud
Shit they tried to make us better but they makin' us worse
Yeah they put in the detectors but that shit didn't work
Kids in the halls messin' up my concentration
I done seen it all—now I'm steady contemplatin'
Halls is full—gotta reason for procrastination
This is bull—They should use it as an indication
All the money they payin'
All the peace that they cravin'
All those things just went to waste
Just like our education . . .

This poem was a response to a prompt. Sixteen-year-old Elizabeth, the club's founder and president, had given them an assignment. "One of the first things that I told them to do is to write about the metal detectors. We wrote about the metal detectors and we wrote about education itself, and everything surrounded itself around metal detectors because that's what we were experiencing and that's what we were seeing." After David finished his piece, his peers cheered, they referenced specific lines and detailed their own stories of interactions with the metal detectors. They laughed about the ever-present pizza for lunch; and swapped sad tales of friends being harassed by security. They referred directly to the writing itself—the use of a particular metaphor, or the sophisticated placements of internal, syncopated rhyme.

David's poem features an abundance of detail that generates a lot of momentum until its rhyme scheme comes crashing down at the end. "Just like our education"—Boom. One of the reasons spoken word and hip-hop-infused poetry is compelling to youth is that it shoots straight, and often does not stray too far into the abstract. This poem's details enumerate so much of the fallout that a school experiences once security protocol becomes the *de facto* solution for a range of problems, including the school's over-crowdedness, its misallocation of resources, its heavy-handed staff or security, irregularly enforced rules such as no hats or keys, lack of school spirit, or the negative stigma attached to schools with metal detectors.

At the same time, this piece of writing has both mood and tone. It captures David's frustration, cynicism, and disappointment. It is both general and specific, but guarded. While poems can express the underlying emotions of a given situation in the way that relaying an experience often does not, David's poem sufficiently *removes* him from the experience of passing through metal detectors daily—an experience of silence and powerlessness—and *allows him to talk back*. It also remains unheard by authority figures.

On a methodological level, such poems were a useful artifact or stimulus with which to gather data from youth participants. When I interviewed a student whose writing I had heard or read, I felt our conversation had already begun. I was able to ask David, for instance, to elaborate on his line about the status of his school gradually decreasing. He spoke at length about how he and other students knew that the consequences of surveillance policy were not just about not having their cell phones and not being able to go out for lunch but about an increase in the rates of violence in this school from one year to the next.

From our interview:

> Jen: Tell me about this line "Yo the status of our school is gradually decreasing."

> David: Students' eyes, teachers' eyes and probably even the Board of Education—now that the detectors are in, the number of students increased. Since they put them in, the number of fights inside the school has increased tremendously. Every day basically there's a fight inside the school cuz you can't go outside to do that anymore. And generally when you have a lot of kids in one area that's going to cause confrontation cuz that's a lot of kids and you don't have like freedom and so that's why I'm saying it's gradually decreasing cuz last year wasn't as bad. There were fights, but they weren't as, you know, as immense as this year.

What might I have lost had I not located the students' writing as a source of data and a form of resistance? In relation to their testimonials about ongoing experiences with surveillance, their writing offered me a sense of their active voice and helped *qualify the powerlessness* I was hearing from them in interviews and was observing as we walked together through the hallways of school or into stores. Student writing was an essential source of data collection and theorizing. Below is Ben's poem on the same topic of *Miseducation*. Although the poems were written independently, here we see how a kind of collective experience gets expressed and shared through student writing. You will notice several overlapping themes. Consider how Ben, like David, documents and catalogues the wrongs committed in the name of security and safety:

Now when I walk into school listen
to what security has to say
"Good morning ladies and gentlemen,
Please take all metal objects out of
Your pockets, this should be done before
You get up to the door, make sure you take
Your belts off, cause if the detector goes off,
To the back you go, don't tell me, 'o mister I ain't know'.
Cause frankly, I don't care, whether you had a bobby pin in
 your hair,
or a cell phone stashed in your underwear, that's on you see?
Cause I guarantee, there's no way through security, so just
Please obey the rules, and you'll have a wonderful day at school."

So one morning I'm about to be walking in,
and they create this vibe like it's me against them,
Looking at me like I got the guns and knives,
But there are real thugs on the streets taking people's lives,
And yet they worried about DWC's[4] crime streak,
Which amounts to eight violent crimes in 43 weeks,
So they started to worry about the weapons kids was wielding,
But yet more than half those crimes didn't occur inside the building,
Wait, so more crimes happen outside the school,
And they go and put more cops inside the school,
Does that make sense to you, cause it don't to me,
But probably, they got other agendas to meet,
Anyway, I go through the detector, and I set the alarm off,
I look at myself like "Damn, what did I forget to take off?"
So they pull me to the side and the guy rudely asks
"Please lift up your hands"
So I reply, "since when did cell phones and c.d. players
become contraband?"
Damn, I can understand, no weapons on the premises,
But you taking our c.d. players and cell phones, and on
What premises?
But they don't stop there,
Telling us we can't wear a shirt with a snowman?
Just because you think it is a cocaine slogan?
Now you see, they trying to stop the profanity,
But most kids don't deal drugs; kids wear it for vanity,
This shit is insanity, where's the humanity?
This is the canopy of neurosis,

Our leaders must have some sort of
Extreme psychosis, but know this,
Our generation does not support this,
Look at my face, does this look like bliss,
This is far from happiness, apparently the
DOE is oblivious, and amiss,
They're nothing but a group of novices,
The Department of Education is full of people
Who don't think,
Millions of public school students uneducated,
Hmmm, What's the missing link?
Maybe it's the mis-education kids are given,
Considering how bad the system is, how
Are kids supposed to grow up and make a living?
Minimum wage don't support two children,
And yeah you got your GED,
But that don't mean shit unless
You got a bachelor's degree,
Cause without both of those,
You ain't getting no fifty g's a year,
So let me make this real clear,
This is a huge problem spreading
Throughout our nation,
Just don't fall victim to our country's
School system of mis-education.

Complicated, abundant in rich detail, sarcastic and informative, Ben's poem unfolds in the way a debate might. His is more of a narrative and helps to take the reader into the experience of passing through metal detectors every morning. At the same time, he indicts everyone in education, letting no one off the hook: security, administrators, the Department of Education (DOE), our national public school system. Ben's tone is sarcastic—"Millions of public school students uneducated / Hmmm, What's the missing link? / Maybe it's the mis-education kids are given . . ."—and helps remind us the way in which writing can function as a buffer between what hurts the writer and how it gets expressed. In fact, the poem sits at a critical juncture between personal experience and explanation. It's a stop-gap between reflection and action.

While it is inevitably true that experiences at the hands of security hurt and mark students, both Ben and David use their poems as a vehicle for diffusing some of the trauma associated with their experiences. Furman, Jackson, Downey, and Bender (2002) studied the mechanisms by which poetry taps into inner resiliencies. They found that engaging in the creative process releases healing energies; breaks down the tasks of healing into manageable parts; and alerts individuals to the self-care skills they need to meet challenges. Tyrone captured this idea well when he told me: "School is stressful for some people, like no matter how you put it . . . some people write about it and it's like 'alright cool, I wrote this down. I'm done. This don't affect me no more.' But some people, they write about it and they see it and they [are] like, 'yo man, this is true, yo fuck this school.' You know, so like, sometimes it works, sometimes it don't. But when it does work, that's a good thing." What Tyrone is saying is that writing can be a form of therapy, but it can also bring to the surface of one's consciousness issues that are difficult to face.

As James Scott's theory of hidden transcripts reminds us, with this level of consciousness come the seeds of resistance and social change; and both poems reflect an individual, as well as a collective consciousness about the ironies and injustices motivating school surveillance policies. While surveillance is often a personal experience, school surveillance policy systematically impacts every student. While it may appear from the outside that students attenuate quickly and conform to standing in a line outside of the school's entrance every day, removing their belts, jewelry, and ignoring the loud shouts from security, it *would be a mistake to observe their seeming willingness to put up with these policies as an acceptance of them.* One of the most crucial meanings of these poems is that they reveal the other side of the appearances of compliance and unearth the seeds of what could eventually be a more sustainable and public form of collective contestation of school surveillance policies.

Writing Binds Youth to Each Other

As the two poems discussed above suggest, writing brings youth together because the content of experience is often shared. But it is not always easy to find communal spaces in which to write. Poems can be figurative spaces where shared experiences get talked about and even felt in the plural. But beyond the page, the students at Baldwin craved a physical and shared space in which they could write together. It was not surprising then that students chose to form a club soon after the walkout failed to bring about the changes they were hoping for. James Scott contends that "far from being a relief-valve taking the place of actual resistance, the discursive practices offstage sustain resistance" (1990, 191).

Within weeks of the walkout, students began to recognize the gradual and seemingly irreversible effects of the metal detectors on their school environment—"it's a very unhappy place and not what you would call a learning place at all," Elizabeth told me. Scott claims that, when faced with domination by powerful groups, subordinate groups perform "feats of imagination" in which they imagine a "total reversal of the distribution of status and rewards." These imagined reversals form what Scott calls "collective hidden transcripts." These collective critiques are not abstract exercises but are "embedded in innumerable ritual practices and . . . have provided the ideological basis of many revolts" (80). Scott insists that for subordinate groups, resistance through political action and struggle are more constraining than through thought, imagination, and ideology (91). He contrasts the "hidden transcript" of a subordinated group with the public transcript, which takes place on the open stage and gives the illusion of compliance. The rebellious transcript containing the critique is often hidden in discourse (27).

It is with Scott's ideas in mind that I consider the significance of the after-school poetry club. Frustrated with the lack of student unity and voice at school, Elizabeth started to talk up the idea of a weekly after-school poetry and hip hop club to her friends. David tells me that: "[Elizabeth] went around and started recruiting kids. There weren't no flyers around the school for poetry club; she wandered around the school. I remember she told me about it 'cause it was like the first day of English class and we had to write an introductory paragraph, introducing ourselves, and in it I said I like to write poetry. So [later] she was like oh, join the poetry club. I was like OK." Although as Adrienne Rich points out, writing has the potential to alleviate the loneliness, frustration, anger, and isolation a situation can present, the opposite is also true. Reflecting on difficult everyday circumstances *in isolation* can lead also to increased frustration, deepening anger and hostility, perhaps even passivity and lassitude. Elizabeth puts it plainly: "having an audience allows me to talk, allows me to express."

Writing can become the glue that binds youth and their struggles to each other. It affords them a reason to become part of a larger cacophony of voiced youth concerns. Adrienne Rich also remarks that "someone writing a poem believes in a reader, in readers, of that poem. The 'who' of that reader quivers like a jellyfish . . . But most often someone writing a poem believes in, depends on, a delicate, vibrating range of difference, that an 'I' can become a 'we' without extinguishing others, that a partly common language exists to which strangers can bring their own heartbeat, memories, images" (1993, 85). This "common language" Rich evokes can also be understood in relation to what James Scott refers to as the hidden transcript—"the privileged site for subversive discourse" (1990, 27)—which takes place off stage, under the nose of those in power. Scott argues that the practice of domination *creates* the hidden transcript. The student writers who founded the club not only used poetry to comment on and speak back to the conditions in their school, but also *transformed for a couple of hours each week a threatening space into one in which collective responses to school-wide surveillance occurred.* Scott contends that social spaces such as these "are themselves an achievement of resistance; they are won and defended in the teeth of power" (119).

Moreover, since this achievement of low-profile resistance takes organization and commitment on the part of the group, it can provide a "rehearsal" for more public collective protest. In order to understand the complexity of the "hidden transcript"—its ever-shifting, cloaked double meanings—Scott looks closely at these organizational "infrapolitics" of subordinated groups—as do Tricia Rose and Robin Kelley, in their documentation of bottom up practices of resistance taken by African American youth. Rose claims, for instance, that rap music is a hidden transcript; that it is "a contemporary stage for the theater of the powerless" (1994, 101). Kelley (1994) argues that historians studying African American history have neglected to uncover the hidden resistance and "infrapolitics" of subcultural groups and have, instead, focused too narrowly on the high profile acts of resistance such as bus boycotts or the freedom riders. The activities and practices of the hidden transcript, by way of contrast, take place off stage, under the nose of those in power. For this reason, they are not always easy to observe, sometime cloaked in apparent conformity.

One of the best ways to locate hidden transcripts and the "infrapolitics" that produce them is to identify spaces that exist "off-stage" that are "actively sealed off from surveillance" (Scott, 1990, 121). Scott provides as an example the secret "hush arbors" where slaves in the antebellum South met to practice an activist religion that defied the passivity of the Christianity slaveholders preached to them. Such secret "social sites" are achievements of resistance and struggle. They are not easily won, nor are they easily defended when breached.

I think we can begin to see the multiple ways in which youth writing, as the examples included in this chapter point to, function as both "hidden transcripts" and "social sites." Indeed, had I stopped my inquiry with the student walkout or the documentation of what de Certeau termed "tactical avoidance," and if I had overlooked the hidden transcripts that were taking place "off stage"—actively sealed off from surveillance—I would have missed some of the richest ways students were choosing to respond to the school's newfound policies.

I would have missed a profound resistance to the surveillance. The writing became a place in which students took refuge from ongoing battles with security guards and school authorities, and from severe overcrowding and increasing violence in the school. Students used the club and their writing to vent, commiserate, joke around, and buffer themselves from difficult experiences in school. They also used their poems to talk back to authority and perceived injustices. While the poem does not eradicate the often painful experiences with school surveillance, the writing—whether in a poetry club, an after-school organization, or a poem—puts youth in dialogue with a wider audience and a shared critique. Students' poems and raps help them to locate and identify an audience comprised of others who refuse to listen, be denied a voice and impact on their educational lives.

Moreover, in settings of pervasive and unjust surveillance, writing may function in its own panoptic way as a place to record what students observe about the authority figures watching *them*. In this panopticism may reside a less obvious, but no less profound role that writing and the after-school poetry club performs in the lives of these students. James Scott argues that there is an important dialectic between the hidden transcript and later public protest—"It would be more accurate," Scott states, "to think of the hidden transcript as a condition of practical resistance rather than a substitute for it" (1990, 191). The ultimate significance of the student poetry and the weekly poetry club meetings may lie within the synergy between the production of the hidden transcripts and the production of the group itself.

The activities maintaining the group—the infrapolitics—offer students a way to rehearse—to implicitly prepare—for more overt, direct protest of the school policies. While the initial student walkout may have failed to generate the kind of change students were hoping for, it is possible that the poetry club and the poems themselves over time will offer students (and teacher allies) a staging ground for what could become the next public display of protest—one that is more sustainable, given the existence and practice of the group and its multiple expressive work together. Scott contends that while hidden transcripts might be denigrated by some as unimportant, they are in fact the building blocks without which "more elaborate institutionalized political action" could not exist (1990, 201).

The "Right" Theory

I have argued that researchers would do well to consider writing by youth as rich and complex sources of qualitative data. The poems and conversations that emerged inside the social space of this writing and in the poetry club itself combined to constitute a rich hidden transcript of critique and resistance—a fecund treasure trove of data specifically addressing student fears and desires related to school surveillance. The writing also provided jumping-off points for further inquiry and theorizing.

Although I had initially felt prepared for my research by several years of immersion in structuralist "high theory," I found that the immediacy of the research site itself—and the needs and activities of my participants—led me to search for other sources to theorize what was occurring. Poet Adrienne

Rich, and "bottom up" theorists de Certeau and Scott provided that access. Scott, in particular, helped me to capture and describe the "immense political terrain [that] lies between quiescence and revolt and that, for better or worse, is the political environment of subject classes" (1990, 199). Scott's lens led me to see that what may appear compliant and quotidian may actually be tactical and significant.

In order to learn more about the culture, subjectivity, internal politics and potential activist role of a subordinated group like urban teenagers of color, researchers need theory that responds to their own questions, methods, and perspectives; theory that accommodates data such as student writing without reducing it. We have to choose the "right" theory; not any theory will do.

Notes

1   Urban Word NYC is an after-school poetry, spoken word, and hip hop organization that provides New York City teenagers free after-school workshops, all-youth open mic spaces, and an annual teen poetry slam. I co-founded the group in 1999.
2   The high school featured in this chapter is populated by close to five thousand low-income youths of color (predominately Latino and/or African American students) from its surrounding areas. It is a large, old, overcrowded urban New York City high school located in the Northwest Bronx. Students are tracked upon entrance into the school; one of the school's specialized programs has a strong reputation even among top-tier public high schools. Some of my research participants were in this program.
3   Sistas and Brothas United is a grassroots, community-based organization that works closely with high schools in the surrounding areas. The high school of mention is one of their projects. It is part of the Bronx Affiliate of Urban Youth Collective, a downtown-based program designed to help urban youth organize and resist unfair school policies. SBU did not organize the walkout but one or two staff from SBU were present. SBU is a youth-based organized and tried to support students in whatever route they chose in addressing the metal detectors.
4   Acronym of the high school.

References

Balmer, S. (2006). *Policing as Education Policy: A Briefing on the Initial Impact of the Impact Schools Program.* New York: National Center for Schools and Communities, Fordham University.

Burawoy, M. (1991). *Ethnography Unbound: Power and Resistance in the Modern Metropolis.* Los Angeles: University of California Press.

de Certeau, M. (1984). *The Practice of Everyday Life.* Berkeley and Los Angeles: University of California Press.

Drum Major Institute (2005, June). *A Look at the Impact Schools.* New York: A Drum Major Institute for Public Policy Data Brief, NY.

Eskanazi, M., Eddins, G., and Beam, J. M. (2003, October). *Equity or Exclusion: The Dynamics of Resources, Demographics, and Behavior in the New York City Public Schools.* National Center for Schools and Communities at Fordham University (NCSC).

Foucault, M. (1979). *Discipline and Punish: The Birth of the Prison.* New York: Vintage Books.

Furman, R., Jackson, R. L., Downey, E. P., and Bender, K. (2002). Poetry Therapy as a Tool for Strengths-based Practice. *Advances in Social Work,* 3, 146–157.

Ginwright, S., Cammarota, J., and P. Noguero. (2005). Youth, Social Justice, and Communities: Toward a Theory of Urban Youth Policy. *Social Justice,* 32: 3, 24–40.

Kelley, R. (1994). *Race Rebels.* New York: Free Press.

McCormick, J. (2004). *Writing in the Asylum: Student Poets in City Schools.* New York: Teachers College Press.

Males, M. (1996). *The Scapegoat Generation: America's War on Adolescents.* Monroe, ME: Common Courage Press.

Mediratta, K. (2006). A Rising Movement. *National Civic Review* DOI: 10.1002/ncr.

Monahan, T. (2006). Questioning Surveillance and Security. In T. Monahan, editor, *Surveillance and Security: Technological Politics and Power in Everyday Life.* New York: Routledge.

Mukherjee, E., and Karpatkin Fellow, M. (2006–2007). *Criminalizing the Classroom: The Over-Policing of New York City Schools.* New York: New York Civil Liberties Union.

Noguera, P. (1995). Preventing and Producing Violence: A Critical Analysis of Responses to School Violence. *Harvard Educational Review*, 65: 2.

Nolan, K. (2007). *Disciplining Urban Youth: An Ethnographic Study of a Bronx High School.* Unpublished dissertation, The Graduate Center, The City University of New York.

Queeley, A. (2003). Hip Hop and the Aesthetics of Criminalization. *Souls*, 5: 1, 1–15.

Rich, A. (1993). *What is Found There: Notebooks on Poetry and Politics.* New York: W. W. Norton.

Rich, A. (2001). *Arts of the Possible: Essays and Conversations.* New York: W. W. Norton.

Rose, T. (1994). *Black Noise: Rap Music and Black Culture in Contemporary America.* Middletown, CT: Wesleyan University Press.

Saltman, K. J. (2000). *Collateral Damage.* New York: Rowman & Littlefield Publishers.

Santos, F. (2005, September 21). 1,500 New York City students protest metal detectors at high school. *The New York Times.*

Schlosberg, M. (2006, July). *A State of Surveillance.* Oakland: American Civil Liberties Union of Northern California.

Scott, J. (1990). *Domination and the Arts of Resistance: Hidden Transcripts.* New Haven: Yale University Press.

Sedgwick, E. (2003). *Touching Feeling: Affect, Pedagogy, and Performativity.* Durham: Duke University Press.

Sullivan, E. (2007). *Deprived of Dignity: Degrading Treatment and Abusive Discipline in New York City & Los Angeles Public Schools.* New York: National Economic and Social Rights Initiative (NESRI).

Personal Reflection

Finding Theory

In 1999, I founded an after-school organization, Urban Word NYC, for teenagers who write and perform their own poetry, spoken word, and hip hop. The organization's policy, painted onto the office walls, comes from one of its former students: "This is a safe space. So say what you want, but don't let your words endanger anyone." Under this banner, I have worked with hundreds of New York City youth in an after-school setting, and also in high schools and colleges as well, always with the goal of holding them and their words accountable to serious thinking. I come to theory because in my years teaching, directing an after-school program, working inside high schools and colleges, and listening to urban youth inside and beyond schools, in poetry workshops, on stages, among their peers, in the hallways between classes, in freestyle battles, on the subways, often out of the earshot of adults they think might be listening, I have not yet found a teenager who isn't in some way engaged in analyzing and theorizing their lived experiences. As one student participant stated in a focus group, "for teens today, one experience is like a lifetime." Further discussion revealed that what he meant by this is that a teenager's lack of years does not prevent them from contending with (and making sense of) the realities of an unstable world. It is their desire to explain and question these realities that makes youth participants such active and important theorizers during the research process. In this personal reflection I attempt to relate my process for choosing those theories that best spoke to my research with and about youth of color in New York City's urban high schools.

Theory Like Poetry

If theory is *a set of statements devised to explain a group of facts or phenomena, abstract reasoning and speculation, or a belief that guides action or assists comprehension,*[1] then I first came to theory as a close reader of poetry. Poetry contains for me a world of speculation and hypothesis, a world that seeks to tell the truth about a given situation, but a truth with no "clear edges" (Rich, 1993, 84). I do not expect an answer to a problem when I read a poem; but I hope to find a new way of looking at something that I have been staring at for a long time. Poet and essayist Adrienne Rich writes: "Take that old, material utensil, language, found all about you, blank with familiarity, smeared with daily use, and make it into something that means more than it says" (ibid.).

When we conduct social research, we can use theory in much the same way—as both a methodological and an analytic tool that helps reveal more than at first appears, because what is close is hard to see. Theory, Stephen J. Ball points out, provides "the possibility of a different language . . . a language of distance, or irony, and of imagination" (2006, 21). The point of theory, Ball continues, "is not that it is simply critical. In order to go beyond the accidents and contingencies which enfold us, it is necessary to start from another position and begin from what is normally excluded" (63).

Though poetry and theory tend to exist in separate spheres of the academy, and many readers of theory may not be readers of poetry (and vice versa), I want to suggest that we consider poetry as a companion and analogue as we move towards choosing the right theories for our research purposes. We would do well to approach a body of theoretical literature as if we were approaching a collection of poems—sifting through both for meaning and clarity, sometimes hope; not rushing to conclusions; waiting patiently for an image, metaphor, or example to resonate with us; and "being alert and ready for unaccountable beauty, for the intricateness or simple elegance of the writer's imagination, for the world that imagination evokes" (Morrison, 1992, xi).

Approaching Theory

Before and during the conduct of my research on youth resistance as a response to high school security and surveillance policies in New York City, I reviewed a broad range of theoretical perspectives: from social theory to literary and performance theory, from contemporary nonfiction and new journalism to post-colonial and critical-race theory. Stacked on my kitchen table or my desk, Toni Morrison's *Whiteness and the Literary Imagination* sits on top of Joan Didion's *The White Album* which hovers next to *Negotiations: Interviews with Gilles Deleuze*. Jose Munoz's *Disidentifications* saddles up against Eve Sedgwick's *Touching Feeling* laid on top of de Certeau's *The Practice of Everyday Life*. James Scott's *Domination and the Arts of Resistance* appears under Jean Anyon's *Radical Possibilities* and beside Judith Butler's *Excitable Speech* and Roland Barthes's *Writing Degree Zero*. Christian Parenti's *Soft Cage* is spread open face down on top of Malcolm Gladwell's *The Tipping Point* and Patricia Williams's *The Alchemy of Race and Rights*. Other books and articles from journals lay open or untouched, in other rooms of my apartment—all with the intention of being part of the conversation I have going with these theorists. Each author becomes an interlocutor of a particular domain of knowledge, offering a unique perspective and interpretation that can also be applied to my field, my area of interest, my particular domain of research.

I am not an obsessive reader: I do not read while eating, watching television, or cooking dinner. I know people like this exist, but I am not one of them. But I have always read widely. Even so, as I began my research process I felt ill-equipped to conduct a worthwhile study with so many savvy and stimulating youth without having a range of theoretical perspectives and open-ended conversations happening in my head at the same time. Oscillating between my practice as an educator and my desire to conduct research towards social change meant utilizing theory outside of my own discipline of education. And looking "from the bottom up" meant considering the multiple ways urban youth contend with and conceptualize the forces that shape their experiences; it has meant approaching research through an inverted spotlight: starting from a broad base of theory which offered me room to consider all the possible ways of framing what I was observing in the field, and then narrowing my focus as I got closer to the analysis and the writing. I found the theories to which I was most drawn were similar to the poetry to which I return often: they did not clarify, except on rare occasions, and instead complicated the ideas I was formulating.

My Job Using Theory

Immersed in the stories of urban youth and the language of high theory, my job has been to make the world of philosophy speak to the world of the urban classroom; to make the urban classroom speak to the world of theory. But theory can take on different valences in the context of research in urban education. Gripped by the hands of those already convinced of their position, theory is often used against those who lack voice or vocal opposition to federal and state-governed policies. It can be used as "finger pointing," Stephen Ball argues (ibid., 21), and can bully those already in a position of powerlessness; it can buttress efforts to pathologize the actions of entire segments of a population; and can serve to over-simplify otherwise complicated and contradictory phenomena. Although I believe that my job as an educational researcher and writer is to put 17-year-old Tyrone West from Brooklyn, NY, and deceased French philosopher Michel de Certeau in the same room together and help facilitate a conversation, I try not to make the meeting a set up for either party.

With these concerns in mind, I have tried to use theory in at least three ways: to facilitate a conversation, not an argument or debate; to listen attentively; and to theorize *with*, not just about, my participants. In doing research with youth who occupy a position of marginality, one must find theory that provides a *complementary* language to what they are already saying. Their stories were already doing important work. My goal was to find theory that could be *juxtaposed* with the thoughts and perceptions of the youth in my study so that they each might hold their own in the conversation. I wanted to avoid what Ball names "a process of concept matching" (ibid.) in which researchers merely apply theory gesturally, simply to boost their findings. Indeed, no matter how applicable a theory might be, its power is in its ability to move us from one position to another—*to unstick us*. No matter how solid or well-known a theory it is, it has to be lived with and remade through the process of research—it cannot be simply applied to a given problem and let go again. It must be worked and reworked, often multiple times.

My chapter in this collection illustrates my decision to work with the theories of Michel de Certeau and James C. Scott. It is worth noting that I spent many years, off and on, reading their work—and was often attracted to other theorists' work. Yet I kept returning to these two during the period in which I was analyzing and writing up my findings precisely because their ideas helped me extend what I was seeing and hearing in the field beyond the sometimes flatness of my observation. For example, James Scott's notion of the "hidden transcript" helped me see the significance of student writing and the poetry club as a tool of resistance in response to heavy policing and surveillance in the urban high school.

In his comprehensive study of de Certeau's oeuvre, Ben Highmore (2006) argues that what we get from de Certeau's work is an "inventive and generative approach to reading and observing . . . a method that values the singularity of close attention to the specific, located object" (7). I found his rare sensitivity to the process of observation and what he calls the "geography of the forgotten"[2] to be of particular importance for understanding my observations of youth resistance.

After years of reading and struggling with de Certeau's work, I believe I am drawn to it because throughout his elaborate theorizing about seemingly mundane activities of everyday life I can sense a delicate and profound appreciation for each activity. He approaches each "located object" in the same way a poet might approach the subject under investigation: "In the wash of poetry the old, beaten, worn stones of language take on colors that disappear when you sieve them up out of the streambed and try to sort them out," writes Rich (1993, 84).

If, as this book argues, theory and research can and must converge for richer, deeper social analysis, we reach for theory in part to "help give name to the nameless so that it can be thought" (Lorde, 1984, 37). In this way theory, like poetry, invites us to be both inventive and generative in our observations, and is concerned equally with the process of conducting research, and the beauty and strength of our claims.

Notes

1   *the·o·ry n. pl. the·o·ries*—1 A set of statements or principles devised to explain a group of facts or phenomena, especially one that has been repeatedly tested or is widely accepted and can be used to make predictions about natural phenomena; 2 The branch of a science or art consisting of its explanatory statements, accepted principles, and methods of analysis, as opposed to practice: a fine musician who had never studied theory; 3 A set of theorems that constitute a systematic view of a branch of mathematics; 4 Abstract reasoning; speculation: a decision based on experience rather than theory; 5 A belief or principle that guides action or assists comprehension or judgment: staked out the house on the theory that criminals usually return to the scene of the crime; 6 An assumption based on limited information or knowledge; a conjecture ("theory", *The American Heritage® Dictionary of the English Language, Fourth Edition* (n.d.)).

2   "beyond, the question of methods and contents, beyond what it says, the measure of a work is what it keeps silent. And we must say that the scientific studies—and undoubtedly the works they highlight—include vast and strange expanses of silence. These blank spots outline a geography of the forgotten. They trace the negative silhouette of the problematics displayed black on white in scholarly books."

References

Ball, S. (2006). *Education Policy and Social Class: The Selected Works of Stephen J. Ball*. London and New York: Taylor and Francis.

Highmore, B. (2006). *Michel de Certeau: Analyzing Culture*. New York: Continuum.

Lorde, A. (1984). Sister Outsider: Essays and Speeches by Audre Lorde. New York: The Crossing Press.

Morrison, T. (1992). *Playing in the Dark: Whiteness and the Literary Imagination*. New York: Random House.

Rich, A. (1986). *Your Native Land, Your Life*. New York: Norton.

Rich, A. (1993). *What is Found There: Notebooks on Poetry and Politics*. New York: Norton.

CHAPTER 3

Theorizing Redistribution and Recognition in Urban Education Research

How do we Get Dictionaries at Cleveland?[1]

MICHAEL J. DUMAS

In capitalist societies, social justice claims have historically been framed as demands for a more equitable distribution of wealth. Increasingly, however, attention has shifted to demands for recognition, as various social groups have come to understand their oppression as rooted in cultural struggles over identity and difference. Some political economists have lamented this shift from the politics of redistribution to the politics of recognition, arguing that it has distracted us from critique of the economic system and has corresponded too conveniently with the rise of neoliberalism (Sayer, 2001).[2] However, as a number of social scientists have argued (Ball, 2006; Fraser and Honneth, 2003; Kelley, 1997), class can not fully explain many contemporary conflicts, which introduce to the field of struggle questions related to the body, voice, affiliation and worth.

Political philosopher Nancy Fraser (1995, 2000) argues that we need *both* a politics of redistribution and a politics of recognition. The politics of *redistribution* are defined by the relations of production. The problem here is the exploitation of the working class by the capitalist (or ruling) class. Social groups that experience *mal*distribution, then, seek reprieve by demanding conditions that will improve their access to the means of production. In political terms, this means that the class structure must be reorganized—dismantled, in truth—so that the lower classes do not shoulder the greatest economic burdens, while others enjoy all the rewards.

The politics of *recognition* denotes efforts to seek redress for forms of cultural disregard, disrespect, and low social esteem. The problem here is one of status subordination, in which a particular group is subject to marginalization, discrimination, intimidation, even death, on the basis of how the society has constructed that group's social legitimacy. *Mis*recognition, then, must be answered by a politics that works for parity in the cultural sphere, to effect a transformation in how despised groups are valued.

Although it is theoretically and politically useful to think about redistribution and recognition as two separate modes of politics, in practice most social groups must engage in both simultaneously. As Fraser points out:

> Even the most material economic institutions have a constitutive, irreducible cultural dimension; they are shot through with significations and norms. Conversely, even the most discursive cultural practices have a constitutive, irreducible political-economic dimension; they are underpinned by material supports.
>
> (1995, 72)

In other words, society is a field of complex relations and institutions in which economic and cultural forms of social order are dialectical and intersecting. In this context, there is no redistribution without recognition, and no recognition without redistribution.

In the area of urban school reform, inequality has been articulated at various times and in certain contexts as a problem of maldistribution, and then in other moments and to varying degrees as a problem of misrecognition. Thus, school desegregation has been conceptualized as a fight for equal access to educational resources *and* as an effort to build bridges of cross-racial understanding (Bell, 2004; Frankenberg, Lee, and Orfield, 2003). Affirmative action is an acknowledgement of historical and ongoing exclusionary practices *and* a statement of support for diversity (Crenshaw, Gotanda, Peller, and Thomas, 1995; Delgado and Stefancic, 2000). And the so-called achievement gap can be interpreted as an opportunity gap (i.e., disparate levels of resources) *and* as the result of low academic expectations of students of color based on their racial/ethnic identities (Fine *et al.*, 2004).

When we—researchers, community organizers, policy-makers, youth—seek to explain persistent inequities, we are, in effect, theorizing the material and ideological roots of educational injustice. Theorizing about redistribution and recognition helps us engage in critical dialogue about which policies and what kind of politics are *substantively* worth pursuing—that is, our imagination of which remedies will make things "right" or "better." Equally important, our theorizing helps us decide which remedies are *strategically* worth pursuing. The question we ask ourselves here is, What is the likelihood that a specific proposed remedy will be palatable to enough people so that it will not be rejected out of hand, or undermined before it has had the opportunity to effect positive change?

What I want to do here is explore a moment of such theorizing in a specific site of contestation over educational inequities within an urban school district. At issue is the absence of dictionaries at Cleveland High School, in the south end of the city of Seattle, and the relative abundance of dictionaries at Roosevelt High School, located in the north end. Decades of racially discriminatory housing policies and practices have ensured that the north end of the city remains overwhelmingly white, while most people of color—and particularly black residents—are concentrated south of the ship canal, a marker commonly used as a racial-geographical dividing line (Orians, 1989). The student population of Cleveland is approximately 90 percent students of color and about 10 percent white, in a city that is 76 percent white, less than 9 percent black and about 13 percent Asian and Pacific Islander. At least half of the students at Cleveland qualify for free or reduced lunch. In sharp contrast, at Roosevelt High nearly 60 percent of the student body is white, and only about 20 percent receive free or reduced lunch (Wright, 2003). The difference in access to dictionaries at the two schools is a mere reflection of more significant disparities: teacher qualifications and experience, breadth of curricular offerings, number of college-preparatory courses, and physical infrastructure.

Why do students in one section of the city have more resources than students in another? What does it mean that Seattle—a wealthy, educated, and decidedly liberal city—has either been unwilling or unable to correct these inequities? What is the responsibility of the state (i.e., city, state and federal government and its agents) to ensure equal access to educational resources? That is, to what extent should (or can) the state mandate that middle- and upper-class communities subsidize the education of poor and working-class students? Or should we instead rely on the compassion and goodwill of individual citizens and corporations? Certainly, social scientists and policy analysts have offered a number of competing and reasonably argued responses to these questions. I am interested in exploring how these questions—and answers—emerge in the narratives of people who are not as detached or abstract as researchers often are, and who view themselves as being in the position to struggle for educational justice in some concrete way. Ultimately, my intention is to provide some insight into how social actors theorize redistribution and recognition, and to identify some implications of a theory of redistribution and recognition for urban education research.

How Students at Cleveland *Did Not* Get Dictionaries

The roots of contemporary urban school reform in Seattle can be traced to the early 1960s, when the school district implemented a voluntary desegregation plan, which offered an opportunity for some black students in the segregated Central District to attend better-resourced schools in the north end. By the mid-1970s, the district, facing the threat of a federal lawsuit, implemented a mandatory busing program that promised to fully desegregate the city's schools. White opposition was immediate and fierce: several families left the city for the suburbs, a substantial number placed their children in private schools, and an anti-busing initiative was placed on the ballot. Although many people in Seattle's black community also opposed busing in the late 1970s (Taylor, 2006), the policy had the support of black leaders, who were convinced that school desegregation would create the social conditions necessary for better days ahead.

Black disillusionment with busing emerged in the mid-1980s, as a number of influential black leaders, educators and activists concluded that the school district's desegregation policy placed a disproportionate burden on children of color, and seemingly did little to improve educational achievement. This decrease in black support coincided with the ascendance of an increasingly conservative federal judiciary, which handed down a number of rulings making it easier for local districts to rescind their desegregation plans (Orfield and Eaton, 1996). During the 1990s, Seattle's municipal and school board leaders worked together to slowly dismantle the unpopular busing program, and, in 1997, abandoned the goal of racially balanced schools altogether.[3]

In place of school desegregation, the district instituted a weighted school-funding formula that allocated extra dollars to schools based on the number of students with special needs (i.e., low-income, bilingual, and special-education). By several accounts, the resources provided by the weighted-student formula have not succeeded in making schools more equal, in part because schools in Washington state are not adequately funded in the first place (Thompson, 2005). To make up for this deficit, some schools in the north end have established endowments which raise monies that are used to hire additional staff, supplement academic offerings, purchase books and supplies, and make improvements to the buildings and grounds. This effort has been aided by the fact that, as Seattle schools rapidly resegregated by race and class, schools in affluent white neighborhoods were able to attract families whose children attended, or would have attended, private schools. For a mere fraction of private school tuition, families can enhance their local public school with little worry that these dollars will be used to subsidize a large number of poor students, who, given their relative academic unpreparedness, are more likely to lower the school's academic reputation and siphon funds for remedial and bilingual programs.

Meanwhile, in the south end, middle-class residents of all racial or ethnic groups are increasingly choosing private schools, leaving a high concentration of poor students, mostly children of color, in the area's public schools. Parents and caregivers of these poor students are the most politically and economically disenfranchised in the city, which makes it more challenging to mobilize for political action. It is not that parent and community organizing does not occur; however, this population has minimal access to the kind of social capital needed to make demands for educational justice (Noguera, 2003).

An Exchange at Rainier Beach[4]

In reading the narrative of the community forum below, I focus not so much on critiquing individual speakers as on examining which remedies for injustice are considered, which are then validated, and which are readily dismissed. I attend to how political actors introduce and engage in discourses on such ideologically informed themes as responsibility, opportunity, empathy, and (white) awareness. As a researcher, I am grateful to all the participants for providing data that allow us to theorize how people who all care deeply about education deliberate over these complex and difficult issues. I will say this again later, but I want to emphasize at the outset that the participants' ideas as expressed at this public event do not reflect the totality of their beliefs. Nor do their statements necessarily reflect their thoughts beyond the moment of this forum, which occurred in 2004.

The evening was almost over. Dr. Caprice Hollins had finished her speech to the audience gathered at Rainier Beach High School. As director of the Seattle School District's relatively new Office of Equity and Race Relations, she had summarized her vision for "ending disproportionality" in the public schools, highlighting three critical areas—multicultural curriculum and instructional materials, communities and family involvement, and culturally relevant staff development. Her role in the district, she emphasized throughout the speech, was to encourage everyone to "look at differences in a positive way, not a negative way." Hollins, who also shared candidly with the audience her own experience as the child of a white mother and black father, had given this speech at community meetings throughout the city, but tonight she was in Seattle's south end, the home of the majority of Seattle's black, Latino, and Asian residents. In fact, of the roughly five hundred students enrolled at Rainier Beach that year, 60 percent were African American, nearly a quarter were Asian, and less than seven percent were white.

One of the final comments was from Karen Jensen, the parent of a middle-school student in the district's highly selective Accelerated Progress Program (APP). Jensen, who is white, recalled an earlier community meeting, where

Roosevelt High students had addressed the disparity between their northend school and Cleveland High. "We had the students from Roosevelt that were there reporting," she explained, "and they had done an exchange program with the students at Cleveland . . . and I was touched by the emotion of one of the students who said that the Cleveland student came to Roosevelt and was just looking around in awe, and said, 'I didn't know it could be this good! Oh my God, is this the same city?'"

The Rainier Beach audience laughed knowingly. Jensen continued, "And a Roosevelt student went to Cleveland and he was like, 'They don't even have dictionaries in their classrooms. Am *I* in the same city?' And I try to think that I'm fairly aware of what's going on . . . I *live* in the southend. But I had no idea that that scope of disparity existed right here in Seattle.

"And I'm saying, well, I'm just a parent, but that's uh, kind of . . . taking the burden off of me, and I'm like, I'm got to own my own—" *Privilege?* Jensen's voice faltered, as if she thought to speak the word, but decided to swallow it instead. She continued, her voice now more pleading, "Do I really just not want to know so I don't go and investigate this and say, why is this happening, and who should do something about it?" She gestured to Hollins, standing behind the podium. "I mean, you're a district person, and [Seattle Public Schools Superintendent] Raj [Manhas] appointed you, so you must have some power, right?" She paused, and then said dryly, "Right. You don't have any staff." The audience erupted once again, the same bitter knowing laughter.

"Why is this, and who makes the change? And is it just funding and what's driving the dollars, and how do we get dictionaries at Cleveland? I have a friend through soccer whose daughter was a freshman at Cleveland, and they're pulling her out and putting her in private school because they don't believe she would *graduate* from Cleveland."

Hollins stepped forward to respond. "The issue with the resourcing," she began, "the allocation of where resourcing is going into programs is definitely something that the district needs to look at . . . If we're talking about closing the achievement gap, we have to think about how our dollars are being spent and where they're being spent.

"But the issue of south end versus north end and what schools have at one end and what schools don't have on another end—for example, what these students witnessed—a lot of the funding that comes into the north end schools comes from the parents . . . So I don't know the quote on this, I've heard it a million times, but we're like, forty-second in the nation in funding,[5] which means that if we were funded just at the average, we'd have $47 million more per year for funding in schools.

"So here's a federal issue about schools not getting enough money to educate all of our students. So the north end schools' parents make up for that. So schools don't have enough money to get dictionaries or they want another teacher or we need a jungle gym or—and their fundraiser looks a lot different than a fundraiser that might occur on the south end.

"So who's responsible?" Hollins asked. She then explained one proposal, which would put a cap on private fundraising at individual schools, and allocate surplus donations to a general fund. Just as quickly, she dismissed the idea and suggested one of her own. "My idea—when we talk about what we can do—to me, here's a great idea of what the community could do, right? The community can talk, the students can talk, the families can talk to one another and say, how are we going to address this issue? Are we going to continue to widen the achievement gap, create more inequities by just caring about our students on this end of the district, or do we really care, are we really about all students? And if so, what does that mean for us, what are our roles and responsibilities as it relates to us having the resources and where we put them? I don't think that's a district decision . . . we can't, I don't believe we have the right to say to a parent, you must partner with this other school over here, and you must help them as well."

At this point, community activist Don Alexander began to grumble. The elderly black leader of Save Our Southend Schools (SOS) had heard enough.

Hollins raised her hand and her voice. "Let me finish, Don . . . But I think we [the district] can support the process of that happening: so how do you connect with that school, if you did want to [support a school in the south end]? I think the district can play a role in that, but not coming to you as a parent and saying, you can not donate your money to this school, you must donate it over there. That's my way of thinking. I think that should come from the families. I think you should get outraged. I think the families should get outraged about the disparities and say, what are we going to do about this, we're not OK with this anymore. It could be a collective kind of community effort and—"

"That's not fair!" Leaning forward on his cane, Alexander interrupted again. This time, Hollins relented. "That's just not fair. It really isn't. Public schools were founded on the basis of equity and equality . . . The district should be held accountable for our children, not just *not* being educated, but *mis*educated. We can't allow the district to say that a school on the south end don't have what a school on the north end have because of the affluence of one compared to the other. We can't afford the district to be able to say that."

It was Hollins's turn to interrupt. The forum had gone on for nearly two hours now. "So Don, I want to stop but I just want to say—"

"There's no way we can accept that!" Alexander said defiantly.

"—This is a perfect example that we have to come together as a community and as a district. Everything is *not* 'you must do this as a district.' If we're going to be serious about closing the achievement gap for our students, we *all* have a role in it. It's not going to work, Don, if it's just, what are *you*, the district, going to do. Everyone is responsible. Everyone is accountable to *our* children in some way or another so . . ."

Alexander continued to make his case, now addressing the audience as a whole.

"Don," Hollins pleaded, "you have access to me all the time. You and I can talk any time. We often do. We can talk about this further, because—"

"Well, Caprice," he said, now more gently, "I want to convince other people—if I can . . ."

"You can," Hollins conceded, with a smile, "but not tonight."

"Why not?" A couple members of the audience asked.

"My son lost his first tooth," she explained, "and I want to get home before he goes to bed."

This brought gentle laughter from the audience, which provided the space for a final speaker, a woman who began, "I just want to say this. I've been to several of the meetings . . . I think the one piece that is so important is that you're going to need the help of other people to continue these conversations, and I know that that's just more talk. What you plan to do, to begin to work with teachers who are good people, but have no or little understanding about how to work with anyone who is different from them—that is *the* key, so we can begin with kindergarten children, to welcome them in the door and really see them as gifts walking in. That's the piece, if we can put our heart into doing that, we won't be talking about this fifty years later, but if we don't, if we continue to rail against the system when we are *all* part of the system, then that's where we will be fifty, sixty, a hundred years from now."

Stepping to one side of the podium, Hollins nodded vigorously.

The speaker continued, "But if we are working with teachers on having them examine white privilege . . . if there is one understanding we have— that there are people who are different than I am and I have to meet them in a different way—that one piece, if we can get that going, and then explore what are the ways of meeting children where they are . . . that's the one piece, and that is all about relationships."

"Yes," Hollins agreed, still nodding. "Yes, that's a nice ending."

Theorizing the Absence of Dictionaries

In the exchange at Rainier Beach, we might imagine that Don Alexander offers a redistribution narrative, while Caprice Hollins (with a number of supporting speakers) offers a recognition narrative. This is incredibly reductive—in my individual interview with Alexander, he also spoke passionately about the cultural dimensions of racism and racial identity. In turn, Hollins is on record critiquing "institutional racism" (Harrell, 2006) which indicates her awareness of structural maldistribution of resources. However, for analytical purposes, let us imagine that each of them represents one of these two interimbricated but theoretically distinguishable political frames.

Alexander, who admittedly didn't get in many words during the forum, nevertheless was very clear about his main point: the affluence of families or neighborhoods should not determine the quality of education that students receive. Doubtless, Hollins would concede this point, but for Alexander, I would argue, the problem of *class* becomes the central political focus. Students at Cleveland do not have dictionaries because the state— represented here by the school district—is shirking its duty to allocate resources so that all children have access to a similar quality of education. Alexander's theorizing leads him to embrace a politics which encourages members of the community to demand more resources from the state, which inevitably means some mandated redistribution from rich to poor.

Hollins makes the argument that affluent communities need to be convinced to care more about those who live in poor communities and attend underresourced schools. If, she suggests, these affluent citizens could reflect on their relative privilege, and recognize that the aspirations of poor people are not so different from their own, we might see a shift in their willingness to become "outraged" by educational inequities. For Hollins, then, the main focus is one of *status*—north end residents must come to understand that poor south end children matter and that they should be regarded as equally deserving of educational opportunity. Students do not have dictionaries at Cleveland because we as citizens do not recognize each other and appreciate our differences. Hollins's theorizing calls for a politics aimed at challenging the public's low valuation of the "other."

Again, let me hasten to say that I doubt that either Alexander or Hollins occupy such a narrow theoretical or political location. In fact, as Fraser points out, social actors rarely articulate or organize around such conceptual axes, at least not explicitly (Fraser and Naples, 2004). However, the narratives of Alexander and Hollins—and their contrasting explanations of educational inequity—provide an opportunity for scholars and activists to think more critically about the "underlying grammar of social conflict" (1112) in everyday education politics. At this point, I want to examine some of the moments of theorizing at Rainier Beach more closely, and place them into conversation with concepts and tensions in Nancy Fraser's work.

"I Don't Think That's a District Decision": The Problem of Displacement

For Fraser, the shift toward the politics of recognition has meant a lack of necessary attention given to the need for egalitarian redistribution (see also

Sayer, 2001). This growing lack of interest in, or perhaps disdain for, policies and politics centered on equitable resource allocation can be attributed to the neoliberal assault on the very idea of social welfare and the absence of a viable socialist vision which might provide an alternative to advanced global capitalism. Within this context, new social movements came to focus almost entirely on recognition, which generally took the form of identity politics along such lines as race, gender, sexuality and ethnicity. These groups often conceptualized politics as a number of related cultural struggles, and attended more to issues of representation and signification than economic inequality and exploitation.

For example, to expound on something I mentioned earlier, in the case of school desegregation, what could be conceptualized in terms of correcting inequitable access to educational resources becomes justified as a struggle for "diverse" racial representation within school buildings. To be fair to myself and others who have advanced certain forms of culturally based identity politics, it was not that we considered economic inequities unimportant. Rather—and Fraser points this out—we tended to explain economic disparities in terms of cultural disregard alone. That is, in discourse and action, many of us tended to suggest that "to revalue unjustly devalued identities is simultaneously to attack the deep sources of economic inequality" (2000, 111). Integrated schools, some proponents argued, would reduce inter-group prejudice, while raising the self-esteem of black students and other students of color. If only it were so. By not having an "explicit politics of redistribution," I would argue, a robust justice never came: School buildings were racially integrated (for a time), but educational resources were and are still not shared equitably *within* those buildings. More fundamentally, a "racial-diversity" approach to school desegregation politics has never adequately addressed the more fundamental issue of the institutional-political power of affluent white communities, and how they have been able to mobilize that power to maintain control over the most valuable educational resources (Bell, 2004; Dumas, 2007).

This is what Fraser calls the *problem of displacement.* Here, "questions of recognition [serve] less to supplement, complicate and enrich redistributive struggles than to marginalize, eclipse and displace them" (2000, 108). Where leftist activists once put forth a vulgar economistic political agenda, in this historical moment they run the risk of advancing a vulgar culturalist agenda, in which the celebration of difference becomes synonymous with, or *the* catalyst for, social justice, rather than a crucial component.

At Rainier Beach, what we see is a kind of "soft displacement." Hollins, in shifting the focus from state culpability to community sensitivity, effectively dismisses redistributive politics without refuting the need for redistribution. Hollins laments inadequate state funding for education and disparate fundraising ability between north and south end schools; she then describes and quickly rejects a plan that would "tax" private donations to affluent schools. Earlier in this chapter, I noted that theorizing redistribution and recognition involved deliberations over the substantive and strategic "worth" of a particular politics. Here, I am not sure if Hollins rejects redistributing funds because it is substantively unjust, strategically infeasible, or perhaps both. From a neoliberal perspective, mandating a sharing of these resources is tantamount to state interference in the market. Schools in the north end have been effective at attracting affluent families and experienced teachers, at least in part because of their private endowments, which have served to enhance their prestige and reputation. Families choose to purchase homes in these neighborhoods with the understanding that (neighborhood) membership has its privileges, including better schools. Forcing these schools to give up some of their resources reduces property values, punishes those with individual initiative and capital, and stunts the kind of competition that could improve all schools by raising the bar of what counts as a "good" school. This, then, is the (neoliberal) argument against redistribution on the basis of substance.

Municipal leaders in Seattle have also expressed concern over the years that various forms of redistribution in the area of education are strategically problematic, because they contribute to white flight, either to the suburbs or to private schools (Kohn, 1996). I am not sure that Hollins is making the argument that the city cannot risk losing the favor of affluent whites in the north end, although that case certainly has been made. For the purpose of this discussion, I am going to assume that the theory advanced by Hollins and others at Rainier Beach is that it is substantively wrong to demand that north end communities share resources, not because they should not share but because it isn't respectful of their individual and neighborhood rights, *and* also because, strategically, an approach that encourages them to "recognize" their neighbors is more likely to lead to some amount of social justice than an explicit politics of redistribution.

Now, then, what to make of Don Alexander's contestation of this argument? Why might he insist that equitable resourcing is a district decision? I would suggest that Alexander does not trust recognition politics to do the job of redistribution politics. Although he probably would agree with the goal of improving cross-cultural dialogue and understanding, he would not see it as a sufficient means to improving educational opportunities for children in south end neighborhoods. And to be clear, I do not think Hollins would make that argument either. The critical difference is that Hollins situates recognition politics at the center of her effort to achieve funding equity; Alexander seems to fear that this focus displaces the struggle for redistribution.

Such fear is not unfounded. As Fraser points out, a cultural approach to rectifying maldistribution would make sense only in a society in which the economic system is totally subordinate and dependent on cultural processes. This, she argues, is not our reality. Although we can easily point to examples where each influences the other, economic processes also operate independently. "Markets follow a logic of their own," Fraser contends. "As a result, they generate economic inequalities that are not mere expressions of identity hierarchies" (2000, 111, 112). It is not clear simply from the narrative of the community forum that Alexander is offering a critique of market forces in education, but, at the very least, he seems to express some wariness of reform efforts which might distract us from a focus on redistribution.

"It Could Be a Collective Kind of Community Effort . . ."

In Nancy Fraser's work, the *redistribution–recognition dilemma* denotes the tension between the contradictory approaches to group difference in redistribution and recognition politics. Redistribution politics, Fraser contends, tend to de-emphasize differentiation between groups, since it is these kinds of distinctions that are seen to legitimize and exacerbate unequal economic arrangements. In sharp contrast, recognition politics highlights group difference. The understanding here is that it is the specificity of a devalued group's identity that makes it a target for social disregard, and the various forms of injustice that follow.

The redistribution–recognition dilemma is not as relevant in social justice claims based primarily in demands for either redistribution or recognition. For example, class-based claims call for redistribution, but have little to do with group identity (at least not in the US, since the new social movements of the 1960s and 1970s). Struggles for lesbian, gay, bisexual, and transgender equality have their bases in misrecognition. Although there may be economic ramifications, the actual basis for oppression is in the sphere of recognition. In the cases of race- and gender-based claims, however, Fraser makes the case that both maldistribution and misrecognition form the bases for injustice. Race and gender, therefore, can be considered *bivalent* modes of social differentiation. The dilemma is that groups engaged in bivalent struggles must claim and deny the significance of difference. Fraser offers some guidance for addressing the redistribution–recognition dilemma, which I will discuss a bit later. For the moment, I want to think about how this dilemma surfaces in the discussion at Rainier Beach.

As should be clear by now, education inequities in Seattle (and throughout the nation) are clearly delineated by race and class. However, race is, and has historically been, the great divide. In Seattle Public Schools statistics, African Americans find themselves on the bottom of nearly every indicator of educational achievement. Other groups at the bottom include Samoans,

Native Americans and certain East African and Southeast Asian immigrants (Wright, 2003). The racial divide is also a spatial divide. Seattle is certainly less segregated today than thirty years ago, although African Americans remain the most residentially segregated racial or ethnic group (Orians, 1989). The other troubling spatial phenomenon is the intensifying gentrification of the historically black Central District, which has had the effect of pushing poor and middle-class black folks out of the center city and, increasingly, out of the city altogether and into low-income inner-ring suburbs. Related to these disparities in education and housing opportunity, black people in Seattle experience about twice the rate of unemployment as whites. Black people are also overrepresented in the state's prisons. Although African Americans are only 3 percent of the population of Washington state, they represent nearly a quarter of those incarcerated (Bureau of Justice Statistics, 1996).

Education politics in Seattle and throughout the nation becomes a "race thing," and specifically a "black thing" precisely because of the history of intentional racial exclusion in education, housing and employment, and ongoing race and class discrimination in the criminal justice system. Each of these reinforces the other, such that it is common for social scientists and policy analysts to speak of them in the same breath (Anyon, 2005; Marable and Mullings, 1994; Wilson, 1996). I would argue that, historically, black leaders, educators, and activists, in surveying this terrain of racial injustices, have placed faith in education as *the* primary way to overcome or transcend, to "uplift the race." In this way, then, education politics becomes an identity-based politics, a politics of (racial) recognition.

What becomes curious about the exchange at Rainier Beach is, first, the lack of discussion about blackness. To be sure, it is there, embedded in the pained, knowing laughter from the audience, and in Alexander's use of the word "miseducation," a discursive referent to Carter G. Woodson's (1933) classic manifesto, *The Miseducation of the Negro*. However, blackness is never named in the discussion after Hollins's speech. Related to this, the second curiosity is the near-confessional narrative on whiteness. Whiteness is very much at the center here, from Hollins's plea for cross-town empathy to Jensen's admission of her own naivety to the final speaker's comment about white teachers' lack of awareness about their own privilege. I describe this as *near*-confessional because, in the face of Alexander's demands for redistributive action, the apologetics of white privilege quickly become the denial of white specificity and culpability. Hollins, who had just suggested that north end schools partner with, or adopt, schools in the south end (read: poor, mostly of color), makes clear that this is a "collective community effort" and that "*everyone* is responsible." There is nothing in her words that is so disagreeable: who would advocate shirking responsibility for young people's educational achievement? It is simply curious that there seems to be such a reluctance to admit the relationship between institutionalized white advantages and the maldistribution of educational resources. At the precise moment when those gathered are asked to consider a corrective shift in the economic arrangement, the language changes from confession about whites' *specific* position in relation to privilege to a *universalizing* discourse that brings everyone equally to the table of responsibility.

This, then, leads to the third curiosity: In an interesting twist on the redistribution–recognition dilemma, here the politics of recognition seem to rely on a *de-emphasis* of difference, whereas the politics of redistribution seek to *highlight* difference. It is Hollins and those who speak in support of her position who focus on cultural valuation and social esteem. Yet they ultimately want to flatten the distinction between communities served by strikingly different schools, and which occupy very different positionalities vis-à-vis social capital and political-economic resources.

Alexander, on the other hand, makes a strong distinction between north and south end schools, and identifies strongly with the communities of color who live in the south end. At the same time, his message at the forum is firmly rooted in the need for redistribution, and he shows little patience for all the laments about intergroup relations and diversity awareness. Instead, Alexander appeals to universal democratic values, such as equality and justice—in a sense arguing that children of color should be treated the same as white children. Of course, neither Alexander's nor Save Our Southend Schools' politics are fully represented in this one narrative. In fact, underlying his redistributive narrative is a subtext of racial group differentiation that would have been obvious to everyone in attendance. Hollins, though, appropriates the language of difference to reframe the politics of recognition so as to effectively deny the validity of a racially or spatially situated narrative, particularly one that dares to demand reallocation of economic resources in response to racial inequities.[6] Thus, in this instance difference is presented as not making a difference at all.

"If We Continue to Rail Against the System . . ."

Chastising Don Alexander, the final speaker at the community forum suggests that the real problem in public schools is not systemic inequities but the quality of relationships, specifically between white teachers and students of color. After all, she insists, "we are *all* part of the system." I would contend that it is the *system*—institutionalized processes of dominance and (dis)advantage—which serves as the mechanism through which inequitable relationships are formed and produced. Maldistribution and misrecognition are, in this sense, instantiations of the system, left unchecked. To be fair, the speaker probably means to imply that, although the system is unfair, the way to change it is to pursue reforms, rather than to critique it. Even so, this reluctance to "rail against the system" tends to silence radical ideas—that is, it dismisses transformative proposals that go to the root of systemic problems.

Fraser makes a useful distinction between what she calls *affirmative* and *transformative* remedies for social injustice. Understanding this distinction also sets us on a path toward resolving the redistribution–recognition dilemma. Affirmative remedies are those that address the outcomes of social inequities without changing the structures that create and reproduce them. In contrast, transformative remedies aim to correct social inequities by changing the institutions, ideologies and processes that generate unequal outcomes. Fraser makes clear that the difference between affirmative and transformative remedies cannot be understood in terms of "reform versus revolution" or "gradual versus apocalyptic change" (Fraser and Honneth, 2003, 74). Rather, the distinction turns on the level at which the respective remedies intervene in social injustice: affirmative remedies respond to outcomes, while transformative remedies address root causes (see Figure 3.1).

Affirmative remedies for educational maldistribution might include allocation of additional funds to schools in low-income communities. Indeed, Seattle's weighted-student formula (WSF), which I mentioned earlier, does just this. Another possible remedy might be to offer special opportunities for low-income students to transfer to better-resourced schools. School desegregation could be an example of an affirmative redistributive remedy, *if* it were pursued on the basis of socio-economic class, rather than race (Kahlenberg, 2006). Efforts to desegregate on the basis of race have historically been based on the assumption that segregated schools damage the self-esteem of students of color and foster intergroup prejudice (see Frankenberg, Lee, and Orfield, 2003). Of course, desegregation advocates have also pointed to the relative lack of educational resources in

	REDISTRIBUTION	RECOGNITION
affirmative remedies	class-based school desegregation supplemental resources for low-income schools	race-based school desegregation multicultural/diversity awareness
transformative remedies	deep-structural shifts in school-funding formulas *(as a result of radical economic shifts outside the sphere of education)*	critical multiculturalism

Figure 3.1 Examples of affirmative and transformative remedies for educational maldistribution and misrecognition

predominantly black and Latino schools, which suggests that desegregation also has a redistributive function. However, given that the redistribution is based on membership in a culturally disregarded group, it is fair to say that racial desegregation is popularly understood as an affirmative remedy for educational *misrecognition*. Other than racial desegregation, the most common remedy of this type has been diversity awareness, which has traditionally focused on fostering appreciation of various group differences.

Transformative remedies for educational maldistribution usually necessitate a systemic change in how resources get allocated, not simply to ensure that poorer children are able to access additional resources but, more radically, to ensure that how resources get allocated is not dependent on who is to receive them. Political-economic analyses of urban education funding (Anyon, 1997; Apple, 2001; Dumas and Anyon, 2006) reveal that middle- and upper-class communities consistently and powerfully exercise their political influence to garner more than their fair share of education dollars. Even when school districts have made some effort to direct more dollars to poor and working-class communities, affluent communities have been able to ensure that a range of federal, state, and local policies are in place so that less of their dollars will be available for redistribution in the first place. For this reason, it may be true that there are no truly transformative redistributive remedies in the area of education *per se*, since the roots of educational maldistribution are beyond the purview of education policy (Anyon, 1997). Still, as I will explain in a moment, it is important to think about what might be done in schools as part of a broader transformative redistributive politics.

With regard to transformative remedies for *misrecognition*, Fraser argues that instead of attempting to raise the self-esteem of devalued groups, we "destabilize existing status differentiations and change everyone's self-identity" (Fraser and Honneth, 2003, 75). In education, this has been at the center of the critical multiculturalist project (Giroux, 1997; Leonardo, 2005; McLaren, 1995). Critical multiculturalism differs from traditional (affirmative) approaches to multiculturalism in that it emphasizes the role of state and market forces in the formation of both esteemed and devalued group identities, and aims to challenge the ideological foundations (and not simply the overt manifestations) of white supremacy, patriarchy, hetero-normativity, and class dominance. Some concrete transformative remedies for educational misrecognition might include ending school tracking, and "revaluing" all students as gifted, or "transforming" the curriculum, which goes beyond adding texts by devalued authors to rethinking what counts as knowledge.

Fraser argues that affirmative remedies are often more palatable because they are more consistent with hegemonic ideas about the liberal welfare state and mainstream multiculturalism. Transformative remedies require a shift toward a more socialist economic structure and a radical re-envisioning of the meaning and function of identity and cultural politics; such remedies, therefore, are more antagonistic to the status quo. I'll come back to this issue in a moment. However, Fraser identifies two problems with affirmative remedies. First, in the area of *recognition*, affirmative approaches tend to reify fixed notions of collective identity. That is, by focusing on one axis of identity, these remedies tend to ignore the complexity of the multiple identities embodied in each individual, and the fluidity and tensions inherent in the processes through which any given group comes to assert its identity and welcome individuals into its collective—or not.

The second problem relates to affirmative *redistributive* remedies. By not addressing the deep-structural causes of economic inequality, the liberal welfare state must continually—and somewhat begrudgingly—transfer resources to poor people. In our present economic system, corporations and the wealthy have any number of tax shelters; therefore, the poor are largely subsidized by the middle class. This creates a situation in which poor people become blamed for their perpetual state of need; they become *culturally* devalued as a result of *economic* policies that are structured to keep a large number of people underpaid or unemployed. Thus, affirmative redistribution remedies can translate into a problem of misrecognition. As Fraser explains, "their net effect is to add the insult of disrespect to the injury of deprivation" (Fraser and Honneth, 2003, 77).

Transformative remedies tend to avoid these problems, and also provide a resolution to the redistribution–recognition dilemma. In this vein, recognition politics challenge *everyone* to re-envision who they are, and redistributive politics focus on the need to systematically eliminate poverty, rather than cast a spotlight on the poor. However, as I mentioned earlier, transformative remedies are more of a threat to the status quo, and, as a result, are less likely to win broad support, at least not immediately. And speaking of immediacy, therein lies the other challenge—poor people and culturally devalued groups have needs for aid and redress that cannot wait until the adoption of more deep-structural economic and social transformations. How can a radical politics—with its focus on envisioning an equitable and just future—speak to those groups who must survive in the inequitable and unjust present?

Fraser contends that the pursuit of what she calls "nonreformist reforms" allows us to respond to immediate needs, while building a foundation for more radical change. That is, we can strategically utilize affirmative remedies to create the conditions for transformative remedies. Again, this is not equivalent to gradualism, in which it is assumed that liberal reforms will naturally and inevitably bring broad social change. Here, affirmative remedies are pursued radically and persistently, in an effort to shift the balance of power, and not as ends in themselves. Fraser presents a number of specific strategies, and complicates these throughout her work. For the purpose of our discussion here, what is appealing about nonreformist reforms is that they address immediate needs for redistribution and recognition as people understand these needs in the present moment, while at the same time "[setting] in motion a trajectory of change in which more radical reforms become practicable over time" (Fraser and Honneth, 2003, 79).

For Cleveland High, then, persistently demanding resources—"railing against the system" of maldistribution—might get a few extra dictionaries in the short term but, if *radically* pursued, could lead to a restructuring of school-funding formulas and, more broadly, call attention to how hegemonic cultural constructions of race and class identities translate into political and economic power in the north end, and disenfranchisement in the south end. This is what Fraser calls "cross-redressing," when we use measures which address one form of injustice to respond to the other. Here, fighting for dictionaries highlights the question of who has dictionaries and who doesn't (and why). In this way, the struggle for redistribution aids in the struggle for recognition.

I am perhaps a bit less convinced that most approaches to diversity awareness help to "cross-redress" maldistribution. However, there is some hope: A critical approach, to, say, teacher professional development might integrate some of the principles of critical multiculturalism in such a way that a foundation is laid for more radical insights. For example, teachers might be asked to explore the experiences of a group of African, Native American, Asian/Pacific Islander and/or African American parents or caregivers as they make meaning of what it means to be an "involved" parent. On the surface, this might appear to be an exercise in appreciating culturally diversity. Indeed, this seems to be what the final speaker at the community forum has in mind. However, we might challenge teachers to consider the question of parent involvement from the vantage point of ethnographic inquiry. This demands that they attend to the range of social, political, economic, and historical factors that inform and to some extent determine how a parent understands and engages their child and their child's school.

We might imagine that, over time, teachers will come to not only "appreciate diversity" but also develop a critical perspective on the relationship between maldistribution and the formation of group identities and experiences. Importantly, teachers might also gain insight into the complexity of these processes (i.e., the fluidity of identity and identity politics), and also examine their own positionality in relation to difference (i.e., understand that their experience is just as "different," just as particular as that of those perceived as Others). Pursued in this way, and pursued aggressively, such an affirmative remedy has the potential of effecting more transformative change in the long run.

Theorizing Redistribution and Recognition in Urban Education Research

"I Want to Convince Other People—If I Can . . ."
Education sociologist Stephen Ball has described theory as "a set of possibilities for thinking with" (2006, 1). By this he means to suggest that the purpose of theorizing is to imagine what may be, to experiment with various explanations for social phenomena, to map out options for political, intellectual or pedagogical intervention. In this way, Ball insists, theory helps us to "chip away at bits of the social, always looking for joins and patterns, but equally aware of fractures and discontinuities" (2). That is the spirit in which I have engaged in my analysis here: Rather than a definitive statement on education politics in Seattle, or an endorsement or indictment of any of the participants in the forum at Rainier Beach, I have used their narratives to unpack some of Fraser's ideas, to wonder about how redistribution and recognition enter our imaginations of urban education reform and renewal. In the end, then, my work offers possibilities, rather than a prescription for getting dictionaries at Cleveland.

I want to suggest three implications of Fraser's theory for urban education research. First, I would argue that it *makes explicit the terrain of struggle in urban education reform*. By highlighting the material and ideological bases of social policy, Fraser offers a theoretical frame for researchers to make sense of how social actors engage education reform, and engage each other in an effort to advance specific interpretations of what has gone wrong in the past, and what must be done to make education "better" now and into the future. What I take from Fraser is that there are rich discoveries to be made at sites of contention over the meaning of policy. Here, the focus is less on education policy *per se*, and more on how policy is imagined in everyday life, and how narratives are constructed in order to mobilize other social actors to coalesce around certain strategies or tactics. Historical and ethnographic research situated on the terrain of struggle complements more traditional policy-driven research by helping to explain the relative strength or weakness of support for certain policies at particular times and in specific contexts and by identifying tensions between the (best) intentions of education reformers and the political and cultural interests of a diverse polity.

Second, and following from this, a theory of redistribution and recognition *provides new ways to think about emerging tensions between race and class in education reform*. As race-based school desegregation and affirmative action lose favor, and as more people of color move into the middle class, some policy-makers and scholars have begun to argue that we need to shift our attention from racial inequities to class inequities (Kahlenberg, 2006). They suggest that class-based policies will be more likely to garner public support and will direct resources where they are most needed—to poor children of all racial or ethnic groups, including poor children of color, who, they would argue, are least likely to benefit from most race-based initiatives. Opponents doubt that shifting our attention away from race will improve opportunities for those who have historically been denied opportunities precisely because of race. What advocates of a class-based approach see as a positive step toward redistributing education resources, critics view as a move toward a new form of racial misrecognition.

I do not mean to resolve this issue here; I simply mention it because it is indicative of the emerging tension between race and class in education reform. Fraser provides theoretical tools to think critically about the limitations of (racial) identity politics, while also cautioning that a strictly redistributionist politics leaves intact those injustices based on cultural devaluation. For researchers, the theory provides a space and a language to explore how various social actors interpret the relative importance of race and class in determining educational maldistribution and misrecognition in their own communities and in others. It also helps us avoid simplistic explanations of racial politics; although race and ethnicity still inform how many of us imagine "community" or "identity," in practice, what that means for collective action is increasingly less certain.

Third, Fraser's theory *complicates what critical (nonreformist) urban education research looks like.* Michael Apple (2001) points out that critical researchers have a responsibility to "[provide] real answers to real practical problems" so that "critical education seems actually 'doable,' not merely a utopian vision dreamed up by 'critical theorists' in education" (227). The example is provided in a number of critical political-economic studies of urban education, by Apple, Anyon and others (Anyon, 1997, 2005; Apple, 2001; Apple & Pedroni, 2005; Lipman, 2003). In their works, they clearly document how capital and the interests of elites shape the trajectory of urban education policy. Heavily influenced by a broad tradition of democratic-socialist thought, their accounts provide a scathing critique of neoliberal economic policy, and advocate a radical redistribution of economic resources. However, when asked to identify concrete recommendations for education reform, they propose a range of things that are arguably more practicable—tax credits for the poor and working-class, additional funding for schools in low-income communities, improvements in compensatory early childhood programs such as Head Start.

Critical education researchers understand, with Fraser, that disenfranchised and devalued communities have immediate needs that are most realistically addressed through affirmative remedies. I would propose that the task for our research now is to examine how such remedies come to have the potential of being "nonreformist reforms." Historical work with this intent might trace the nonreformist impulses of specific campaigns for educational equity. Ethnographic and other qualitative research could focus on how community organizers and teacher-activists understand the gap between their educational dreams and what they understand as the current educational reality. This is the scholarship we all need: research rooted in a critical understanding of injustice and imbued with a sense of hope that transformation is indeed possible.

Notes

1   This research was made possible by dissertation fellowships from the Spencer Foundation and from The Graduate School and University Center of The City University of New York.

2   Neoliberal ideology advances the idea that inherent individual and group differences explain inequality, as opposed to the practices of the market. Since identity politics also call attention to, and celebrate group differences, the critique is that this inadvertently provides justification for the neoliberal project.

3   The US Supreme Court is currently reviewing the constitutionality of Seattle's so-called "racial tiebreaker," a policy that offered a racial preference for underrepresented groups at oversubscribed high schools. The policy has not been in effect since 2001, soon after the case, *Parents Involved in Community Schools v. Seattle School District No. 1*, was first filed. The district has indicated that it may not reinstate the policy even if it wins the case. In any case, the racial tiebreaker, which affected admission at only five of the city's ten high schools, does not constitute a plan to racially balance the public schools.

4   The description of the community forum is based on a video-recording of the event (Hollins, 2004). Given that the camera is fixed on Caprice Hollins at the podium, some details (e.g., racial identities of participants, Alexander leaning on his cane) are based on other sources of information and, in the case of Alexander, some literary license based on my observations of him on other occasions.

5   This is an often-repeated statistic in Seattle. See, for example, Thompson, 2005.

6   Elsewhere (Dumas, 2007) I argue that growing class divisions within black communities and transformations in the collective imagination of black affinity and solidarity have precipitated a shift in contemporary black education politics such that we can no longer assume that black leaders, educators, and activists (most of whom are middle-class) will identify with, or accurately represent, the interests of black students in urban public schools (who tend to come from relatively poorer families). In this context, we might see an unsettling of traditional recognition politics, a renewed focus on economic concerns, and, as a result, a more class-conscious articulation of priorities in black education activism. This neither resolves nor invalidates Fraser's redistribution–recognition dilemma. However, it complicates matters a bit, which from Fraser's perspective is certainly preferable to the kind of displacement of redistribution politics we have witnessed in recent years.

References

Anyon, J. (1997). *Ghetto Schooling: A Political Economy of Urban Educational Reform*. New York: Teachers College Press.

Anyon, J. (2005). *Radical Possibilities: Public Policy, Urban Education, and a New Social Movement*. New York: Routledge.

Apple, M. W. (2001). *Educating the "Right" Way: Markets, Standards, God, and Inequality*. New York: Routledge.

Apple, M. W., and Pedroni, T. C. (2005). Conservative Alliance Building and African American Support of Vouchers: The End of Brown's Promise or a New Beginning? *Teachers College Record*, 107: 9, 2068–2105.

Ball, S. J. (2006). *Education Policy and Social Class: The Selected Works of Stephen J. Ball*. London and New York: Taylor & Francis.

Bell, D. (2004). *Silent Covenants: Brown v. Board of Education and the Unfulfilled Hopes for Racial Reform*. New York: Oxford.

Bureau of Justice Statistics (1996). *Correctional Populations in the United States, 1996*. Washington DC: US Department of Justice.

Crenshaw, K., Gotanda, N., Peller, G., and Thomas, K., editors. (1995). *Critical Race Theory: The Key Writings that Formed the Movement*. New York: The New Press.

Delgado, R., and Stefancic, J., editors. (2000). *Critical Race Theory: The Cutting Edge*. Philadelphia: Temple University.

Dumas, M. J. (2007). *Sitting Next to White Children: School Desegregation in the Black Educational Imagination*. Unpublished doctoral dissertation, City University of New York Graduate Center, New York.

Dumas, M. J., and Anyon, J. (2006). Toward a Critical Approach to Education Policy Implementation: Implications for the (Battle)field. In M. Honig editor, *New Directions in Education Policy Implementation: Confronting Complexity*. Albany: State University of New York.

Fine, M., and *et al.* (2004). *Echoes of Brown: The Faultlines of Racial Justice and Public Education*. New York: The Graduate Center, City University of New York.

Frankenberg, E., Lee, C., and Orfield, G. (2003). *A Multiracial Society with Segregated Schools: Are We Losing the Dream?* Cambridge, MA: Harvard University Civil Rights Project.

Fraser, N. (1995). From Redistribution to Recognition? Dilemmas of Justice in a "Post-socialist" Age. *New Left Review*, 212, 68–93.

Fraser, N. (2000). Rethinking Recognition. *New Left Review*, 3, 107–121.

Fraser, N., and Honneth, A. (2003). *Redistribution or Recognition: A Political-philosophical Exchange*. London: Verso.

Fraser, N., and Naples, N. A. (2004). To Interpret the World and to Change It: An Interview with Nancy Fraser. *Signs*, 29: 4, 1103–1124.

Giroux, H. A. (1997). *Pedagogy and the Politics of Hope*. Boulder: Westview.

Harrell, D. C. (2006, June 2). School District Pulls Web Site After Examples of Racism Spark Controversy. *Seattle Post-Intelligencer*.

Hollins, C. (2004). Ending Disproportionality in Our Schools: The Seattle Channel (www.seattle channel.org/videos/video.asp?ID=3307).

Kahlenberg, R. D. (2006). *A New Way on School Integration*. New York: The Century Foundation.

Kelley, R. D. G. (1997). *Yo' Mama's Disfunktional*. Boston: Beacon.

Kohn, L. (1996). *Priority Shift: The Fate of Mandatory Busing for Seattle and the Nation*. Seattle: RAND/University of Washington.

Leonardo, Z., editor. (2005). *Critical Pedagogy and Race*. Malden, MA: Blackwell.

Lipman, P. (2003). *High Stakes Education: Inequality, Globalization and Urban School Reform*. New York: RoutledgeFalmer.

McLaren, P. (1995). *Critical Pedagogy and Predatory Culture*. New York: Routledge.

Marable, M., and Mullings, L. (1994). The Divided Mind of Black America: Race, Ideology and Politics in the Post Civil Rights Era. *Race & Class*, 36: 1, 61–72.

Noguera, P. (2003). *City Schools and the American Dream*. New York: Teachers College Press.

Orfield, G., and Eaton, S. E. (1996). *Dismantling Desegregation*. New York: The New Press.

Orians, C. E. (1989). *School Desegregation and Residential Segregation: The Seattle Metropolitan Experience*. Seattle: University of Washington.

Sayer, A. (2001). For a Critical Cultural Political Economy. *Antipode*, 33: 4, 687–706.

Taylor, Q. (2006). Into the 21st century, 1951–2000: The Black West in the modern era, *African Americans in the West*. Seattle: University of Washington.

Thompson, L. (2005). Schools Renew Push in Olympia. *The Seattle Times*.

Wilson, W. J. (1996). *When Work Disappears: The World of the New Urban Poor*. New York: Vintage.

Wright, S. F. (2003). *Seattle Public Schools: District Data Profile Summary*. Seattle: Seattle Public Schools.

Personal Reflection

Early Lessons

My introduction to critical theory came at the age of seven, when my mother sat me down to instruct me on the ways of white folks. Because I was a Black boy, she explained, some white teachers would assume that I was less intelligent, and would be more likely to find fault in my work and my behavior. I needed to keep my head down and concentrate on my schoolwork, she advised, but I also had to be vigilant, keeping my eyes open for the injustices that I would inevitably endure.

"If you have a problem in that school," she told me, "you come home and tell me, and I'll be up there the next day." ("However," she warned, "if you've caused the problem, I'm gonna be on your behind.") Most importantly, my mother insisted, I must never, ever believe the lies I would hear about myself, and about Black people in the second grade, or in the many years of schooling to follow.

Decades before I encountered theories of social and cultural reproduction, critical race theory, or whiteness studies, my mother offered me the necessary theoretical framework not only to discern (individual) acts of prejudice but to actually map the ideological terrain of willful ignorance and presumptuous arrogance which is the foundation of white racism. On some level, to be sure, my analytical maps were only as sophisticated as one might expect of a second grader. But I was also able to comprehend, if only in nascent form, some of the theoretical complexities of race: the difference between white friends, whom one may grow to love and trust, and *whiteness*, which could neither be loved nor trusted; the otherness of Black skin in the public imagination, which situated us as other-than-deserving, other-than-intellectual, other-than-civilized; and the link between racial oppression and "money problems."

All theory is, and what theory is, at its best, is a way to make systematic sense of "what's goin' on," as Marvin Gaye would say. I do not mean to dismiss the intellectual labor that goes into developing formal theory, much of which I have found quite useful (more on that in a moment); but I want to acknowledge that the roots of my love for theory were planted not in the academy but in the kitchen and at the barber shop and in the back seat of the church van, eavesdropping on adult conversations. And of course, in what my mother taught me to help me survive the experience of schooling.

I took from my childhood experiences in the 1970s and 1980s three lessons for engaging in theoretical inquiry. First, *no one theory will ever do.* As I heard adults deliberate on the issues of the day—the difference between how Black and white people responded to *Roots*; in exactly how many ways Ronald Reagan had it in for Black folks; why Vanessa Williams got her crown taken away; who brought crack into our neighborhoods—I might find myself swayed by this or that argument. For some time, that argument would provide the totalizing explanation, at least in my own mind. Then I might hear another conversation, or read an article in *Ebony* or *Jet* or our own local Black newspaper, that either countered that argument with another, or suggested a more complicated analysis that incorporated the earlier argument into a new one. Later, I would learn to identify some of these arguments as liberal or Black-nationalist or socialist, or some combination thereof. But most importantly, I learned that the richest, and most believable social explanations drew from a range of theoretical traditions. Those people who consistently espoused rigid allegiance to one theory always seemed to be the least sane, and the most illogical.

The second lesson is that *no theory is ever too radical for consideration.* Growing up, I always heard that "you could never put anything past white folks" because "there's no telling what they will do" to maintain their racial advantage or assert their superiority. In other words, one always had to remain open to the possibility that the seemingly ridiculous may, in fact, be true. More than a generalization about white people, this is a statement on how power is exercised and, more specifically, the extreme measures taken to concentrate power within certain groups. Understanding the material and ideological working of power requires not only more than one theory but also theories that uncover the structural "root" (the meaning of the Latin word from which the word "radical" evolved) of injustice. No suggested explanation can be prematurely dismissed, since—and I learned this from Granny, not Gramsci—those in power have us thinking *we're* the crazy ones.

Radical theories push back against this hegemonic "common sense," even if they are not always correct.

Third, I learned as a child that *theory is too often the nonsense of a bunch of people just interested in running their mouths.* Historically, Black people have been the objects of countless academic and government studies. The persistent "Negro Problem" has created a profitable industry in which experts offer explanations of who Black people are and why we do the things we do. On several occasions, I remember grown-ups laughing as they watched scholars and politicians pontificate about "Blacks" on the evening news, or discussed an article in the newspaper that sought to explain why unemployed young Black men sell drugs or why Black people were still so angry.

These mainstream interpretations of Black life failed to ring true usually because the proposed theory was offered with no believable supporting data. Instead of evidence, instead of anything that might connect ideas with Black lived experience, we were offered a rambling treatise on why such-and-such was so. We were to believe it simply because the speaker was Dr., M.D., Ph.D., M.S.W. the III, and more, the Director Professor President of the American Association Department of Whoknowswhatology. "A bunch of nonsense!" I would hear someone shout back at the TV screen.

Black folks could also be called to task for such pontification. I remember times in the barbershop, particularly, when one brotha or another would be going on and on about this or that issue. People would listen attentively for a while. Some might even nod in agreement. But if he seemed to get a little too cocky, a little too certain of the superiority of his point of view, someone would begin, "So, are you tryin' to say . . .?" If the response sounded too defensive or too simplistic, folks would start to laugh and slap their knees. "Man, you had me for a minute, but now you just talking mess" (or "bullshit," depending on the barbershop's profanity rules). "Yeah," another would say, "he just runnin' his mouth." Sometimes this would even make the pontificating brotha laugh and admit that no, he didn't have it all figured out.

These lessons on the uses and abuses of theory followed me throughout my graduate work. I became interested in Black discourses on education. I began to construct this idea of something I termed *the Black educational imagination,* which I took to denote "the polyvocal cultural processes through which Black political actors make meaning of schooling, knowledge and social mobility as paths toward (and perhaps spaces of) Black freedom" (2007, 6). In conceptualizing the Black educational imagination, I was influenced by my reading of such theorists as Antonio Gramsci, W. E. B. DuBois, Carter G. Woodson, Stuart Hall, Paul Willis, bell hooks, and Toni Morrison, among others. The very idea of a Black *educational* imagination actually came from Robin D. G. Kelley's concept of "the Black radical imagination" in his book *Freedom Dreams* (2002), in which he honors the diverse traditions of Black liberation thought.

However, what I want to emphasize here is that my interest in and passion for the Black educational imagination did not come from my reading of formal theory, as invaluable as that theory has been in my analysis. Rather, I had in mind the theorizing of organic intellectuals—to use Gramsci's term—that I heard as a child. Education was, and remains a central theme in nearly every narrative on Black freedom, whether the aim is garnering collective political power or simply making ends meet. From my mother's cautions about white teachers to the broader deliberation over school desegregation, I witnessed (and participated in) the Black educational imagination on the ground.

My concern in subjecting it to research and formal theorizing was that I might end up like the pontificating brotha in the barbershop, either spouting nonsense or simply using bigger words to describe what most (Black) folks already know. And beyond that, how could such a project offer a radical vision of education and Black cultural politics in an era in which the very idea of radical theorizing is viewed as passé, and a distraction from the seemingly more important task of educational measurement?

The answer did not come to me until I was already in the field, in Seattle, where I had decided to collect data for my dissertation research. My inquiry focused on how Black leaders, educators, and activists imagined and engaged school desegregation policy in the city from the mid-1970s to the present. I had interviewed a number of people already, and as much as they were interested in recounting past events, every single one of them indicated that they expected my research to offer direction for the future. However, the theories I had used to conceptualize the Black educational imagination focused primarily on critical analysis of the problem and a vision of what could be. They did not theorize how we might get from here to there. And that is what folks wanted to know.

So one day I was riding the bus and I pulled from my backpack political scientist Michael Dawson's book *Black Visions*, which provides a critical analysis of Black political ideologies from liberalism to Marxism to feminism to nationalism. I came across a section on the "Black counterpublic sphere." To explain the Black counterpublic and why it became so useful as a theoretical concept in my work, I have to first explain the idea of the counterpublic sphere, which Dawson explained comes from the work of political philosopher Nancy Fraser. Fraser contends that, in highly stratified societies like ours, discourse does not take place in a single public sphere. Rather, there are parallel discursive spaces in which subordinated groups construct oppositional interpretations of history, politics, and daily life. The Black counterpublic, Dawson explains, emerged not only because Black people were excluded from the broader public discourse and from other counterpublics (e.g., feminist and labor organizations) but also because Black people came to desire and believe in the need for alternative spaces in which to advance specific Black political ideologies and wrestle with questions of Black liberation outside the gaze and influence of whites.

My chapter in this volume is somewhat tangential to the dissertation, and evolved as I considered Fraser's work on the politics of redistribution and recognition, which directly takes up the question of how we theorize *remedies* for social injustice, in both public and counterpublic spaces. Her focus on the deliberate process of political theorizing again resonated with what I had witnessed happening informally, in the counterpublic spaces within the Black community in which I grew up and first encountered critical theory. Fraser's perspectival dualism recognizes the need for more than one theory, or even two theories. Her attention to the cultural and political-economic roots of social injustice keeps us necessarily open to *radical* explanations. And her insistence on identifying radical, or at least nonreformist, remedies provides a potentially more meaningful use of theory than simply running our mouths.

Reference

Dumas, M. J. (2007). *Sitting Next to White Children: School Desegregation in the Black Educational Imagination.* Unpublished doctoral dissertation. New York: The City University of New York.

PART II

Theorizing with Research Participants

CHAPTER 4

Theorizing Back

An Approach to Participatory Policy Analysis

EVE TUCK

Think of our work like that of a potato in the dark, complicating our perception and sensory surfaces by spreading out in search of something real we can use to survive.

Craig Gingrich-Philbrook, 2005

In February 2006 I co-founded a New York City-based research collective of high-school-aged youth, the Collective of Researchers on Educational Disappointment and Desire (CREDD). Though initially founded to conduct research on New York City public high school practices that push students toward the GED rather than the high school diploma, the group has decided to continue working as a collective, filling a gap in New York City's terrain of youth activists and organizers, researchers, and policy advisors. Now having completed our first research endeavor, the Gateways and Get-aways Project, CREDD is in the design stage for our next study while also training and collaborating with other youth participatory research collectives, and offering community workshops to share our findings and our methods.

This chapter addresses the complexity of the use of theory in educational research and policy analysis by describing how CREDD's Gateways and Get-aways Project has utilized Gilles Deleuze and Félix Guattari's theories of the rhizome, to critique policies regarding the GED. The chapter has in its sights the nexus of participatory action research and social theory. This is indeed a grappling with theory, with the practice of theorizing and the practice of contending with it. I see these as trajectories, flows where theory goes, the anticipated and unanticipated directions that knowing can take. The possibilities are exponentially cultivated when working within a collective, particularly a collective that may not be part of a theory's intended audience. By describing the ways in which my co-researchers and I have repositioned ourselves not only as the audience but brazenly also the co-theorists and counter-theorists of theories unintended for us, I detail an approach of *researching and theorizing back.*

Researching and Theorizing Back

Researching back is the practice of reclaiming and recovering knowledge and narratives that have been used against us by becoming researchers, while also contending with what research is and does and what knowledge is and can do. Researching back involves an inherent critique of the ways in which Indigenous scholars and Indigenous peoples have historically been excluded from researching while at the same time being open targets for being researched on. Researching back, a concept and methodology of recovery, knowing, analysis, and struggle gifted to us in Linda Tuhiwai Smith's *Decolonizing Methodologies* (1999), inspires the concept of *theorizing back* offered in this chapter. Theorizing back, a sister component in a larger decolonizing project, contains a critique of the ways in which whitestream[1] voices are constructed as rigorous, logical, reasoned, and valid while voices outside of the whitestream are considered experiential and emotional, representing devalued ways of knowing. Theorizing back, borrowing from Sandy Grande's notion of dialogical contestation (2004) involves a demystifying and de-deifying of grand theory in order to revise, resist, and refuse stereotypical or erroneous analyses of us and our communities.

CREDD's approach to researching and theorizing back arises from the range of frameworks and theories that each of us has brought to the collective. For example, CREDD researcher Jamila Thompson has deepened our understanding of researching and theorizing back by drawing parallels to Maroon societies. CREDD researchers Jovanne Allen and Alexis Morales linked researching and theorizing back to ideas of healing and proving the limitations of the reasoning of those who doubt us, while Maria Bacha has helped make explicit the connections to theories of community organizing. This chapter could have mapped researching back and theorizing back in relation to (in rhizome to) any of those traditions. But before I say more about our various traditions and experiences, let me provide a bit more background on who CREDD is and how we came to be.

The Collective of Researchers on Educational Disappointment and Desire and Participatory Action Research

I founded CREDD along with eight New York City youths to initiate a participatory action research project that would examine the lived value of the General Educational Development (GED) credential and the policies and practices within New York City public high schools that put particular youth on the path toward the GED rather than a path that leads to a high school diploma. Existing studies of the GED are in most cases stunningly void of youth and GED earners' or seekers' voices. Further, many studies focus on the depleted educational and/or market use-value of the credential (Boesel, Alsalam and Smith, 1998; Smith, 2003). For these reasons, the existing narrative of the GED, a narrative that documents both the increased numbers of youth who pursue a GED and the depleted value of the GED in higher education and employment, contains a major contradiction: Why are so many rushing toward a seemingly washed-up credential?[2]

This is a question that has anchored our research; without it, GED seekers, especially youth GED seekers, can too easily be perceived as having been duped or self-defeated. CREDD's research indicates that many students are, by implicit and explicit measures initiated by school administrators, teachers, school policies, and rules, *pushed* toward the GED and are misled about their rights to attend school or make a choice to attain a GED (Tuck, 2007; Tuck *et al.*, forthcoming; see also Advocates for Children, 2002). The GED's greatest lived value in the lives of students may be in being an alternative to schooling in a national and local climate where few true alternatives to test-based curricula exist; the GED may be more appreciated by students in New York City public schools not as a gateway to higher education and employment, but as a get-away from schools that fetishize standardized testing, that undermine student self-worth, and owing to political and economic pressures have harried, patched together visions of schooling's purpose (Tuck *et al.*, forthcoming).

A diverse group, my co-researchers represent a range of educational experiences, and most consider themselves push-outs. Most importantly, all of us bring to the collective an experience of feeling disenfranchised by schooling and unwelcome in our former educational institutions. Given our way of identifying and coming together, our process of research and method took on particular importance.

CREDD is a participatory action research (PAR) collective. PAR is best described as an epistemology and a politic rather than a determined set of methods or tools (Fine and Torre, 2006, 2004; Fals-Borda, 1997; Torre and Fine, 2006, 2003). As such, PAR supports the process of theorizing back. Its legacy in communities all over the globe, PAR calls upon both quantitative and qualitative methods to crack open access to knowledge-building and meaning-making often carried out behind the closed doors of the academy, the corporation, or government office (McTaggert, 1997; Fals-Borda and Rahman, 1991). In PAR, "people can choose or devise their own verification system to generate scientific knowledge in their own right. An immediate objective of PAR is to return to the people the legitimacy of their own knowledge systems as fully scientific, and the right to use this knowledge— including any other knowledge, but not dictated by it—as a guide in their own action" (Rahman, 1991, 15).

There are a variety of methods that can be modified to be participatory, and indeed, participatory research falls within a spectrum—not all sites and circumstances can support fully participatory research. However, many maintain that increased participation of stakeholders in research is a worthy goal across sites and disciplines (see the Participatory Action Research Collective at The City University of New York website: http://web.gc.cuny.edu/che/start.htm). Increased participation of stakeholders inverts power relationships of domination, and electrifies commonly held attitudes about knowledge, especially how knowledge is generated, held, shared, and used.

PAR is a praxis, and is made of many praxes, weaving theories and approaches. PAR includes five elements that differentiate it from other methodologies and from other participatory designs: (1) Questions are co-constructed; (2) The design is collaboratively theorized, negotiated, and co-constructed; (3) There is transparency on all matters of the research; (4) Analysis is co-constructed; and (5) The products of the research are dynamic, interactive, and are prepared and disseminated in collaboration (Tuck *et al.*, forthcoming). These five points serve not only as guideposts for those wanting to engage in PAR, but it is through these elements that we were able to develop our practice of *theorizing and researching back*.

Though other writings on CREDD's work have been collaborative and multi-authored (Tuck *et al.*, forthcoming; Collective of Researchers on Educational Disappointment and Desire, forthcoming), I write this chapter as a single author so that I am best able to discuss how I have, as a scholar, as co-researcher, as co-founder, brought an array of theories about which I am curious and passionate to my co-researchers. For me, as an Aleut woman from a working-class background, the project of researching and theorizing back is a mainstay; and for my co-researchers who are young women, who are of color, and who are working-class and who have in a range of ways been discouraged, disappointed, and excluded in their schooling, researching and theorizing back is profoundly resonant.

Purpose and Rationale

It is my hope that this discussion will demonstrate not only the multiple uses of theory in research—to destabilize and decenter conventional thinking that speaks against our experiences, to refuse to sit still and be researched, to rehistoricize our relationships to the colonizer and domination, to escape a "logic" that runs counter to our own knowing—but will also demonstrate the multiple participants (participatory audiences) of theory. It is in this interfacing of use and participants that theory unfurls most radically. Gilles Deleuze writes that when reading a book, the only questions that matter are, "Does it work, and how does it work? How does it work for you? If it doesn't work, if nothing comes through, you try another book" (Deleuze and Guattari, 1987, 8). Roland Barthes has said that reading is what happens when we look up from the page (Barthes, 1989). Deleuze's and Barthes's takes on reading leap easily to theory: what is powerful about theory is that kernel or universe of it that resonates; and, for me and for CREDD, powerful theories are those that resonate somehow even with unintended audiences. This resonance is at the crux of theorizing back: when we theorize back, we are aiming to understand what is at the heart of this resonance, and are working to articulate but not always resolve those (political, historical, powered) parts of a theory that do *not* resonate. Theorizing back is not about neatly packaged reconciliations, but *articulation* (speech and anatomy) of unlike parts.

Holding that theorizing and theory use are not contained only in the analysis phase of any research project, I will focus on the planning stage of the Gateways and Get-aways Project, in order to offer an example of educational research design as practical theorizing, or theorizing in the real.

Deleuze and Guattari are not the only theorists whose work we have negotiated in the Gateways and Get-aways Project, and by focusing on their work in this chapter I do not want to overrepresent the power of their theoretical work on CREDD's theoretical work. It is easy to become honorific with theorists and theories, easy to be—or at least feel like we should be—subservient to grand ideas and their masters. In many ways, my work with CREDD has taught me to give that up. Participatory work cannot be by invitation only, and though much of our collective's work as theorists may be as uninvited guests, our attendance or attending to these ideas can deepen the work of all of those at the table.

Rhizome

In this section I will address one of the many Deleuzian and Guattarian concepts that have come to life in CREDD's work—the rhizome. Much of the theory considered here can be found in their 1987 book, *A thousand plateaus*.

Though the theories of Deleuze and Guattari may be among the most underutilized in educational scholarship (Kamberelis and Dimitriadis, 2005) the rhizome is often the concept that theorists and researchers gravitate towards. The rhizome, the underground stalk or stem system of plants such as irises, asparagus, and ginger, but also of pervasive and invasive plants such as forest ferns and ivies, is used by Deleuze and Guattari as an epistemological and ontological model that is decidedly different from *roots and trees.* Of trees, they write, "All of arborescent culture is founded on them, from biology to linguistics" (Deleuze and Guattari, 1987, 15). Deleuze and Guattari critique aborescent culture or root-fetishizing culture as fascist, linear, one-dimensional, and uni-causal.

Encountering Deleuze and Guattari

I first read Deleuze and Guattari's work in a doctoral course on anti-oedipal psychologies with Eve Sedgwick. Not sure where my reading of their work was going, I read them with the open-handed hold that I use in my reading of poems—suspending disbelief, generous, ambivalent. My reading of their work spread out and out, beyond the course and over the months that followed. As I moved through preparations for my second doctoral exam, I noticed that many conversations with friend-scholars returned to the ideas that happened behind my eyes while on Deleuze and Guattari's pages, and, as I readied myself for my work with CREDD, I allowed the rhizome to be a quiet companion to my thinking.

I was eager to bring Deleuze and Guattari's work (along with the works of many other theorists, such as Taiaike Alfred, Gloria Anzaldúa, Marie Battiste, Kimberle Crenshaw, Vine Deloria Jr., Sandy Grande, Avery Gordon, Julia Kristeva, Cherrie Moraga, Edward Soja, Graham Smith, Linda Tuhiwai Smith, and Patricia Williams) to my co-researchers. Their first responses to the chunks of text on the rhizome were tepid; they found it interesting, but moved on to the next idea, the next task, the next flashpoint. It was several months later, when theorizing our dissatisfaction with one of our methods, when it made sense for us to return to Deleuze and Guattari's work.

In the Gateways and Get-aways Project, we used the "problem tree," an exercise in the popular education tradition, extensively in our project design process, in our data gathering in focus groups, and in our data analysis. In the problem tree exercise, a group begins with the identification of a problem. Then, the group dialogically maps the leaves, or the everyday symptoms of the problem. Next, the group maps the trunk, or the attitudes and beliefs that support the leaves. Finally, the group maps the roots, or the ideologies and structures that anchor the problem, unseen (for more on the problem tree, see Ferreira and Ferreira, 1997). We have seen the ways in which this tool has powerfully aided our mapping and understanding of the relationships between everyday experiences, hidden ideologies, and mainstream perceptions and attitudes.

However, while the tree is useful in excavating otherwise unseen linkages, it is decidedly unhelpful in plotting a course of action for political or social change. Must the roots of a problem be addressed in order to alleviate the stresses and pitfalls of the everyday expressions of the problem? Or, should the immediate goal be to address the symptoms of the problem in order to prevent ongoing suffering, which might leave little energy to make the structural and ideological changes needed for change to be sustainable? For CREDD, it made sense for us to escape from this chicken-or-the-egg-like conundrum, because it was linked to the very metaphor of the tree, and thus the very theory of relationship and change that we were using and trying to critique. "Nothing is more beautiful or loving or political aside from underground stems and aerial roots, adventitious growths and rhizomes" write Deleuze and Guattari (1987, 15). CREDD researcher Jodi Ann Gayle described the rhizome as "connections we can unearth and see."

Frustrated by arborescent, tree-like theories of social reproduction, youth and community "development," and deficit models of colonized peoples and non-whites, we have utilized the metaphor or paradigm shift of the rhizome to mark a departure from these root-fetishizing, tree worshipping theories toward interconnected, ever-seeking paradigms of relationships of knowledge, power, and practice. A part of the draw of the rhizome is the precise, poetic way in which Deleuze and Guattari describe it:

> a rhizome as subterranean stem is very different from the tree or root which plots a point, fixes an order.
>
> (1987, 7)

> a rhizome can be broken, shattered at a given spot, but it will start up again on old lines or on new lines.
>
> (ibid., 9)

> a rhizome ceaselessly establishes connections between semiotic chains, organizations of power, and circumstances relative to the arts, sciences, and social struggles.
>
> (ibid., 7)

> the method of the rhizome involves decentering (a power center) onto other dimensions and registers.
>
> (ibid., 8)

The metaphor of the rhizome reciprocally complements participation—and participatory action research—in a way that the tree as a metaphor cannot: the importance of ideas is dependent not on their origin but, rather, on their directions and distances. The collective moves in and out of ideas based on its needs, not a predetermined list of procedures, and, when making a misstep, it can retrace its paces and make a new choice, or leap and land, initiating a new path from which many other paths will now grow. Purposefully participatory spaces are spaces of ever-seeking linkages between peoples, places, subjectivities, histories, languages, texts, memories, and knowings. Deleuze and Guattari write, "Make a map, not a tracing. The orchid does not reproduce the tracing of a wasp; it forms a map with the wasp, in a rhizome. What distinguishes the map from the tracing is that it is entirely oriented toward an experimentation in contact with the real . . . A map has multiple entryways, as opposed to the tracing, which always comes back to the same. The map has to do with performance, whereas the tracing always involves an alleged 'competence'" (ibid., 12).

Sandy Grande describes Indigeneity as containing a "paradox of the tension between the urgency to border-cross and impulse to border-patrol" (2004, 95); the interfacing of Indigenous theory and theories of the rhizome demonstrates this paradox. When confronted by the US-sponsored, globalized, tree-narrative of colonization as a fixed event in time that is now over, that affirms only the historical tellings that coincide and reify first contact fantasies of the 13 colonies and "our" forefathers, that casts Native people as extinct or on the verge of extinction, I agree that "We're tired of trees. We should stop believing in trees, roots, and radicals. They've made us suffer too much" (Deleuze and Guattari, 1987, 15).

However, theories of rhizome run counter to Indigenous worldviews in some significant ways, primarily in the divergence of embracing a project that abandons roots for map-making of subterranean *stems*. Our senses of ourselves as Indigenous people are often intimately connected to our everyday tracing of passed-down stories and knowledge, to strengthening our links to the past and future, to attending to old ways in our new lives, and new ways in old lives. In this way, a sense of competence *is* involved, not mere performances of our identities or community binds, but rather and for the sake of future generations, a knowing that is bodied, explicit, lived, and passed on.

I raise this not because I believe that the rhizome and Indigenous worldviews need to be reconciled (a futile task) but rather to make explicit the ways in which theory use is complicated. This is not a rare instance; it happens at every nexus of theory, experience, culture, and memory. In pottery, when bringing two pieces of formed clay together, the potter makes scratches, or "roughs the clay" on each piece at the locations they will be joined. In theory use too, we rough the clay in order to hinge unlike, unfired textures and shapes. In the sections that follow, I describe how we in our design of the Gateways and Get-aways Project have roughed the clays of participatory theory, rhizome theory, and Indigenous theories of balance and interconnectivity.

Theorizing Back: Rhizoming Inquiry

Our theorizing back was an organic but self-aware, intentional process, that occurred in spurts and starts in CREDD's meetings, but also on the subway rides to focus groups or survey sites, during breaks from data entry, or in walks and long talks on the street corners of Manhattan, before we parted ways and went home for the night.

For example, early on in our reading from Deleuze and Guattari's introduction to *A Thousand Plateaus*, we talked about the barriers that limited the effectiveness of the rhizome as a metaphor. One of the researchers said, "We're city people, we've never seen a rhizome." I had grown up in a rural area, and I let the group know that the rhizome didn't charge any images in my brain either.

"A metaphor is supposed to help you explain things," another researcher said. "I can't go home and my mother asks how the project is going and I tell her, 'Oh we rhizomed this today,' she's not going to know what I'm talking about."

"It's not like we can go to the kids we are doing our survey and interviews with and say schools are trees and we have to make them be rhizomes. They'll look at us like we're crazy." The conversation shifted to roots.

"It's hard because all my life as a Black woman I've been told, 'go back to your roots,' 'don't forget your roots,' 'look to your roots.' My roots are important to me."

"Since we've been reading and talking about this stuff I've noticed how often I use roots in my everyday thinking. It doesn't work to just swap out roots and put in rhizome," another researcher commented. I shared with the group my similar concern, that as an Indigenous woman I had been raised to tend to my roots, and that I was suspicious of anything that told me that my roots aren't important.

It was several meetings later, when we were discussing something completely different that CREDD researcher Maria Bacha asked, "But maybe there's something to the rhizome's aerial roots?" In a prior session all of us had experimented in making and mapping our own rhizomes: on rolls of paper we drew the balances and imbalances of relationships among one another, our communities, our current and former schools, policy, theory, practice, and memory. These made for elaborate drawings. We used the internet to cull images of rhizomes, and when CREDD researcher Sarah Quinter found a series of up-close underground images of rhizomes, we were captivated by the presence of aerial roots. "We deepen our theorizing of aerial roots so that it's not as though our model has no roots, but a different *kind* of roots. The aerial roots are our personal and our people's histories. This is how we are reconceptualizing Deleuze and Guattari," Bacha continued. "This is how we are making the rhizome *our* work." This is theorizing back.

In many scenarios, communities, families, and disenfranchised individuals are forced to use data collected against them, indeed speak against themselves, to gain a "win" from powerful institutions. To protest a corporation's wrongdoing, for instance, a community has to prove that it has been *damaged.* For hundreds of years, Indigenous people in the US have been told by scientists that they are savage, under-civilized, simplistic, and inferior; and, in order to gain access to needed resources that are otherwise denied us, our communities have had to use these same words to describe ourselves.

Theorizing back requires us to reprove and reclaim theories that have been used against us, theories that we have mis/believed about ourselves, that have fed our own self abnegation, theories that have made us rely upon, cater to, offer gratitude to, and even congratulate the colonizer, and theories that, as one CREDD researcher has said, "paint us as lazy, crazy, and stupid" (Tuck *et al.*, forthcoming). Researching back and theorizing back are refusals to speak against ourselves, shifting the scrutiny off of our own bodies and rightly placing it upon the institutions that naturalize racism, misogyny, gross disparities of wealth, homophobia, and neglect.

Four Areas of Inquiry

A further example of CREDD's theorizing back through and with the rhizome is our approach to social inquiry. As a space of contestation, a major component of CREDD's project has been our refusal to concede to existing analyses of the GED, GED-seeking and earning youth, and pushed-out, exiled students *a priori.* To praxes rhizoming or delinking these circuitous, causal analyses from their objects, CREDD's approach to designing the Gateways and Get-aways Project was a tactic of complexity through inquiry.

Owing to the participatory and dialogical nature of our decision-making and design processes, CREDD decided to house our questions within four *areas of inquiry*, and I believe that this is one of the things that really worked about our process. The areas have served as a placeholder, a tie around a finger to be sure to carve out enough space for our project to be complicated and comprehensive.

Like other researchers, we believed that our study would only be as strong as our research questions. However, after spending full days during our first retreat trying to tame our dynamic, divergent yet inter-connected ideas into one to three research questions, we decided to reconcile with being unreconciled, to stop ourselves from the tree-like, arborescent task of streamlining, and hang out in the complexity. We moved our attention and energy to another element of our design. In the weeks that followed, we were a bit sheepish about the fact that, when asked about our research questions, all we could provide was a lengthy description of the complicated ins and outs of our research questions, and how we had, when compared to experiment-based research, organized our wonderings around four connected hubs. In rhizome fashion, we followed our hunches.

It was when we were deeper into our research, and when we had further developed the metaphor of the rhizome for our work, that we were able to fully appreciate our decision to work within areas of inquiry rather than one to three precise research questions: our areas of inquiry have helped us build involvedness, reflexivity, nuance, generosity, and I would say, reliability into our project. The rhizome, non-causal, ever seeking and ever linking, is a way for us to communicate how and why the GED means.

Further, as a strategy of cultivating and sustaining participation, having areas of inquiry rather than set questions has allowed us to reframe our questions depending on our audience or own subjectivities, while not losing what is salient about them in relation to the rest of our research.

Area of Inquiry One: The Value of the GED

This area is concerned with taking the existing literature that describes the GED as a depleted credential to task, primarily by seeking to understand the *lived value of the GED*. By engaging in PAR, which positions those upon whose back research has been historically done instead as knowers and experts, this project rejects depictions of youth GED seekers as being duped or self-destructive. Beyond these depictions an alternative possibility emerges: The value of the GED is not only in its being a *gateway* to employment to higher education; more importantly, its value is in its being a *get-away* from dehumanizing high schools.

Area of Inquiry Two: Push-out Practices in New York City Public Schools

This area is concerned with the implicit and explicit ways that students are (or are made to feel) unwelcome in schools. CREDD's research documents that students are most often encouraged to seek a GED in the second semester of ninth grade, and some students have been told by school personnel that they will likely "end up getting a GED, if anything," as early as seventh grade, two years before they set foot in a high school (Arenson, 2004, 3).

This area of inquiry seeks to determine exactly how this message comes across, and to understand what practices and policies specifically thwart student attendance. Dubbed "Operation Shove" by CREDD, public school push-out practices are a violation of students' legal rights to attend school until the age of 21 or obtain a high school diploma. By pushing and prodding very particular students out towards the GED, schools shirk their responsibility to develop real alternatives to schooling based on standardized testing.

Area of Inquiry Three: Alternatives to Standardized-Testing-Based Schooling

This area of inquiry is informed by our mistrust of most school leadership to adequately inform the public of alternatives to standardized-test-based schooling. Because I was aware of small New York City public schools that had lost the authority to utilize their own (portfolio) graduation requirements in lieu of standardized tests, I think I may have been too cynical to ever consider the issue of testing to be a crucial area of inquiry. However, my co-researchers smartly insisted that it be structured into our design. Though in its original version there was need and hope to document existing models that confound the testing model, the depressingly few examples we found inspired us to revise our inquiry plan in rhizome style, to instead document what GED seekers and earners *imagine* as good schools.

Area of Inquiry Four: (False) Meritocracy: How the GED Exposes the Myth of the American Dream

This area of inquiry is concerned with the widely held fantasy that the United States, particularly through its schooling, is a meritocracy (Carnoy, 1994; Hochschild, 1995; Labaree, 1997; Livingstone, 1998; Olsen, 1997; Persell, 1977). CREDD's theorizing of the GED as implicated in an escape from insulting school experience moves towards a score of complicated relationships to meritocracy: agnosticism; being bound (and gagged) to it; riding the horseback, coattails, wave, underbelly or bandwagon of it; being magnetized; sucked in; covered up; thwarted; tripped up and stuck with the bill (Fine and Burns, 2003).

Jennifer Hochschild's work on meritocracy and the American dream offers us a view of these narratives as being incomplete, entirely lacking a provision for failure, as "those who do not fit the model disappear from the collective self-portrait" (1995, 26). The lived experience of failure in schools is exceedingly vulnerable to a meritocratic narrative which individualizes and pathologizes failure. This serves to splinter both the spirit and communities of outrage that might otherwise convene.

Researching Back: Rhizoming Design

Our design planning process centered on playing out our ideas of what *research* should be—from developing and voicing a counter-narrative to tree-like and deficit theories, to the decolonizing project of researching back, to theorizing what it means to be recognized, and to soldering research to a legacy of rebellion. CREDD's design of the Gateways and Get-aways Project sought to put into practice anti-imperialist, anti-hierarchical ethics and epistemologies. At the same time, as a group women, mostly of color, including youth who might be perceived by others to have been "dropouts," we were aware from the very beginning that our work would need to stand up to intense scrutiny. One of our first design decisions was that our study would give the most space and credence to the voices and experiences of youth GED earners and seekers. Contending that it is those at the bottom of social hierarchies who understand most critically those institutions (in this case those who have been implicitly or explicitly pushed out from schooling *via* the GED) we made this choice not only because this perspective is missing from the existing literature but because we believe that this perspective is invaluable to our hard look at schooling in NYC (Fine and Rosenberg, 1983; Fine, 1991). It was a choice representing our politics, but also revealed who we saw as experts and knowers, and whose experiences would most fully inform our research. The Gateways and Get-aways Project included over thirty interviews with youth GED earners and seekers, and ten interviews with GED earners who had earned their GEDs as youths, but were in their thirties at the time of the interview. These interviews began by asking the interviewee to share "anything that you want to make sure I know about the GED and the GED experience," and moved through a series of semi-structured questions that ask the interviewee to theorize the GED alongside us. The material that came from the interviews often refuted mainstream views of the GED and the value of the GED; for instance, all of our interview participants maintained that the GED was an intensive, rigorous exam, while many outsiders may believe that it is an easy credential to achieve (Galloway, Stroble, and Tharp, 1999).

The design of the Gateways and Get-aways Project sought to expose and theorize back against mainstream perspectives on dropouts and pushed out students as nihilistic, self-destructive, unmotivated, and dull (Tuck *et al.*, forthcoming), and against perceptions of young urban women of color as uncomplicated, unthoughtful, and untheoretical. CREDD thinks of design as *practical theorizing*; we see our research design as a contribution to the ways in which knowing, lived value, meritocracy and desire, and educational options can be theorized.

We crafted our design to be dynamic and pedagogical in order to be mutually beneficial to those who participated in our interviews and surveys. Further, we wanted our design to be provocative, to consist of a series of small actions, to be pointing all the way along to embedded injustices, to demand that those who maintain the power to cloak themselves in silence speak, and to amass so many stories, so many tellings that audiences might be compelled to listen.

The Gateways and Get-aways Project utilized over 18 different methods, including focus groups, interviews, surveys, cold (unannounced) calls to employers and colleges, mapping, memoir, and organizing-research hybrids such as popular theater and popular education exercises, slam books, and school yard games (ibid.). The methods have worked rhizomatically to triangulate our quantitative data, our qualitative data, and our personal experiences.

For example, two CREDD researchers used their experiences as youths who had been pushed-out toward the GED to generate questions for several of our methods. On our survey (which would eventually be completed by over five hundred youths) we asked, "Some people say that some students are better off getting a GED rather than staying in high school until graduation; do you agree or disagree and why?"[3] We also asked, "Some people think that high schools benefit by getting rid of students who don't get good grades, don't pass Regents [New York state mandated exit exams], and/or don't attend classes regularly; do you agree or disagree and why?"[4] Then, in our interviews we asked, "Some people think that seeking a part of the value of the GED is that it is a way to avoid sitting in school for four years. What do you think about this idea?" Finally, in our focus groups with youths earning and seeking GED, we asked, "Some people say that getting a GED rather than completing high school is a cop out. Was this the case for you? Why do people think of it as a cop out?" The personal experiences of members of our collective inspired the lines of questioning, and then we developed statistical (from the survey), narrative (from the interviews), and dialogical (from the focus groups) data.

In another example, we interfaced our archival research of newspaper articles, scholarly articles, and NCES data with a series of two hundred cold calls to college admissions counselors and human resources representatives of well-known employers. In CREDD researchers' and our focus group and interview participants' experiences, youth are advised by school personnel to get a GED as an equivalent to a high school diploma, and as a route to higher education and employment. Many of those who participated in our study emphasized higher education as a goal (See also Boesel, 1998). However, the journalistic and scholarly literatures suggest that the GED does *not* work in higher education or employment as an equivalent to the high school diploma (Boesel, 1998; Marriott, 1993; Galloway, Stroble, and Tharp, 1999). One study found that the GED is likely to work as an equivalent to a high school diploma in employment for white men, but unlikely to work as an equivalent for men of color, women of color, and white women (Rivera-Batiz, 1995).

Wanting to update these data, CREDD used a combination of research participants' concepts of "dream jobs," local city and state employers, and Forbes' 2006 list of *Top 100 Companies to Work For* to compile a cold call list of approximately one hundred employers. Similarly, we crafted a cold-call list of approximately one hundred colleges drawing from research participants' "dream schools," local city and state colleges, and the 2006 *US News and World Report's* top hundred colleges. In our cold calls, we inquired about the employers' or colleges' acceptance of GED applicants, the frequency of acceptance of GED applicants, resources available to GED accepted applicants, and stories of success of GED applicants.

In our cold calls to employers, 50 percent indicated that an applicants' ability to fit into the company cultures was the most important factor in hiring decisions, and 35 percent indicated that the most important factor depended on the position sought. When we asked what degree they most preferred for a successful applicant to have, 64 percent indicated that it depended on the position sought, and 14 percent indicated a high school diploma, and 14 percent indicated a high school diploma or GED. When we asked if employers prefer for successful applicants to have a high school diploma or GED, 42 percent declined to answer, 33 percent indicated that they do not differentiate, and 25 percent indicated that they prefer a high school diploma. No one answered that they prefer a GED. Our finding that 33 percent of employers do not differentiate between the high school diploma and GED complicates the results of the prior studies described above.

In our cold calls to college admissions officers, 87 percent of those who agreed to participate indicated they accept GED earners, 11 percent accept GED earners as transfer students (often from community colleges), and 3 percent did not accept GED earners. However, when we asked about the most important factor in a prospective student's application, 38 percent answered the applicant's transcript, 27 percent answered the applicant's "whole file" of transcripts, GPA, SAT, etc., and 15 percent answered the applicant's high school GPA (totaling 80 percent). Admissions offices' reliance on these factors put GED earners at a disadvantage: a GED earner can be admitted on paper, but our findings reveal that it is rare for a GED earner to be admitted to these desired schools in practice. Ninety percent of those who participated in our cold calls indicated that one percent or fewer of their incoming students were GED earners. One private Northeastern college did state that GED earners' applications were reviewed in consideration of factors that were different from high school diploma earners, such as "work history." However, this school had not admitted a GED earner in the past ten years.

Re-visioning Change: Rhizome as a Unit of Analysis

The rhizome "connects any point to any other point, and its traits are not necessarily linked to traits of the same nature" (Deleuze and Guattari, 1987, 21). Concerned not only with rhizoming as an activity or as a way to describe behavior or performance, CREDD and I have thought together about the use of the rhizome as a unit of analysis, especially as a unit of policy analysis. Rather than looking in arborescent, tree-like style—for "causes"—we studied *relationships*. The rhizome as a unit of analysis has had a major impact on CREDD's design of the Gateways and Get-aways Project, and is at the heart of our decisions to carve out and work within our four areas of inquiry and to craft methods that would help us better understand the relationships involved between students, institutions, and communities, *rather than the origins or causes of the trend* of pushing students towards the GED rather than a high school diploma.

Learning from and building upon Jean Anyon's (1997, 2005) work in the political economy of education policy, in which she looks at social policy to help understand disproportionate outcomes in schooling, our view of the school system is in rhizome with:

- federal, state and city social policies around healthcare, homeland security, welfare, housing, policing, and prison
- federal, state and city education policies such as No Child Left Behind, state-mandated exit exams, and mayoral control
- mainstream attitudes and messages about the value of the GED in nexus with the lived value of the GED from the perspectives of GED earners and seekers and their communities
- school rules and practices that implicitly teach students that they are unwanted and that higher education was not intended for them in the first place
- school curricula and instruction that replicate racism, misogyny, homophobia, and the criminalization of poor people
- the unclear purpose of schooling anyway
- the shrinking number of real alternatives to testing-based curricula in attaining a high school diploma and the abuse of the GED as a cover for this lack of alternatives
- meritocracy as the dominant paradigm explaining the results of schooling and capitalism within a newly re-energized effort to maintain the legitimacy of an American dream that had no provision for failure.

A mouthful certainly, each of these hubs is ceaselessly in relation to the others, ceaselessly in connection with other rhizomes. "The rhizome is reducible neither to the One nor the multiple . . . It is composed not of units but of dimensions, or rather directions in motion. It has neither beginning nor end, but always a middle from which it grows and which it overspills" (Deleuze and Guattari, 1987, 21, *ellipses added*). In the more usual approach to education policy analysis by elites, recommendations are made to address the *symptoms* of the problem, relying on a tree-like symptoms-causes-roots model of change. Some *critics* of education policy, on the other hand, condemn policies that mitigate the surface structures rather than deep structures of inequality, inverting the model of change to roots-causes-symptoms. Both are hierarchical, aborescent schema, however.

A critique of policy analysis informed by the rhizome, such as CREDD's, breaks from this hierarchical schema by spotlighting the *relationships* among individuals, communities, and institutions; the shift to the rhizome as the guiding metaphor involves rethinking cost-benefit, cause-effect, input-outcome approaches toward a new object-relation that focuses on the space *between* institutions, communities, and families. In other words, the rhizomatic approach to educational policy analysis is concerned not with tracing problem to their roots but rather with mapping the relationships of a problem; thus, recommendations are geared not towards the origin or inversely the symptom but on improving, reworking, or upending the relationships upon which or within which inequity thrives.

As researchers, reorienting prior perceptions of a trickle-down vs. ground-up power dichotomy toward a vision of power that is generating, sweeping, shattering, in multidirectional motion, has resonated with the experiences that we have brought and have cultivated in our collective. Further, attending to the middle, to the space and relationships between and among students, institutions, rules, attitudes, implicit and explicit practices and policies has been exhilarating rather than daunting. Our design of in-rhizome areas of inquiry and pedagogical or interactive methods has yielded a clear construction of what is and is not working, what is triumphed and what is undermined, what is announced, voiced over, and silenced across and within these relationships. The policy recommendations that will come from the Gateways and Get-aways Project will be toward strengthening and dissolving existing relationships between current and exiled students, communities, schools, institutions of higher education and employment, media and policy-makers, and toward initiating new relationships.

This is CREDD's radical contribution to education policy analysis, an emphasized shift in object relations that focuses on relationships.

Closing

CREDD's theorizing back to the valuation of the GED and policies surrounding it, to assumptions regarding exiled students, and to Deleuze and Guattari's theories of the rhizome and relationships aided us in breaking apart the binaries of success-failure, cause-effect, reproduction-resistance, damaged-unaffected. Further, through our theorizing back of these concepts and our commitment to participatory action research, we have deepened these concepts, marked them by our use.

I close with the emphasis that theorizing back is messy, and complicated. It does not suffice to use theory and append a list of caveats. The caveats must be practiced, explored, and teased toward entering a conversation that has not included us, has silenced us, or has previously happened with Indigenous people, people of color, and poor people as the objects. Theorizing back requires that we shift the language or narrative of theory and policy so that they do not speak against us, and so that we in using them do not speak or act against ourselves. Further, we must reconsider our prior notions of change and rearticulate our relationships between and within knowledges, institutions, and practices. It is ongoing and ever-seeking, but profoundly rewarding work.

Notes

1   I use the term "whitestream" in the tradition of Claude Denis (1997) and Sandy Grande (2004) to signal the idea that while American society is not "white" in socio-demographic terms, it remains principally structured on the basis of the Anglo-European, "white" experience" (Grande, 2004, 9).

2   During the Second World War, and in response to critics of drafting teenagers into war and interrupting students' education for military time, the first GED exam was crafted in 1943 as a credential for veterans (Smith, 2003; Quinn, 1997). The GED, based on the Iowa Test of Educational Development, was used by colleges and universities as major tool for evaluating the 2.2 million veterans who entered higher education under the GI bill (Smith, 2003; Quinn, 1997). The GED quickly became an exam for civilians rather than veterans, particularly through the push of the American Council on Education, the GED's sponsor and lobbyist for college and universities' interests (Boesel, 1998; Smith, 2003). While it was established as an exam for adults, the rise in market value of a high school degree coupled with increasingly higher regimentation in secondary schooling has contributed to the growing population of teenagers who opt out of a traditional high school diploma for a GED. Between 1975 and 2000, the percentage of GED test takers ages 19 and below grew from 32 to 43 percent, while the percentage of GED test takers ages 25 and older fell from 41 to 33 percent (Smith, 2003).

While about one in seven diplomas in the United States was a GED in 1993, in 2001, about one in five diplomas in the United States was a GED. While about one in seven diplomas in New York City was a GED in 1993, in 2001, one in four diplomas in New York City was a GED. In the 2000s, more than a million people in the US, Canada, and US territories take the GED exam each year (Smith, 2003).

Although anecdotal evidence (Arenson, 2004) supports that school-aged youths are flooding GED programs traditionally designed for adults, there are few, if any, quantitative studies that effectively document this trend. As the current debate in New York state over graduation reporting standards suggests, we cannot appreciate the measure to which this is affecting New York City youth without uniform, transparent reporting practices (Ruglis, 2007). "There are no counts of how many students are in GED programs nationwide, but GED directors say that their programs are overflowing and that the number of young people has shot up" (Arenson, 2004, 2). In New York City, there were 25,500 school-aged students documented as enrolled in GED programs in 2001. This number rose to 37,000 school-aged students by 2003 (ibid.).

3   To be eligible to take the survey, participants had to be ages 16 to 22, and were current or former New York City public school students. Forty-three percent agreed that some students are better off getting a GED rather than staying in high school until graduation and 57 percent disagreed.

4   Forty-four percent agreed that high schools benefit by getting rid of students who do not get good grades, do not pass Regent's tests and/or do not attend classes regularly, and 56 percent disagreed.

References

Advocates for Children and Goldbaum, B. (2002). Are the Children Being Left Behind?" www.advocatesforchildren.org/pubs/pushout-11-20-02.doc. Last accessed June 2007.

Alexie, S. (1996). How to Write the Great American Indian Novel. In *The Summer of Black Widows*. Brooklyn, NY: Hanging Loose Press.

Anyon, J. (1997). *Ghetto Schooling: A Political Economy of Urban Educational Reform*. New York: Teachers College Press.

Anyon, J. (2005). *Radical Possibilities: Public Policy, Urban Education, and a New Social Movement*. New York: Routledge.

Anzaldúa, G. (1987). *Borderlands: The New Mestiza = La Frontera*. San Francisco: Spinsters/Aunt Lute.

Anzaldúa, G., and Moraga, C. (1981). *This Bridge Called My Back: Writings by Radical Women of Color*. Watertown, MA: Persephone Press.

Arenson, K. (2004, May 15). More Youths Opt for GED Tests, Skirting the Hurdle of High School. *New York Times*, 14.

Barthes, R. (1989). *The Rustle of Language*. Berkeley: University of California Press.

Billig, M. (1995). *Banal Nationalism*. London and Thousand Oaks, CA: Sage.

Boesel, D. (1998). The Street Value of the GED Diploma. *Phi Delta Kappan*, 80: 1, 65.

Boesel, D., Alsalam, N., and Smith, T. (1998). *Educational and Labor Market Performance of GED Recipients*. Washington DC: U.S. Department of Education Office of Educational Research and Improvement, National Library of Education.

Carnoy, M. (1994) *Faded Dreams*. Cambridge: Cambridge University Press.

Collective of Researchers on Educational Disappointment and Desire (Forthcoming) *The Youth to Youth Guide to the GED*. New York: CREDD.

Deleuze, G., and Guattari, F. (1977). *Anti-Oedipus: Capitalism and Schizophrenia*. New York: Viking Press.

Deleuze, G., and Guattari, F. (1987). *A Thousand Plateaus: Capitalism and Schizophrenia*. Minneapolis: University of Minnesota Press.

Deloria, P. J. (1998). *Playing Indian*. New Haven: Yale University Press.

Denis, C. (1997) *We Are Not You: First Nations and Canadian Modernity*. Peterborough: Broadview Press.

Fals-Borda, O. (1997). Participatory Action Research in Colombia: Some Personal Feelings. In R. McTaggert, editor, *Participatory Action Research: International Contexts and Consequences*. Albany: SUNY.

Fals-Borda, O., and Rahman, M. (1991). *Action and Knowledge*. New York: Apex Press.

Ferreira, E., and Ferreira, J. (1997). *Making Sense of the Media: A Handbook of Popular Education Techniques*. New York: Monthly Review Press.

Fine, M. (1991). *Framing Dropouts: Notes on the Politics of an Urban Public High School*. Albany, NY: State University of New York Press.

Fine, M., and Burns, A. (2003). Class Notes: Toward a Critical Psychology of Class and Schooling. *Journal of Social Issues*, 59: 4, 841.

Fine, M., and Rosenberg, P. (1983) Dropping Out of High School: The Ideology of School and Work. *Journal of Education*, 165: 3, 257.

Fine, M., and Torre, M. E. (2004). Re-membering Exclusions: Participatory Action Research in Public Institutions. *Qualitative Research in Psychology*, 1, 15–37.

Fine, M.. and Torre, M. E. (2006). Intimate Details: Participatory Action Research in Prison. *Action Research*, 4: 3, 253–269.

Fine, M., Tuck, E., and Zeller-Berkman, S. (2007). Do You Believe in Geneva? Methods and Ethics and the Global/Local Nexus. In C. McCarthy, A. Durham, L. Engel, A. Filmer, M. Giardina and M. Malagreca, editors, *Globalizing Cultural Studies: Ethnographic Interventions in Theory, Method, and Policy*. New York: Peter Lang, 493–526.

Galloway, J., Stroble, W., and Tharp, M. (1991, March 1). Not in the Army Now. *US News and World Report*, 126: 8, 14.

Gingrich-Philbrook, C. (2005). Autoethnography's Family Values: Easy Access to Compulsory Experiences. *Text and Performance Quarterly*, 25: 4, 297–314.

Gordon, A. (1997). *Ghostly Matters: Haunting and the Sociological Imagination*. Minneapolis: University of Minnesota Press.

Grande, S. (2004). *Red Pedagogy*. Lanham, MD: Rowman and Littlefield.

Hochschild, J. L. (1995). *Facing Up to the American Dream: Race, Class, and the Soul of the Nation*. Princeton, NJ: Princeton University Press.

Hochschild, J. L., and Scovronick, N. B. (2003). *The American Dream and the Public Schools*. New York: Oxford University Press.

Kamberelis, G., and Dimitriadis, G. (2005). *On Qualitative Inquiry*. New York: Teachers College Press.

Labaree, D. (1997). *How to Succeed in School without Really Trying*. New Haven: Yale University Press.

Livingstone, D. W. (1998). *The Education Jobs Gap*. Boulder: Westview Press.

McTaggert, R. (1997). *Participatory Action Research: International Contexts and Consequences*. Albany: SUNY.

Marriott, M. (1993, June 15). Valuable Diploma or Meaningless Piece of Paper? *New York Times*, 1.

Olsen, L. (1997). *Made in America*. New York: The New Press.

Perl, S. (1980). Understanding Composing. *College Composition and Communication*, 31: 4.

Persell, C. (1977). *Education and Inequality*. New York: The Free Press.

Quinn, L. (2002). *An Institutional History of the GED*. http://www.uwm.edu/Dept/ETI/reprints/GEDHistory.pdf. Last accessed February 21, 2008.

Rahman, M. A. (1991). The Theoretical Standpoint of PAR. In O. Fals-Borda and M. A. Rahman, editors, *Action and Knowledge: Breaking the Monopoly with Participatory Action Research*. New York: Apex Press, 12–23.

Rivera-Batiz, F. (1995). Vocational Education, the General Equivalency Diploma, and Urban and Minority Populations. *Education & Urban Society*, 27: 3, 3–13.

Ruglis, J. (2008). Dropouts. In S. Mathison and E. W. Ross, editors, *Battleground Schools*. Westport, CT: Greenwood Press.

Smith, G. H. (2000). Protecting and Respecting Indigenous Knowledge. In M. Battiste, editor, *Reclaiming Indigenous Voices and Vision*. Vancouver: University of British Columbia Press, 209–224.

Smith, L. T. (1999). *Decolonizing Methodologies: Research and Indigenous Peoples*. Dunedin, New Zealand: Zed Books.

Smith, L. T. (2005). On Tricky Grounds: Researching the Native in an Age of Uncertainty. In N. Denzin and Y. Lincoln, editors, *Handbook of Qualitative Research*. Beverly Hills: Sage Publications, 85–107.

Smith, T. M. (2003). Who Values the GED? An Examination of the Paradox Underlying the Demand for the General Educational Development Credential. *Teachers College Record*, 185: 3, 375–415.

Torre, M. E., and Fine, M. (2003). Youth Researchers Critically Reframe Questions of Educational Justice. Harvard Family Research Project's *Evaluation Exchange*, 9: 2, 6 and 22.

Torre, M. E., and Fine, M. (2006). Researching and Resisting: Democratic Policy Research by and for Youth. In S. Ginwright, J. Cammarota and P. Noguera, editors, *Beyond Resistance: Youth Activism and Community Change*. New York: Routledge, 269–285.

Tuck, E., and Fine, M. (2007). Inner Angles: A Range of Ethical Responses to/with Indigenous and Decolonizing Theories. In N. Denzin and M. Giardina, editors, *Ethical Futures in Qualitative Research: Decolonizing the Politics of Knowledge*. Walnut Creek, CA: Left Coast Press, 145–168.

Tuck, E., Allen, J., Bacha, M., Morales, A., Quinter, S., Thompson, J., and Tuck, M. (forthcoming). PAR Praxes for Now and Future Change. In J. Cammarota and M. Fine, editors. *Revolutionizing Education: Youth Participatory Action Research in motion*. New York: Routledge.

Personal Reflection

Reading and Writing Theory

For new scholars, myself included, reading and writing theory can be a project of stomach-quivering anxiety and trepidation. My first brushes with grand theory were uncomfortable, intimidating, uninviting. Though I have always been an almost obsessive reader, for many years I was so resistant to theory I even thought of myself as being *anti*-theory, in what I now understand was an attempt to reject a conversation that I was sure would reject me. Much of this had to do with assumptions that some of my prior teachers had about theory, and about me as someone without potential as a theorizer.

I reveal this about my first encounters with theory to illuminate what is necessary in the praxis of reading and writing theory (and theorizing back): a dedication to demystifying theory and its texts. Philosopher Gilles Deleuze has been crucial for me as a new reader of theory and an even newer *writer* on theory. I am affirmed and emboldened by his analysis of reading:

> There are, you see, two ways of reading a book; you either see it as a box with something inside and start looking for what it signifies, and then if you're even more perverse or depraved you set off after signifiers. And you treat the next book like a box contained in the first or containing it. And you annotate and interpret and question, and write a book about the book, and so on and on.
>
> Or there's the other way: you see the book as a little non-signifying machine, and the only question is "Does it work, and how

does it work?" How does it work for you? If it doesn't work, if nothing comes through, you try another book. This second way of reading's intensive: something comes through or it doesn't. There's nothing to explain, nothing to understand, nothing to interpret. It's like plugging in to an electric circuit . . . This intensive way of reading, in contact with what's outside the book, as a flow meeting other flows, one machine among others, as a series of experiments for each reader in the midst of events that have nothing to do with books, as tearing the book into pieces, getting it to interact with other things, absolutely anything . . . is reading with love. That's exactly how you read the book.

(1997, 7–9)

Extending Deleuze's strategy for reading books to theory (not a far stretch), the questions of "Does it work?" and "How does it work?" are useful criteria for engaging in a body of theory in order to further, contextualize, deepen, and contest your own research and scholarship. Deleuze's questions crack open for me elitist assumptions of who can and cannot grapple with theory, who should and should not have access to theory, what can be considered theory, and who can be considered a theorist; his questions challenge who is allowed as an audience of theory, what constitute the subjects and objects of theory, and the very project of theory. Applying Deleuze's strategy for utilizing books to reading and thinking theory also assists in penetrating the inner circle of who has "owned" theory—and supports access to theory for those who have historically been denied it, and upon whose backs some social theories have been mounted.

As an Indigenous woman, my own coming to theory is very much a part of that opened-up access, and has been facilitated by mentors who have encouraged me to speak and write aloud what I previously only appreciated as reader response. It is still at times almost excruciatingly unnerving to read and write high theory, requiring a vulnerability that chips away at the ad hoc practices of self-protective perfectionism I cultivated over my years as a student. Working through high theory requires a willingness to make public ideas and analyses that are pre-verbal and in many ways feel like a part of my being: there are things I want to express, but they are *mesas*, with sharp drops following any misstep or underestimation of the terrain.

From composition study, Sondra Perl's notion of the felt sense, "the feelings or non-verbalized perceptions that surround the words, or what the words already present evoke" (1980, 367), is bound to the ways in which I approach theory: through my own experiences and my own body, through the experiences and bodies of my grandmothers and mother and sister, through the stories of my Aleut people. "The felt sense is always there, within us. It is unifying, and yet, when we bring words to it, it can break apart, shift, unravel, and become something else" (ibid.).

Writing and negotiating theory by attending to the felt sense, and by reading with love as Deleuze offers, feels strikingly similar to how I approach the page as a poet—with an attention not to the objects but to the space between them, a curiosity in regards to scale, a spread towards new and forgotten words and images. Theorizing through the felt sense involves moving and pausing and seeing what resonates.

And theorizing *back*, out of response to other theorists, is also risky and humbling. For those of us who have been taught to be compliant to theory, critiquing and reworking theory can feel hazardous and sacrilegious. The punishment for talking back for Indigenous peoples and other disenfranchised groups in the United States is not confined to slaps and pinches, but is forced removal, dispossession, neglect, deportation, and imprisonment. Talking back in one's own language, for many of my elders, has had lifelong repercussions.

There are repercussions too for Indigenous people and people of color who engage in theory as if there were no difference, as if the ontologies and epistemologies employed in whitestream theory really can wash us with sameness. This washing only serves to reduce Indigenous people to the status of "whites without technology" (Grande, 2004, 64).

I write this to point to an obvious element of theorizing: the way we do it is in the way that we do other risky things in our lives. For me, this means that I approach theory with a firm belief in our rights of complex person-hood (Gordon, 1997; Fine, Tuck, and Zeller-Berkman, 2007; Tuck and Fine, 2007). It means that I approach my own theorizing with the responsibilities of preparedness and listening, reflection, and reparation (Tuck and Fine, 2007). Finally too, I approach theory with a steadfast commitment to group participation, as the risk of theorizing is mitigated and put in balance by working in a collective.

References

Deleuze, G. (1997). *Negotiations 1972–1990.* New York: Columbia University Press.

Fine, M., Tuck, E., and Zeller-Berkman, S. (2007). Do You Believe in Geneva? In C. McCarthy, editor, *Globalizing Cultural Studies.* New York: Peter Lang Publications.

Gordon, A. (1997). *Ghostly Matters: Haunting and the Sociological Imagination.* Minneapolis: University of Minnesota Press.

Grande, S. (2004). *Red Pedagogy: Native American Social and Political Thought.* Lanham, MD: Rowman and Littlefield.

Perl, S. (1980). Understanding Composing. *College Composition and Communication,* 31: 4.

Tuck, E., and Fine, M. (2007). Inner Angles: A Range of Ethical Responses to/with Indigenous and Decolonizing Theories. In N. Denzin and M. Giardina, editors, *Ethical Futures in Qualitative Research: Decolonizing the Politics of Knowledge.* Walnut Creek, CA: Left Coast Press, 145–168.

CHAPTER 5

Low-income Latina Parents, School Choice, and Pierre Bourdieu

MADELINE PÉREZ

On a cold evening in December 2006, hundreds of New York City parents gathered at the offices of Governor-elect Elliot Spitzer to deliver written pleas by public school students for better middle schools and a more equitable high school admissions process. Although the protest had an air of holiday cheer, the families of the students were chanting—not cheering.

> *Jingle bells, jingle bells*
> *Jingle all the way,*
> *All we want is good schools*
> *So our children can gradu-ate.*[1]

The protest was led by parent members of the NYC Coalition for Educational Justice (CEJ)—a collaborative effort of 12 community groups and unions representing tens of thousands of New York City parents. The group was organizing to end inequities in the city's educational system. On this December day, a top demand was for the creation of a position of Deputy Chancellor to revamp the public high school choice process, during which a hundred thousand eighth grades vie for spots in nine elite and hundreds of other high schools.

It is not difficult to understand why parents wanted changes in the high school admissions process. Two years earlier Schools Chancellor Joel Klein had stated during a press conference that "Eighty-six percent of the high schools in New York City are undesirable" (Herszenhorn, 2004). That so many schools were deemed inadequate would have been of concern to any New York parent—but felt even more urgently by low-income parents of color, most of whom could not exit the public school system into expensive private schools. Moreover, there had been evidence of ugly racial steering in the New York City schools, in which researchers documented widespread practices as a result of which white parents were informed of gifted programs available to their children, while Black and Latino parents were not (ACORN, 1996, 1997, 1998; Center for Immigrant Families, 2005; see also Brantlinger, 2003).

The parents demonstrating knew that people of color are often excluded from educational opportunities by virtue of their race and working-class or poor status. And multiple studies have shown that low-income Black and Latino students are overrepresented in special education classes, poorly resourced schools, general-equivalency degree programs (GED), and as high school dropouts or push-outs (see Fine, 1991 and Kozol, 2005, among many others). These students are also underrepresented in honors and advanced placement classes, college prep programs, and colleges and universities (Oakes, 1985; Lucas, 1999; Auerbach, 2002). One important educational opportunity that is sometimes available to low-income parents, however, is when children and families can choose the district school which the child will attend—especially important being high school choice (Price and Stern, 1987; Wells, 1993; Willie and Alvez, 1996; McGroarty, 2001; Scott, 2005).

As Noguera and Wing point out, high school is the last opportunity for young people to acquire the knowledge and skills they need to achieve life goals (2006). "It is the final destination for all students who make it to the ninth grade, and it is the place where future trajectories—to Ivy league colleges, to state and community colleges, to dead-end jobs, or to prison—are determined" (15). Aware from experience that the well-paying manufacturing jobs formerly available had all but disappeared (see Anyon, 2005), the parents demonstrating in December 2006 understood that their children needed college degrees; and they wanted the district to improve its capacity to educate students well enough for them to attend college.

Choice in New York City

The New York City Department of Education describes its high school application process as one of "choice and equity" (NYC Department of Education, 2005). However, the low-income Latina parents I worked with in my ten years of community organizing knew that race and class often entered into the selection process to disadvantage them. Research was in congruence with their understandings. Studies by ACORN, a national and local community-based organization, documented a high degree of exclusion of students of color from the district's elite high schools. ACORN found in 1998, for example, that although the NYC district was 39 percent Black and 34 percent Latino, the student body of the elite Stuyvesant High was less than five percent Black and four percent Hispanic. At Bronx Science High School, fewer than 11 percent of students were Black and nine percent Hispanic (1998). (By 2006, the percentage of Black students at Stuyvesant had dropped to 2.2 percent [Gootman, 2006].) ACORN researchers also discovered that the majority of students who attended the city's elite high schools in the late 1990s came from only three of the city's many districts (1996).

Other studies described practices that prevented Black and Latino students in New York City from exercising choice. In 2005, the Center for Immigrant Families, a parent organizing group, documented that in District 3, under a choice plan where parents and students were to chose a middle school, office personnel and administrators in some schools encountered by low income parents of color were dismissive or insulting, and frequently provided information that was erroneous and that prevented parents of color from applying to that school (2006). In response to this and other research—and to parent organizing efforts—the city was moved to implement a policy reform in District 3 that addressed the racial and economic inequalities in that district's schools (ibid.).

Questions that guided the project I report in this chapter include the following: How can low-income parents and children of color negotiate a choice program in an environment where race and class exclusionary practices influence the process? How is school choice operationalized for those whose schedule inflexibility (from, say, multiple jobs, language unfamiliarity, or lack of information) deny them access? What are the schooling options for students who do not successfully navigate the complex admissions process? And what are the conditions that enable families to challenge central office allocations?

A Participatory Action Project

In order to think about these questions with some of the Latina parents I had been working with as a community organizer, I asked them to join me in researching and creating a handbook for parents that would describe all the high school options. Over a period of six months we worked together to research the schools. We made joint decisions about the content and design of the guide. The book we produced provided an overview of the city's high school admissions process, presented findings about what low-income families want in a high school, and gave detailed information about each school. This handbook described the public high school admissions process through a parent's perspective. We made it available city-wide.

In order to prepare material for the book, parents and I engaged in three main activities. First, the parents shared their successes and struggles in navigating Board of Education bureaucratic processes (I discuss these in some detail below). Second, we created profiles of each high school by visiting them, observing classes, and interviewing school staff, students, and families. This allowed us to describe each school in the voices of parents, the main stakeholders, instead of as bundles of statistics, which was the format of district descriptions. Third, parents and I created and disseminated a survey to families of all high schools. Parents were provided with training on how to create a survey and how to analyze the data we obtained. To make the guide attractive and reflective of the communities it sought to serve, we recruited the talents of James De La Vega, a Nuyorican artist and educator, who illustrated the book.

My decision to shape the guide as a participatory action project led by parents was informed by Pierre Bourdieu's theories of social and cultural capital—specifically his view that high-status social networks and cultural knowledge and skills are valued and therefore useful in social interactions with bureaucratic and other social institutions. The parents in my group, who had grown up in poor and immigrant families, did not possess these networks or skills, and I thought they might profit from understanding the power of, and acquiring some of, these attributes (Noguera, 2003). As a doctoral student, I was reading many theories, and was struck by Giroux's edict to "take theory to the people" (1983). I thought that Bourdieu's concepts or "thinking tools" as he described them, might be useful to the parents in their educational advocacy work.

Indeed, it pained me to me to hear the mothers—many of whom had spent long hours trying to deal with their children's teachers and school administrators—blame themselves and their children's lack of success on their own previous educational inadequacies or their children's behavior and alleged linguistic and other deficits.

Following sections of this chapter delineate Bourdieu's theoretical constructs, describe how I shared his theory with parents, and offer evidence that knowledge of the power of activated high-status social and cultural capital assisted the parents in more systemic, structural understanding of the admissions process and the way it worked. In some cases their new knowledge allowed the parents to act more efficaciously as their children's advocate. Indeed, I learned from the parents during our time together. Discussing high-level theory with people who had not encountered it before broadened and deepened my own understanding of Bourdieu's work, and affirmed my respect for the nascent theories parents had already developed.

Cultural and Social Capital

Pierre Bourdieu's notions of social and cultural capital have been fruitful constructions for scholars exploring family–school relations (e.g., Reay, 1998; Noguera, 2001; Brantlinger, 2003; Lareau, 2003; Andre-Bechely, 2005). For Bourdieu, capital includes resources that are invested and utilized in hopes of achieving a certain goal. For my purposes, his (1983) descriptions of economic capital, cultural capital, and social capital were useful. Economic capital of course, involves financial and material possessions one owns. One important distinction Bourdieu makes is that he sees all symbolic capital as disguised economic capital. "Economic capital is at the root for all the other types of capital, including social capital." And, "every type of capital is reducible in the last analysis to economic capital" (252). Bourdieu used cultural and social capital as lenses with which to explain the educational success of children of various social classes:

> The notion of cultural capital initially presented itself to me, in the course of research, as a theoretical hypothesis which made it possible to explain the unequal scholastic achievement of children originating from different social classes by relating academic success, i.e. the specifics profits [sic] which children from the different classes and class fractions can obtain in the academic market, to the distribution of cultural capital between the class and class fractions.
>
> (243)

Cultural capital as advanced by Bourdieu is defined as relatively rare, high-status cultural and linguistic knowledge, skills, and dispositions passed from one generation to the next. An important note is that these dispositions consisted of a set of dispositions and competencies legitimated and valued by dominant strata of society. Bourdieu saw cultural capital as existing in three main forms: in the embodied state (in the form of long-lasting habits of mind and body); in the form of cultural goods (certain kinds of art work, literature, or sculpture); and in the institutionalized state, a form of objectification, as certificates and degrees (ibid.). Educational researcher Annette Lareau finds that Bourdieu's concept of cultural capital "has the potential to show how individual biography intersects with social structure, a potential that theoretical and empirical work must take advantage of" (1989, 179). The concept of cultural capital is useful for researching families' relationships with schools, because educators tend to perceive the cultural capital of those who control the economic, social, and political resources as the "natural and proper sort"; thus they favor students (and families) who posses the cultural forms of the dominant groups (Harker, 1984). Cultural capital is a relational concept and cannot be understood in isolation from other forms of capital that constitute advantage and disadvantage in society.

Bourdieu defined social capital as "the mobilization of actual or potential resources, which are linked to possession of a durable network of institutionalized relationships of mutual acquaintance and recognition—or in other words, membership in a group. [Social capital] is made up of social obligations or connections" (1983, 248). Economist Nan Lin clarified for me that social capital can include two types of resources an individual can gain access to and use—personal resources and social resources (1982, 21). Lin sees personal resources as "resources possessed by an individual and may include ownership of material as well as symbolic goods [e.g., cultural capital]." Examples of these include academic credentials and/or degrees. On the other hand, he defines social resources as those "accessed through an individual's social connections" (ibid.). Thus, social and cultural capital can be exchanged for each other and for economic or other gain.

James Coleman pointed to ways actors attempt to control social and cultural capital resources in which they have an interest—for example, as education researcher Ellen Brantlinger found, in a district in which middle-class parents mobilize to ensure that school choice programs exclude lower-income families of color (2003). Sometimes, in order for individuals to gain interest from the outcome of an event, actors participate in exchanges or transfers of resources (Coleman, 1990, 302). Bourdieu describes this as members in a group gaining a "credit" which provides the backing of the collectively owned capital in the group. Research supports the notion that parents' social capital—specifically leading to collaborations between teachers and families—plays a role in producing high achievement of children (Lareau, 2003; Noguera, 2004).

Valenzuela (1999), Noguera (2001), and Stanton-Salazar (2001) recognize that poor people have their own social and cultural capital. These authors describe the networks and cultural resources that low-income urban parents and residents of color create and utilize as they negotiate to good effect in their community environments. As Valenzuela points out, however, although the low-income Mexican families she worked with did have access to forms of capital that facilitated their activity in their social circles, these resources were no match for the exclusionary tracking practices and deficit discourses in the schools their children attended. The unequal playing field of types of cultural and social capital haunted me as I worked with parents over ten years of education organizing. And it played a major role in my decision to take Bourdieu to the people I worked with.

Using Bourdieu to Talk with Parents about School Choice

I spent the second weekend of March 2007 in a conference room at a local public college with the ten parent advisory committee members of the Parent Guide project. Before I could tap into the expertise of these parent leaders and relate it to Bourdieu's ideas, I needed to create the conditions where parents felt comfortable sharing their experiences with formal schooling. Then we could explore what information they felt needed to be included in the parent guide and explore Bourdieu's notions of capital as a lens through which to view their experiences navigating school bureaucracy and public school choice. I wanted Bourdieu's work to confirm and extend insights the parents already had developed as they had negotiated school bureaucracies.

Despite the fact that the women on the advisory committee had long advocated for their children (in both successful and unsuccessful ways), most of them had a difficult time believing that they had valuable expertise or knowledge. Research has documented low-income parents' feelings of inadequacy, sometimes leading to their adopting a passive role and leaving education decisions to the schools (Liontos, 1992; Christenson and Hirsh, 1998, among others). Christenson and Hirsh emphasize how educational jargon or "teacher talk" often dominates low-income parent/teacher conversations, and facilitates the passivity of such parents.

In order to ensure that the parents would be active agents in the weekend retreat, I invited an educational researcher and a bilingual school teacher who shared racial and class attributes of the parents to share the first day of the retreat with us. I wanted these visitors to demystify scholarship as well as public school teaching, and to engage parents in conversation about what constitutes knowledge and expertise. The speakers shared stories of their own childhood growing up in low-income immigrant neighborhoods, and highlighted important educational moments on their journeys to higher education. Working with this researcher and teacher also created a situation in which transmission of academic cultural capital from the professionals to the parents could occur.

I asked parents to reflect on and share their own educational memories—positive or negative—and to tell us how they think their own educational experiences might have shaped what they wanted for their children's education. To stimulate their thoughts, parents took part in what participatory action researcher Michelle Fine calls "The Writing's on the Wall" (personal communication, March 23, 2006). During this exercise the parents were asked to write their stories, fears, misconceptions, and questions about high school admissions on huge pieces of chart paper that covered all the walls in our conference room.

The women shared positive stories ("My child's teachers helped me and my child with high school choice. I felt supported"), questions and confusions ("Are there zoned high schools or not? I don't understand the process and no one has answers for me"), and negative experiences ("When I tried to tell the guidance counselor about my child's strengths and abilities, she told me to leave the decisions to the professionals"). Parents also shared memories of their own childhood, being praised and protected by teachers, as well as painful misunderstandings in interactions with educators.

Negative experiences were most common. In fact, I heard a flood of anecdotes about exclusion and injustice while interacting with the public schools. I used the concepts of social and cultural capital to provide explanations for their bitter experience. "The right networks, knowing the people in charge, or being acquainted with their friends and colleagues are how white middle- and upper-middle-class parents can get their children in." "Our accents, the way we dress, our inflection: everything alerts school personnel to who we are and what they think our kids will be like. And they want students who have parents with money to buy art supplies for the school; they want kids who they think will score high on the standardized tests."

We also talked about what we had learned from our research for the parent guide in terms of cultural and social capital. One conversation centered on the mothers' observation of classrooms during our school visits. The mothers had been made painfully aware of the differences in the "hidden curriculum" in various schools (Anyon, 1980). These seemed to differ by the race and socio-economic status of the students, and it provided an opportunity for further discussion of the power of social and cultural capital. For example, in one school where all the students were Latino and Black and 92 percent of the students were eligible for free or reduced price lunch, teachers seemed to have very little patience when students were disruptive. Parent committee members observed a teacher yell at a student for 20 minutes because he spoke out of turn in class. Matilde stated, "I found it strange that the teacher was so upset by the student taking away two minutes of class time when he spoke out of turn and responded by yelling to the point were she then eliminated 20 minutes of instructional time. I don't think the student heard what she was saying. Her tone said, 'I hate you.'"

Later in the week, Matilde visited another school with a student population that was more economically and racially mixed, with a preponderance of middle-class Caucasian students. She reported that, "A boy was shouting in class. The teacher ignored him, but praised him right away when he engaged with the class again. Afterwards, she asked the student if everything was OK. It turned out that he was having a bad day and shared that with her. That boy probably heard, 'I care' from the teacher." Parent guide members had not visited upper-middle white classrooms before, and had not observed how teachers handled such students. After our visits they concurred with

Bourdieu that schools do seem to reward students and their families who possess certain embodied cultural capital attributes and penalize others who have different attributes.

The parent stories and my own "structural anecdotes"—in which I described their stories so that they were seen as "incidents in which the key structural elements are revealed"—demonstrated to the parents how "institutional and organizational forces converge around what on the surface may appear to be an individual, personal or idiosyncratic matter" (Duster, 1989). I was also able to employ the structural anecdotes provided by parents and our discussion of "The Writing's on the Wall" to facilitate conversations about the themes of high-status social and cultural capital as facilitating parent–school interactions.

To take our discussion further into Bourdieu's emphasis on the power of elite social networks, I asked the parents who had already gone through the high school admissions process with their children to tell us from whom they had gotten information they needed, and who had given them the most helpful information. It became clear that in most cases school personnel had not been helpful. We discussed how the neighborhood or country where one was a child, where one lives now, the job one has, and where one attended school (or not) strongly affect what people become a part of your social networks. These are the people who you contact when you need information. Yvette, the only parent who was a professional (a lawyer—and whose social capital therefore included high-status acquaintances), shared how she obtained information and strategized about the high school admissions process for her sons.

> My husband and I reached out to our law school colleagues when it was time to think about applying to high schools. They were able to introduce us to their own kids who were alumni from [elite] schools in the city such as Stuyvesant and Hunter. One of the parents was involved in the state-wide campaign for better school funding, as well. Because of this she knew many of the principals. We got our advice from these people and they told us what we needed to do.

Yvette's possession and activation of social capital was very different from Hilda's, who as a recently arrived immigrant from the Dominican Republic did not have the networks to orient her in how to make choices or how to navigate the bureaucracy. She was not able to obtain helpful information about the admissions process from officials, nor did her friends have the information she sought; she was forced to rely on the occasional letters her son brought home from school. Hilda shared that, in her homeland of the Dominican Republic, teachers are viewed as extended family—a second set of parents for the child. Therefore, families demonstrate their trust for the teacher and their involvement in the education of their child by *deferring* to the teacher. She told us that because of her trust in the education process in her country, when she came here and her daughter was going through the application process, she tended to accept "the luck of the draw" in what school she was assigned (see also Calabrese Barton *et al.*, 2004). Other parents concurred that, though they took part in demonstrations and protests, they too had often accepted their child's placements without question—"*esa es la que le toca*" ("that's the one he/she gets"). Hearing the lawyer-parent's experiences as she described her powerful networks and strategies cemented for the other parents an understanding of the importance of race and social status in a process of ostensibly equal choice. Yvette shared with us a chart she and her husband had constructed to help them decipher differences between the schools (Table 5.1).

We contrasted the difference between Hilda's and some of the others' responses to Yvette's mobilization of her lawyer friends and the chart she had created, and parents agreed that she had engaged powerful cultural skills and social networks. She provided a model for the parents. Annette Lareau (2003) found that middle- and upper-middle-class parents, like Yvette, typically utilize social networks and cultural skills to advocate for their children and, for example, rarely hesitate to challenge an educator's decision around what is best for their children. Lareau describes the resulting "personalized education" middle-class children receive, and contrasts this to the "generic education" that working-class and poor families receive. I discussed this research with the parents.

In spite of occasional unwillingness to challenge educator decisions, several of the parents had developed their own theories about why inter-action with the schools was difficult. Laura, for example, a recently arrived Latina immigrant from Colombia, had previously theorized the power of social capital. She said she had described her experience navigating public school choice in New York by telling others that she knew she might have problems because "Yo no tengo padrino aqui" ("I do not have a godfather here"). Maria sympathized. She said she had explained to her husband the treatment she had received from district officials in terms of *power.* "I went over there to ask about transferring my daughter, and they ignored me. They knew I had no power, I was somebody they didn't care about. They knew nothing would happen to them if they ignored me. They probably threw it [my daughter's application] away."

As I write this chapter, a full year has elapsed since the creation of the parent guide and my weekend with the parents. I have recently reunited with them—as they are now serving as the parent advisory committee for my dissertation on the NYC high school admissions process. During our reunion

TABLE 5.1 Notes about schools we are interested in:

Characteristics that are important	School 1	School 2	School 3	School 4
Location				
Distance/travel time (Within borough? Near bus/train?)				
How long has the school been in existence?				
Size of school				
Number of students per class				
Student–teacher ratio/student–guidance counselor ratio				
Student support services				
Where do most teachers get their training?				
Is there a test requirement for applying?				
If so, is there a cost for the test?				
Deadline for test application/test date				
Specialization (art, music, dance, etc.)				
How diverse is the school? (students, teachers, curriculum)				
School tour—date of tour				
Is an interview required? If so, when?				
Are there tuition costs or any other fees?				
If there are tuition costs or fees, does the school offer scholarships?				
What is the school's graduation rate?				
What are some of the colleges that students attend after graduation?				
What is the "feel" of the building?				
Does the school share space with other schools?				
If so, are the schools able to do this in a mutually beneficial way?				
Other deadlines/factors				
Overall impression of the school—score 1 through 10				

meeting, I asked for their thoughts on the production of the guide and our "theory" retreat. It became apparent that the use of Bourdieu's theorizations over the weekend of our time together—and the experience of researching and writing the school guide—had sharpened parents' understanding of the system, and in several cases had improved their advocacy practices.

Several stated that producing the guide and discussing social and cultural capital empowered them as researchers and advocates, providing them with the confidence to question their child's teachers and school principals in ways they had not before. Matilde described how she had shared with other parents in her neighborhood the chart that Yvette had made. Another parent took Bourdieu's notions further, extending them into an acknowledgement of the value in the capital that families and children in her working-class Latino neighborhood held. She decided to pursue a career in a Bronx school as a parent advocate. "I realized that I have a lot of social capital with the families in the school. And I know about high-status capital now. I can serve as a bridge between the school and the parents. This makes me a valuable resource in ways I didn't realize before."

The mothers also reported that as a result of our weekend retreat they were better able to problematize the limitations of "choice" in a city where 86 percent of the schools are deemed undesirable by district leaders. They saw that, if their children did not get accepted at a good school, reasons might inhere in the inadequacies of the school system rather than in their culture or their children's inadequacies.

And I learned a lot, as well. I understood in a concrete manner that theory can be a tool for the empowerment of poor and working-class people. I saw that it was possible to extend parents' insights, to strengthen their resolve, and to improve their capacities by offering them high-status knowledge that mirrored and magnified their own.

Note

1   Thanks to Educational Justice Organizer Milli Bonilla for sharing the parent chants with me.

References

ACORN. (1996). *Secret Apartheid: A Report on Racial Discrimination against Black and Latino Parents and Children in the New York City Public Schools.* http://www.acorn.org.

ACORN. (1997). Secret apartheid II: Race, Regents, and Resources. http://www.acorn.org.

ACORN. (1998). Secret apartheid III: Follow up to Failure. http://www.acorn.org.

Andre-Bechely, L. (2005) *Could It Be Otherwise?: Parents and the Inequities of Public School Choice.* New York: Routledge.

Anyon, J. (1980). Social Class and the Hidden Curriculum of Work. *Journal of Education,* 162: 1, 67–92.

Anyon, J. (2005) *Radical Possibilities: Public Policy, Urban Education, and a New Social Movement.* New York: Routledge.

Auerbach, S. (2002). Why Do They Give the Good Classes to Some and not to Others? Latino Parent Narratives of Struggle in a College Access Program. *Teachers College Record*, 104: 7, 1369–1392.

Bell, L. and Ribbens, J. (1994). Isolated Housewives and Complex Maternal Worlds? The Significance of Social Contacts between Women and Young Children in Industrial Societies. *Sociological Review*, 42: 2, 227–262.

Bempechat, J. (1998). *Against the Odds: How "At-risk" Students Exceed Expectations.* San Francisco: Jossey-Bass.

Bourdieu, P. (1983). The Forms of Capital. In J. G. Richardson, editor, *Handbook of Theory and Research for the Sociology of Education.* Westport, CT: Greenwood Press, 241–58.

Brantlinger, E. (2003). *Dividing Classes: How the Middle Class Negotiates and Rationalizes School Advantage.* New York: Routledge.

Calabrese Barton, A., Drake, C., Gustavo-Pérez, J., St. Louis, K., and George, M. (2004). Ecologies of Parental Engagement in Urban Education. *Educational Researcher*, 33: 4, 3–12.

Center for Immigrant Families. (2005). *Segregated and Unequal: The Public Elementary Schools of District 3 in New York City.* New York: Center for Immigrant Families.

Christenson, S. L. (1995). Supporting Home-School Collaboration. In A. Thomas and J. Grimes, editors, *Best Practices in School Psychology III.* Washington, DC: National Association of School Psychologists, 253–267.

Christenson, S. L. and Hirsh, J. (1998). Facilitating Partnerships and Conflict Resolution Between Families and Schools. In K.C. Stoiber and T. Kratochwill, editors, *Handbook of Group Interventions for Children and Families.* Boston: Allyn & Bacon, 307–344.

Coleman, J. (1977). Choice in American education. In Coleman *et al., Parents, Teachers, and Children: Prospects for Choice in American Education.* San Francisco, CA: Institute for Contemporary Studies, 1–14.

Coleman, J. (1990), Choice, Community and Future Schools. In W. Clune and J. Witte, editors, *Choice and Control in American Education.* London and New York: Falmer Press.

Duster, T. (1989). The Structured Anecdote in Social Analysis. Unpublished manuscript presented at the August 9 meeting of the American Sociological Association, San Francisco, CA.

Edwards, E. B. (1977). Why a Harlem Parents Union? In J. Coleman *et al., Parents, Teachers, and Children: Prospects for Choice in American Education.* San Francisco, CA: Institute for Contemporary Studies, 59–66.

Fine, M. (1991) *Framing Dropouts: Notes on the Politics of an Urban Public High School.* Albany: State University of New York.

Fine, M., Torre, M.E., Boudin, K., Bowen, I., Clark, J., Hylton, D., Martinez, M., "Missy," Rivera, M., Renes, R.A., Smart, P. and Upegui, D. (2003). Participatory Action Research: Within and Beyond Bars. In P. Camic, J. E. Rhodes, and L. Yadley, editors, *Qualitative Research in Psychology: Expanding Perspective in Methodology and Design.* Washington DC: American Psychological Association, 173–198.

Fine, M., Roberts, R., Torre, M. and Bloom, J., Burns, A., Chajet, L., Guishard, M., and Payne, Y. (2004). *Echoes of Brown: Youth Documenting and Performing the Legacy of Brown v. Board of Education.* New York: Teachers College Press.

Fuller, B., Elmore, R.F., and Orfield, G. (1996). Policy-Making in the Dark: Illuminating the School Choice Debate. In Fuller and Elmore, editors, *Who Chooses? Who Loses?: Culture, Institutions, and the Unequal Effects of School Choice.* New York: Teachers College Press.

Giroux, H. (1983). *Critical Theory and Educational Practice.* Geelong: Deakin University Press.

Gootman, E. (1997, November 20). Action filed over school admissions. *New York Times.*

Gootman, E. (2006, August 18). In Elite N.Y. Schools, a Dip in Blacks and Hispanics. *New York Times.*

Grenfell, M. (1998). *Bourdieu and Education: Acts of Practical Theory.* London: Falmer Press.

Harker, R. R. (1984). On Reproduction, Habitus, and Education. *British Journal of Sociology*, 5: 2, 117–127.

Henderson, A.T., Johnson, V., Mapp, K.L., and Davies, D. (2007). *Beyond the Bake Sale: The Essential Guide to Family/School Partnerships.* New York: New Press.

Herszenhorn, D. M. (2004, November 19). Council Members see Flaws in School-admissions Plan. *New York Times.*

Jackson, B., and Cooper, B. (1989). Parent Choice and Empowerment: New Roles for Parents. *Urban Education*, 24: 3, 263–286.

Kozol, J. (1992). *Savage Inequalities: Children in American Schools.* New York: Harper Perennial.

Kozol, J. (2005). *The Shame of the Nation: The Restoration of Apartheid Schooling in America.* New York: Random House.

Lareau, A. (1989). *Home Advantage: Social Class and Parental Intervention in Elementary Education.* Landham, MD: Rowman and Littlefield.

Lareau, A. (2003). *Unequal Childhoods: Class, Race, and Family Life.* Berkeley, CA: University of California Press.

Lawrence-Lightfoot, S. (1978) *Worlds Apart: Relationships between Families and Schools.* New York: Basic Books Inc.

Lin, N. (1982). Social Resources and Instrumental Action. In P. V. Marsden and N. Lin, editors, *Social Structure and Network Analysis,* 1–45. Beverly Hills, CA: Sage Publishers.

Lin, N. (2001). *Social Capital: A Theory of Social Structure and Action.* Cambridge: Cambridge University Press.

Liontos, L. B (1992). *At-risk Families and Schools: Becoming Partners.* Eugene, OR: ERIC Clearinghouse on Educational Management, College of Education, University of Oregon.

Lucas, S. R. (1999). *Tracking Inequality.* New York: Teachers College Press.

McGroarty, D. (2001). *Trinnietta gets a Chance: Six Families and Their School Choice Experience.* Washington DC: The Heritage Foundation.

New York City Department of Education. (2005). *Directory of the New York City Public High Schools: 2005–2006.* New York: NYC Department of Education.

Noguera, P. (1999, May 20) Transforming Urban Schools Through Investments in the Social Capital of Parents. *In Motion Magazine.*

Noguera, P. (2003). *City Schools and the American Dream: Reclaiming the Promise of Public Education.* New York: Teachers College Press.

Noguera, P., and Wing, J. Y. (2006) *Unfinished Business: Closing the Racial Achievement Gap in Our Schools.* San Francisco, CA: Jossey-Bass.

Oakes, J. (1985). *Keeping Track: How Schools Structure Inequality.* New Haven: Yale University Press.

Price, J. R., and Stern, J. R. (1987). Magnet Schools as a Strategy for Integration and School Reform. *Yale Law and Policy Review,* 5, 299–300.

Procidano, M. E., and Fisher, C. B. (1992). *Contemporary Families: A Handbook for School Professionals.* New York: Teachers College Press.

Putnam, R. (1993). The Prosperous Community: Social Capital and Public Life. *The American Prospect,* 4:13.

Putnam, R. (1995). Bowling Alone: America's Declining Social Capital. *The Journal of Democracy,* 6:1, 65–78.

Reay, D. (1998). *Class Work: Mothers' Involvement in Their Children's Primary Schooling.* London: Taylor & Francis.

Rosso, D., and González, P. (2006, November 2). Las Voces de los Padres Cuentan/Parents' Voices Matter. OPINIÓN, *El Diario/La Prensa* (New York City).

Scott, J. T., editor. (2005). *School Choice and Diversity: What the Evidence Says.* New York: Teachers College Press.

Stanton-Salazar, R. (2001). *Manufacturing Hope and Despair: The School and Kin Support Networks of U.S.-Mexican Youth.* New York: Teachers College Press.

Valenzuela, A. (1999). *Subtractive Schooling: U.S.-Mexican Youth and the Politics of Caring.* Albany: SUNY Press.

Wells, A. S. (1993). *Time to Choose: America at the Crossroads of School Choice Policy.* New York: Hill & Wang.

Wells, A. S. and Crain, R. L. (2005). Where School Desegregation and School Choice Policies Collide: Voluntary Transfer Plans and Controlled Choice. In Janelle T. Scott, editor, *School Choice and Diversity: What the Evidence Says.* New York: Teachers College Press, 59–76.

Willie, C. V., and Alvez, M. J. (1996). *Controlled Choice: A New Approach to Desegregated Education and School Improvement* (A publication of the Education Alliance Press and the New England Desegregation Assistance Center). Providence, RI: Brown University.

Personal Reflection

My Relationship with Theory

For years, I resisted scholarship, theory, and doctoral studies. Despite encouragement from professors in undergraduate Psychology and Masters of Social Work programs, I refused. After all, I was making a much bigger contribution to society by pursuing a career as a community organizer than I would as a detached, disconnected scholar. I felt I was most useful working with the people in low-income neighborhoods in New York City and Oakland, California. We carried out political campaigns around affordable housing, ending domestic violence, access to affordable healthcare and pharmaceuticals, and school reform. Together, residents, parents, and I felt that we were influencing policy, increasing the skills and confidence of people in the community, and sparking public awareness of problems that prevent equity and social justice.

Some of the concrete outcomes of our campaigns included construction of a new school building for Cypress Hills Community School, a dual-language parent-led school in Brooklyn, NY; the involvement of local elected New York City officials in proposing policies that better protect survivors of domestic violence from their attackers; a bilingual guide to school admissions designed and written by parents; and a commitment from several landlords in Park Slope, Brooklyn, that despite their right to demand market rents, they would not displace long-time residents.

Although I knew that it was important to document the work we were doing, and to embed such activity in a larger framework of thought about issues of social change, I didn't believe that scholarship or theory made much of a difference in the world. And carrying out research on people I worked with made me uncomfortable. Why would I interview Doña Juana about her experience with neighborhood gentrification? How would that improve her situation? A sympathetic professor in my Master's program even referred to research in poor neighborhoods as "rape and run." He critiqued scholars who go into communities and exploit the people they meet. The knowledge that researchers gain in these communities fuels and feeds their theory and their careers. And the community remains just as it was before—with nothing gained.

Other professors in my Master's program assigned theory. The more theory I read, the angrier I became. Theories and scholarship that were racist, classist, and sexist prevailed (Oscar Lewis and the "culture of poverty" leap to mind). Studies that were conducted with little regard for human beings and disdain for their culture were cited as truth. My response was to continue to disengage from scholarship even though I continued in the program; I delved deeper into grassroots community work.

Several progressive professors in the School of Social Work became aware of my neighborhood initiatives, and in my final year of the program asked if I would take part in developing an organization called the Latino/a Community Organizer's Network—a marriage between local grassroots organizers, professors from the city university's Hunter College, and the college's Center for Puerto Rican Studies. Despite initial reservations I agreed, and soon learned that these professors wanted to carry out what they called Participatory Action Research (PAR)—a linking of academic study with grassroots organizing that allowed local residents to define the problems to be studied and to partner as co-researchers.

As we prepared for our work together, relevant course readings replaced the racist, classist, and sexist readings that had haunted my previous study. We read feminists of color such as Patricia Hill-Collins, Angela Davis, Cherie Moraga, and Gloria Anzaldua. These women were people of color like me— and they argued that race and class cannot be studied in isolation from each other or from people's experiences, but must be explored together. I was grateful for their work, and wanted to read more.

Several years later, working in New York City with Mexican immigrant mothers who were part of a school planning team, I read *Ghetto Schooling*. I decided to email Jean Anyon. I felt connected to her vision of research that exposes injustice; she seemed to be an ally, someone who wanted to change conditions that were hurting kids in schools and their families. I shared with her my commitment to community work and my recent experience in joining grassroots work with the academy. Jean was supportive, and encouraged me to apply to the Doctoral Program in Urban Education. Subsequently in academia in New York City I met other allies—Michelle Fine and Pedro Noguera—scholars who were committed to research that would have the purpose of transforming urban public schools and the experiences of students.

When I took Jean's theory course, I was introduced to the writings of French sociologist Pierre Bourdieu. I was first attracted to Bourdieu's work because it had been useful to other scholars concerned about relationships between schools, communities, and families. But then I read *about* Bourdieu and his life. Born in a remote village in the mountains of southwestern France, Bourdieu was the grandson of a sharecropper, and the son of a farmer who became the village postman. Although Bourdieu trained as a philosopher under Marxist philosopher Louis Althusser at the Ecole Normale Superieure in Paris at the same time as Jacques Derrida and Michel Foucault, he never completed a doctorate. And this, along with his origins in the provinces, gave him an "outsider" status among the French intellectual elite. He was also a severe critic of the academy (see Webb, Schirato, and Danaher, 2002; Eakin, 2001). I came to the frightening (and amusing) realization that Pierre Bourdieu was in many ways like me.

Bourdieu had long argued that scholars should bring their expert knowledge to bear responsibly on social and political issues. He professed discomfort with the role of an ivory-tower social scientist and intellectual, and said he felt more comfortable working "in the trenches." During the 1990s he was involved in community campaigns for railway workers, undocumented immigrants, and unemployed persons, and against globalization (Pollitt, 2002). He was committed to connecting his theoretical ideas with empirical research grounded in everyday life. His contributions to the field of sociology were both empirical and theoretical. And I was hooked; I read his theories voraciously.

Now, as I am guided in my dissertation project by the group of Latina mothers I describe in my chapter for this volume, I look not only to them but to Bourdieu (and to Anyon, Fine, and Noguera), as models of scholarship that is importantly theoretical yet aimed at empirical study and that wants to affect social and educational policy and practice. I have come to terms with theory, scholarship, and doctoral studies, and celebrate its confluence with the goals of the community members whose lives remain of deep concern to me.

References

Eakin, E. (2001, January 6) Social Status Tends to Seal One's Fate, Says France's Master Thinker. *The New York Times*.

Lewis, O. (1996). The Culture of Poverty. In G. Gmelch and W. Zenner, editors: *Urban life*. Prospect Heights, IL: Waveland Press.

Pollitt, K. (2002, March 18). Subject to Debate: Bourdieu 1930–2002. *The Nation*.

Webb, J., Schirato, T., and Danaher, G. (2002). *Understanding Bourdieu*. Crows Nest, NSW: Allen & Unwin.

CHAPTER 6

Queer Theory and Teen Sexuality

Unclear Lines

DARLA LINVILLE

Depending on whom you ask, teens are said to be very comfortable with a flexible and fluid understanding of sexuality or, conversely, among the most rigid part of the population regarding gender and sex. The popular press has recently seized on research that reports the ways that lesbian, gay, and bisexual youth are finding it easier to be out at younger and younger ages (Cloud, 2005). At the same time, the stories of non-gender-conforming and same-gender-attracted teens assaulted or killed for daring to pursue sexuality in their chosen body have regularly appeared in the news over the last 15 years (a few of the fatal examples include Brandon Teena in 1993, Matthew Shepherd in 1998, Gwen Araujo in 2002, and Sakia Gunn in 2003). Clearly, those who are reporting on popular culture in the news media find the attitudes of youth toward gender and sexuality compelling.

This chapter reports interviews and journal data collected from, as well as through the research activities of, a group of teens in a New York City after-school program. The teens talk about sexuality in their schools and the beliefs, language, and practices of students, teachers, and school administration about queer youth. Their responses are analyzed through the lens of queer theory, which provides a conceptual resource for moving beyond the binaries of schools as either safe or unsafe places for lesbian, gay, bisexual, transgender, and queer and questioning (LGBTQ) youth, and LGBTQ youth as either "normal" or "deviant." Student responses, and the emphases they place on different elements of the conversation, tend to speak *back* to the theory, contesting in their speech the priorities of queer theory's political application.

I began this research with both theoretical and empirical questions: How does queer theory help explain the narratives of high school students, both LGBTQ and heterosexual-identified, and the contradictions and counter-narratives that they expose in the policies, practices, and pedagogies of their schools? Do queer theory's prescriptions resonate with students' wishes for their schools? I also wondered if there is a "best way" for schools to make their hallways and classrooms more welcoming environments for LGBTQ students. I utilized queer theory to design the research project, the interview questions and other data-gathering strategies, and later to identify and categorize themes in the teens' responses.

My reading of the literature on homosexuality and education is that education researchers have engaged with queer and post-structuralist theories previously (for excellent examples see Kumashiro, 2001; Rasmussen, 2006; and Rofes, 2000), and some have suggested educational innovations that would queer education; however, most of the changes being made in school districts do not question the fundamental assumptions of education and leave in place the current curriculum, pedagogy, policies, and teacher preparation (Aleman, 2004; Szalacha, 2004). Their inclusivity merely adds a week or day or chapter on homosexuality to the curriculum. Education researchers engaging with queer theory have not involved current high school students in order to analyze the applicability of queer theory to teens' experiences. In this piece, I want to use queer theory to interrogate and challenge educational discourse and practice. The following sections set my work in the education literature, then explicate queer theory as I used it. Then I describe schools' interactions with LGBTQ students as other students see them. The final section explores the intersection of the students' discourses and precepts of queer theory. I attempt to think through what the student responses reveal that queer theory offers and what they see as its political limitations.

Education, Homosexuality, and Queer Theory

This section lays the groundwork for how I used theory in my study. Recent research has sought to disrupt the conventional portrayal of LGBTQ youth as perpetual victims, psychologically tormented by their inability to fit in and at risk for the pathologies of drug and alcohol abuse and suicide. These newer studies declare that older work used data primarily from teens who sought psychological treatment—a pre-selected group exhibiting patho-logical behavior or feelings (Savin-Williams, 2005). The argument is that, in the larger teen population, the feelings about non-heteronormative sexuality are much healthier. On the other hand, national organizations such as the Gay, Lesbian and Straight Education Network (2005) and Human Rights Watch (2001) have published recent nationwide survey data describing the harassing comments and behavior that middle and high school students hear and see in the halls and classrooms of their schools. Respondents report that anti-gay and anti-girl slurs (such as "slut" or "bitch") are heard most often, and nearly all reported hearing the phrase, "That's so gay," as an insult. Students also described feeling unsafe in schools where there is no extant policy giving students a process for redress against these types of harassment.

My work with teens, described below, leads me to believe that the experience for most teens perhaps lies between these two extremes. Although they may feel less conflict about sexuality than previous generations, they do not feel that sexuality is a simple choice, nor do they accept that one can feel happy without naming oneself or picking a category. Most teens feel that they can make room for friends who come out and they can think about their own sexuality (or sometimes even claim to be questioning their sexuality) without fear. They may still use heteronormalizing speech to police one another, but will defend the flamboyant gay boy who is their friend. LGBTQ teens may sense that school is fine and free of homophobia and, at the same time, that the least safe place they find themselves is school, without this being a contradiction. Because school is the place where they are known and out with their sexuality, but also a place where social dynamics can change from day to day as teens struggle to define themselves and their beliefs, the stakes are high for being visible as Other.

In this chapter, lesbian, gay, bisexual, transgender, queer or questioning (LGBTQ) will be used interchangeably with "queer" to speak about students who are exploring non-heteronormative sexuality and non-normative gender. The term "sexuality" refers to romantic attractions, sexual behaviors, sexual identity and desires, as well as to the presumed embodied existence of these characteristics. "Gender" is the behavioral characteristics that attach to binarily sexed bodies—feminine to female bodies and masculine to male bodies—as determined by secondary sex characteristics and hormonal or genetic factors. Many labels are affixed to persons who sexually or romantically desire someone of the same gender or biological sex, or who do not conform to heterosexual or binary-gendered categories. The labels above are but a small number of the possible categories a young person can subscribe to when deciding to describe him/herself and his/her gender or sexual desires. Many of the labels used by young people are not known to adults; and all have shifting boundaries of inclusion and exclusion.

Education scholars (Birden, 2005; Blackburn, 2002; Dilley, 1999; Epstein *et al.*, 2000–2001; Kumashiro, 2001; Leck, 2000; Letts and Sears, 1999; Loutzenheiser and MacIntosh, 2004; Quinlivan and Town, 1999; Rasmussen,

2006; Rofes, 2000) have already begun to explore queer theory's application to education. Most uses of queer theory in studies of education policy and practice focus on complicating and decentering both gender and sexuality, disrupting identity politics, and understanding heteronormativity. Because queer theory developed in response to some of the essentializing tendencies of lesbian and gay studies and earlier women's studies, it questions the categories of the subjects of its studies—even as it seeks to say something about those persons and about the material conditions of being viewed as belonging to a marginal category. "Queer studies is largely a deconstructive enterprise, taking apart the view of a self defined by something at its core, be it sexual desire, race, gender, nation or class" (Gamson, 2000). These theoretical positions allow space for an education researcher to understand the complex field of statements by students about sexuality and gender and to situate them in the context that creates them.

Disruption of Gender and Sexuality Categories

Following the social constructionist move which revealed gender and sexuality categories as socially created and culturally contingent, queer theory, notably in the work of Michel Foucault (1978) and Judith Butler (1990), argued that gender and sexuality were negotiated categories, reworked and restructured in each encounter—constantly being perfected, adjusted, and refined. In the understanding of biological sex, gender, and sexuality in the writings of Foucault and those who come after him, the presumed binary categories were disrupted. No longer is the ontological status of the male or female body secure. The many possibilities for bodies outside of the two normalized categories have been explored, as have the discursive powers—medical institutions and doctors—that place ambiguously gendered (often babies') bodies into one of the binary categories.

Foucault demonstrates (1973a, 1977, 1978) how the body came to be understood differently in the modern era with the Enlightenment and the rise of objectivity and observation as part of medical practice. In eighteenth-century medicine the body had been conceived as similar for both women and men. Differences were described mostly in terms of function, what the body could do, rather than in form or essential parts. A woman was a woman because she could bear children rather than because she had a certain anatomy. The anatomical differences between men and women, and the "normal" and "abnormal" iterations of that anatomy, had not yet been delineated as the critical mark of sex difference (Foucault, 1973a). During the Enlightenment, medical observation increased and knowledge was created through anatomical exploration and repeated observations of the same phenomenon, in attempts to understand the usual range or appearance.

The body came to be seen as normally constituted and constructed in certain ways and variations came to be understood as abnormalities. The world of humans could be decisively divided among women and men and those persons born with undifferentiated or out-of-range anatomical parts could be medically fixed to fit within the normal categories (ibid.).

As humans came to understand themselves as subjects during the Enlightenment, they saw themselves as limited by or tied to the materiality of their bodies (ibid.; also Foucault, 1978). With the rise of modern governmental structures, too, emerged "biopolitics," which Foucault (1977, 1978) describes as arising in Europe in the seventeenth century. As populations increased and ruling transformed from local dictate to larger and then democratic societies in which death and torture were no longer accepted as the normal means of social control, government became more interested in regulating bodies through bio-social control over the population's growth and functions—marriages, births, deaths, production, reproduction, and sexuality—and the state-istics needed to control these—became the accepted means of governing behavior and maintaining control. New discourses aimed at bodies arose about, for example, how, at what age, and under what rules bodies were engaging in sexual practices and reproducing.

Foucault is extremely critical of this "disciplining" of the body. He chastises medicine, psychology, and religious morality for the limitations they place on the gender and sexual expressions of the body, and demonstrates the variance and contingency of "natural" bodies, "natural" sexualities, and "natural" gendered positions in society (1978). His work delineates discourses that have created the categories in which human activity has come to be understood and known. As with biological sex and the medical establishment, the categorization of sexuality into heterosexual (normal) and homosexual (abnormal or pathologized) limits human subjects' knowledge of themselves and their desires. It is impossible for a subject to know him- or herself except through the discursive lens of the era and the culture (Foucault, 1977). "Discursive knowledge regulates, among other things, what can be said and done, what constitutes right and wrong, and what counts for knowledge in the first place. In short, discourse establishes and controls knowledge" (Dimitriadis and Kamberlis, 2006, 113). However, within discourse and everyday practice the subject can resist various subjections, and through resistance and transgression can push the boundaries of possible subject positions. One is limited by the materiality of the time and place in which one lives, but within that time and place one has choices about acceding to or resisting sexual and gender regulation.

The primacy of biology and biological discourses in creating gendered presentation and positions in society is further questioned by queer thinkers following Foucault. Judith Butler, for example, changed the way that postmodern scholars understand the "natural" gendered behavior that people in different bodies exhibit (Butler, 1990, 1993, 2004; Butler and Salih, 2004). Butler (1990) claimed that gender is a *performance* that the subject is required to repeat over and over in interactions with others, and through this performativity the body is structured and the self is created as gendered. "There is no gender behind the expressions of gender ... identity is performatively constituted by the very 'expressions' that are said to be its results" (25). Although a subject is created by the expressions of gender, subjects are not limited to this performance. In fact, since no one can perfectly perform gender (because it does not exist prior to its enactment), and since gender has to be renegotiated and reiterated in each interaction, the agency of the subject is quite apparent (Butler, 2004). Yet each subject performs gender to a greater or lesser extent in conformity with society's gender expectations.

Clearly, this understanding of sex, gender, and sexuality counters what is regularly taught in schools (Landry *et al.,* 2003) and what is commonly accepted as scientifically normal in society (Fausto-Sterling, 2000). Schools do not teach about biological sex in a way that questions the categories, and educators do not attempt to disrupt gendered differences between girls and boys. Binary gender is built into the architecture, the policies, the curriculum, the pedagogy, the social interactions and the publications of the school (Chesir-Teran, 2003).

Identity Politics

Identity politics advocates organizing around one facet of a person's being, such as ethnicity, gender, race, class, or sexuality, in order to win benefits for persons who claim to or can prove they fall within that category. Identity organizing and politics have been very successful in gaining civil rights for various groups in the United States. However, the exclusions inherent in identity organizing have been criticized by queer theory, and in a continuation of the effort to disrupt identity categories, queer theory has denounced simple identity politics as a way to advocate for change in schools (Birden, 2005; Rasmussen, 2006). Queer theory challenges the essential bases of identity categories. Basing political movements in identity categories codifies and hardens the lines that separate insiders from outsiders. Because movements have to specify for whom they are advocating and who will be the recipient of benefits won, a cutoff point must be decided upon and artificial boundaries around socially constructed categories must be erected (Birden, 2005; Butler, 1993; Young, 2000).

Identity organizing has been very successful in schools in advocating for gay–straight alliances (GSA). Using research that has shown LGBTQ students to be at risk for suicide, alcohol and drug abuse, and psychological problems, advocates and school system allies have pushed for clubs based on gay and lesbian identity for students in high schools. The clubs are designed to provide a social space for LGBTQ students and their straight friends to meet safely in school, and to increase the tolerance for these students within the student population by making them visible. However, educational queer theorist Mary Louise Rasmussen has argued against an essentializing identification of LGBTQ students as victims who need safe spaces in schools. In this kind of essentializing, students may be excluded from spaces in schools even without declaring themselves LGBTQ, based on the assumptions that other students make about them. Also, students who are non-heterosexual and non-gender-conforming, but who do not conform to the standards of lesbian, gay, bisexual, transgender or queer identities, may be excluded from the spaces that are created by schools to protect them. Schools may decide that LGBTQ students are a "disruption" to the order or discipline of the school, or decide that queer students' behavior is "inappropriate" or puts them in danger and remove the student to a more safe environment. This kind of "safety transfer" abdicates responsibility for addressing the heterosexism in the schools and removes the student against whom malice or violence is directed. LGBTQ students are then quietly excluded from their regular schools in the name of their "protection". The political moves based on identity that gain students "safe spaces" in schools also work to control their gender expression and sexuality and to confine them to certain understandings of their desires and their subjectivities.

Rasmussen describes spaces in schools that are defined as serving LGBTQ students as heterotopic (Foucault and Miskowiec, 1986). "Utopias permit fables and discourse: they run with the very grain of language and are part of the fundamental dimension of the *fabula*; heterotopias desiccate speech, stop words in their tracks, contest the very possibility of grammar at its source; they dissolve our myths and sterilize the lyricism of our sentences" (Foucault, 1973b, xviii). Language is heterotopic when it mixes elements that don't belong together in what results in "monstrous" (xvi) language. Foucault defines several ways in which spaces may also be heterotopic (Foucault and Miskowiec, 1986). Heterotopias are the various spaces in which one lives or which define one's existence in which individuals experiencing bodily changes and changes in status once experienced rituals, such as one marking the transition from childhood to adulthood. More often, now, these experiences have become private, or shameful, and heterotopias are spaces of "deviation" (ibid., 25), where those who are not considered normal are placed by society. Foucault cites prisons and psychiatric hospitals as examples. An example of heterotopic space in schools is one in which a person is relegated to involuntarily or to which it looks like there is free and voluntary entrance but certain rules or codes must be followed in order to be allowed to be there. The space, which seems like an entrance, is itself an exclusion (Rasmussen, 2006). This concept of heterotopias helps disrupt the unquestioned outcomes of politics based on identity by exposing the ways sexuality and gender identity categories both include those who feel ambivalent about being included and risk excluding those who desire to be included.

Queer theory has been used by education researchers to argue against these spatial enforcements that students may encounter in schools. LGBTQ students must be served by the school in some way, because they cannot *be* otherwise, meaning they must be recognized as legitimate students and eligible citizens (Butler, 2004). However, in the current structure the deviance and pathology becomes located in the body of the student, not in the school or the heterosexual students. The problem is identified, and if it cannot be concealed or normalized by the LGBTQ students, then the student is removed from sight for her inappropriate behavior. Engaging with queer theory gave me new tools and language with which to discourses about LGBTQ students and schools—including student safety, heterosexism, and "natural" gender—and a way to listen to students' voices and experiences.

Queer Theory and My Research

I wanted to obtain the input of high school students on the attitudes of young people toward LGBTQ students in their schools. I had been reading queer theory, and found it compatible with my interests and relevant to my empirical quest. Ultimately, I used queer theory to design my study, frame my questions, and analyze the data.

I received a small grant from my institution and devised a method[1] for asking students questions about their schools. The students who participated come from four of the five boroughs of New York City and represent six high schools, two small schools and four large comprehensive high schools. Student participants were recruited from an after-school leadership program run by a community-based after-school human rights education program. The leadership program met once a week for the entire school year, and the curriculum focused on social justice issues. Students in this program were considered good candidates for this project for several reasons: (1) They had already discussed difficult issues during the school year and had an ethic of group participation based on respect for others' ideas; (2) They had information about related issues, such as gender inequity, global health issues, and HIV/AIDS, but had not necessarily discussed LGBTQ and non-normative gender issues; (3) They had applied a social justice lens to other issues in their schools and issues affecting their peers. These attributes made it easier for them to discuss difficult issues with thoughtfulness in a safe setting. Thus, although they have a somewhat different educational background from other New York City teens owing to their participation in this after-school group, in other ways they are quite typical. They come from various ethnic backgrounds, they live in diverse neighborhoods. Some qualify for financial assistance for school lunches based on their family income. They are all students of color between the ages of 15 and 18 years old. Three of the twelve students identified as non-heterosexual, and none were transgendered. Four of the students were boys.

I created questions with a strong anti-essentialist idea in mind, yet I tried to elicit student understandings of the discourses and interactions in schools without imposing a structure in which I wanted them to answer. I heard from them in several formats: I encouraged them to share their thoughts and to reflect upon and restudy their school with eyes made more critical by conversations that took place in focus groups. Each student wrote a letter to an imaginary LGBTQ person new to their school. They were to describe for this person what he or she would find upon arrival and participation in the school. Second, each student participated in a focus group or a one-on-one interview. The focus groups ranged from two to five participants with two single-participant interviews. Finally, each student took home a notebook in which they journaled their thoughts at the end of each school day. In the focus groups and interviews, participants were asked:

1. Are there lesbian, gay, bisexual, transgender, queer, or questioning students or teachers at your school? How do you know?
2. Is any place in your school considered safer for these students? Is any place less safe?
3. What would happen if:
   • A boy took a boy to the prom?
   • Two girls walked down the hall holding hands?
   • A boy (or girl) came to school dressed or acting like a girl (or boy)?

For the week of journaling, the students were asked to record anything they thought was interesting in light of the focus group conversation. They were invited to respond to the topic and any questions that it raised for them in any form that they wanted to. All responded with daily journal entries. Responses to the focus groups and journals will be reported here; data from the letters will be reported at another time.

These questions are "queer" in that they ask students to think about how they identify those in their schools who are LGBTQ. Queer research questions "why, how, and who determines that those lives are queer" (Dilley, 1999, 460). Queer theory also directs students to think about multiple levels of power—the institutional spaces provided for students' safety and the discourses around those spaces and the rest of the school that regulate the feeling of safety or necessity of safe spaces in the school. Finally, by asking "what would happen if," I request that students place themselves in the space of a transgressive moment in their school and imagine the reactions of their friends, the teachers, the administration and their parents.

Most of the students participating in this study identified as "straight" or heterosexual according to their self-disclosures about sexuality. They therefore gave the perspective of those who inhabit the normative spaces in the school of the school's acceptance of those who inhabit the "othered" spaces. Even if they do not have this experience in their school they can imagine it, and register the emotional responses of members of their school community. Research is queer, Dilley says, if "it is about questioning the presumptions, values and viewpoints from those positions (marginal and central), especially those that normally go unquestioned" (1999, 462). Peer and parental reactions would be based on many factors, including the social standing of those who decided to cross the heteronormative lines and the beliefs of their families, as well as the gender expression and perceived sexual explicitness of the behavior of the transgressing students.

The data and discussion presented below suggest that the overwhelming message from the students was, "it's not too bad." The presence of out LGBTQ students in their schools reassures them that things must be OK in their schools, since those kids are out (or since the participants themselves are out—in the cases of a bisexual girl and a gay boy). Students reacted to the questions in three ways that exhibit how they are questioning the gender and sexuality norms that exist in society. They questioned the ways that people represent themselves as LGBTQ or pass as straight in high school and outside of school in the city. They questioned which expressions of self constitute "real" gender. And they questioned valuing a person based on his or her sexuality, and asked for acceptance of people based on their "real" worth. In these ways the students sometimes use post-structuralist discourses to describe their understandings of the construction of gender and sexuality, and sometimes rely on a binary understanding of the differences between girls and boys—for example to show what is real or unreal about a person's performance. As I argue below, these seemingly conflicting messages do not discredit the testimony teens give; the conflicts simply highlight the ways in which teens struggle with the various messages they receive from church, school, after-school activities, family, friends, and popular culture as they attempt to understand themselves and gender and sexuality.

Disrupted Categories: Gender and Sexuality are [Somewhat] Fluid

Eleven of the twelve participants reported that there are students who are crossing gender lines in their schools. They acknowledge a range of gender identities—girls who dress as boys, boys who dress as girls, those who wish to be seen as the other gender and those who keep the pronoun of their birth—most of these stances find some acceptance in their schools. Philip[2] says, "There's like a few girls who act masculine, but they're girls. But they'll walk, talk, act like a boy. But when they turn around, you see their chest, like, 'Oh, that dude is a girl.' But it's good in my school" (interview 5/12/06). Philip claims not to have a problem with girls dressing in clothing that is marketed as boys' clothing, and to respect the gender signifying of these girls. He acknowledges that they are girls, but that they are also making themselves unavailable to boys through dressing as not-girls.

Emma also reports, "There's a boy in my school who's openly gay, he wears female clothes . . . He has hair extensions . . . He wears tight clothes, female cologne. Like most people comment on him, but he doesn't really care, and most people just accept him as who he is" (interview 6/15/06). The boy in Emma's school finds friends among the girls, but he experiences some discomforts that are visible to other students. He appears uncomfortable being scanned by the male security guards, although he does not get a choice about who scans him upon entry into the school. Also he is sometimes called "she" by the boys in the school, and he takes this comment as an insult or a taunt. Although he dresses in girls' clothing, he does not identify himself as a girl. Participants in the study affirm the ways that peers of these students are accepting and inclusive of them, not shutting them out of the social circles, even when this acceptance by some occurs in conjunction with obvious incidents of harassment by other peers at school.

Participants also report sexuality experimentation and an acknowledgement from some of their LGBTQ friends that they are trying on different sexualities. Veronica's friend told her that "she'll never marry a woman, but she just doesn't want to be with a guy right now" (interview 5/19/06). Veronica understands her friend to be "going through, like, her phase. Now she's kind of bi" (ibid.). She also thinks, however, that the girl is looking for emotional fulfillment that is a replacement of her mother's love, and that she can find that in a relationship with another woman, rather than with a man. Katherine, too, sees that in her school "a lot of girls . . . turned, like, bi or fully lesbian, and in my school it seems like it's a trend to be gay now, openly gay" (interview 6/2/06).

In some ways this experimentation is seen to be inauthentic sexuality, or a rebellion that is like taking drugs, as Annabelle asserts, but there is also an acknowledgement that each person should get to name his or her own identity. Veronica points out, "That's for, up to you to handle your sexuality as anything like that, so, you know, how some people are like, 'I get this feeling that he's kind of—,' but, you know, like, if he is, he'll figure it out" (interview 5/19/06). Additionally, Philip rejects his peers' insults of the non-gender-conforming behavior of a boy in his school, stating that "life is all about being different. Would you like it if you look like your friend, talk like him, and dress like him?" (interview 5/12/06). With this comment he makes discursive space for his friend to perform gender and sexuality as it best suits him. Philip confirms the assertions of his focus group that teens struggle to understand themselves and the discursive categories into which they are placed by others or by themselves. They seek identities that fit and ways to meet their needs, desires, and pleasures, and in order to do that they sometimes must differentiate themselves from the hegemony of the group.

Participants in the research project expressed a sophisticated under-standing of gender and the ways that it works in society and their lives. They were able to clearly discuss the way that gender interacts with sexuality to create more spaces for girls to transgress sexuality boundaries than for boys. Girls—lesbian and bisexual—in their schools are much more able to be out and are generally much more visible in higher numbers than boys. One participant (Emma, interview 6/15/06) estimates that 30 percent of girls in her school identify as lesbian or bisexual, while she knows of only one boy who claims to be gay. While these numbers may not be accurate, the differences between boys and girls in her school makes a large impression on her. This difference is explained in many different ways, but most participants agree that the eroticization of lesbianism and bisexuality in women that can be found in pornography makes lesbian and bisexual girl peers seem sexy to boys (Omar, interview 5/19/06; Philip, interview 5/12/06).

The approval (or lesser disapproval) by boys creates a social space in which girls can declare themselves non-heterosexual. Girls' approval of boys' homosexuality and boys' feminine attributes was also widely reported by participants as is seen in Emma's comments earlier about the boy in her school who wears girls' clothing. This approval did not confer the same social openness to boys, who do not "come out" at the same rates that girls do. Boys are generally disapproving in these students' schools of other boys' feminine behavior and are verbally derisive, if not physically threatening, to boys who declare themselves gay. In only one school was it reported that girls responded in anger and disgust at a girl who had been passing as a boy. Omar reports, "but the girls were like, 'This bitch.' Like they wanted to kill her, and I'm like, 'How the fuck?' You know, it was like she betrayed their race or something, or their gender" (interview 5/19/06). In this quote Omar shows his understanding that sexuality, gender, and racial identity categories all compel young people to behave in a correct way that defines the category. This intersectionality (Collins, 2003) sometimes causes complications for the teens where behavioral codes conflict. The focus group participants could see how gender is constructed through a behavior code of acts called feminine and masculine, and accepted the stated gender, for the most part, of their classmates who transgress gender boundaries. They have begun to deconstruct for themselves the concept of gender.

Remember that queer theory proposes that sexuality and gender are not fixed categories but are historically contingent and continually negotiated in relational interactions. Teens, like everyone else in early twenty-first-century US society, understand the imperative to be easily legible as one or the other gender and to be able to pass as heterosexual. For those teens in their schools who choose not to appear to fit into acceptable gender and sexuality categories, there are risks. But many teens seem willing to take those risks in exchange for the greater freedom achieved through pursuing their desires and pleasures. Foucault suggested that the normative discursive understandings of sexuality and gender limit the possibilities of human expression (1978). However, within those limitations there exist ruptures where the boundaries can be expanded, where transgression and resistance are possible, and where new subjectivities can be formed. Teen girls, especially, are taking advantage of these ruptures to engage with their sexuality and gender expression in high schools in New York City, to explore their desires and bodily pleasures in the social spaces provided by their peers' tacit or explicit approval.

I would argue that many LGBTQ teens' attitudes toward gender and sexuality reflect the cultural struggles between modernist ideas and postmodern ideas of the body, that is, between a body that is ontologically real and knowable and biologically natural and a body that is discursively created and knowable only through the discourses actually put into practice. Teens in this study believe both in the natural, biological basis of sexuality and gender, and also in the right of a person to declare his or her own sexuality and gender and to live in a way that meets personal desires. For those students who transition from one gender to another, or who signify gender in a way that does not conform to gender binaries, teens appear willing to accept the declared gender of their peers. However, they do not use a language that moves beyond binary gender or troubles gender hegemony. Teens who feel secure in their gender do not question the natural, biological basis of gender performances and categories. Their peers' questioning does not necessarily lead teens to question their own gender and sexuality performances.

Politics Based on Justice and LGBTQ Student Voices

Participants in this study emphasized strongly that being LGBTQ does not and should not disqualify a person from being accepted within his or her peer group. Katherine began her interview by declaring, "I accept it. Like, it's nothing to me, because it doesn't change who you really are, or what your personality is" (interview 6/2/06). Several other participants echoed this sentiment and made the case that at their school a person is not judged based on their sexuality. Omar's school, which has a Gay–Straight Alliance, says the club advocates with the school community on behalf of the LGBTQ students to remedy any ignorance in the school community. "It's very easy to be afraid of—for people, what they don't know and what they haven't experienced, it's very easy to say that and make that a taboo. And I think once they started this organization [the GSA] in our school, and people were like, 'Okay, you know what? They're just another human person'" (interview 5/19/06). Participants also thought that LGBTQ students do not have to act in any certain way, that they could just be regular teens. Vanessa's friend who is a lesbian is "herself . . . she's loud. She's crazy. She's like how any other teenage girl would be, and no one harasses her. No one bothers her" (interview 6/9/06). These participants assert that being an LGBTQ teen in their school is no different from being anyone else.

However, Annabelle tempers Vanessa's comment slightly with the warning that she offers three times over the course of the focus group. She is very concerned that

> when you proclaim yourself gay or lesbian or questioning or whatever, once you put that status over your head, you put yourself out here for criticism . . . I mean, you go through life, and you want to be different, and you want to be accepted for who you are if you're different, but that's not the case, because some people are like that, afraid of the unknown, and they don't want to know the unknowns inside.
>
> (interview 5/19/06)

Annabelle offers a warning to LGBTQ students that once people see a person as queer they may only see the queer, not seeing the rest of the personality or character of the person but only the stereotype. She sees this status as similar to her teacher's decision to wear her hair in dreads. The teacher was worried that no one would see the English degree or the teaching job, they would just see her as a Black woman in dreads and dismiss her according to the stereotype they have about people with dreadlocks.

In addition to Annabelle's concern about the stereotyped view that others may have of students who declare themselves gay, Veronica also worries that queer students may become enveloped in "being gay" and let the subculture dictate their lifestyle, attitudes, personal presentation, and ways of thinking. She sees the performances that are expected of persons who are claiming a queer identity, and declares, "I think it just went past your sexuality, like they try to make it seem like it's your religion. It's your life. It's the way you act. It's the way you dress. It's the way you do things. It's . . ." Annabelle completes her thought, "It's becoming like a culture" (interview 5/19/06). Veronica later reiterates, "It's because basically I think that being who you are, your sexuality and how you come out with it, hinders your individuality. I don't think there's a lot of individuals in the world. I think everybody conforms to a 'norm' or what you should be" (interview 5/19/06). She clearly sees that norms exist, not just for heterosexuality and heteronormativity, but that those norms police the boundaries of gay identity as well, and that those who are coming out and declaring themselves gay feel the need to fit the norms to be found a legitimate member of the queer community. The strength of norms around gender and sexuality are subject to discussion among these teens, and they recognize transgressions among their fellow students. Teen participants see both the stereotypes that others have and the norms of the queer community as essentialist ideas about queerness that do not fit all persons and advocate for the acceptance of LGBTQ students in their schools, without requiring that they conform to the norms.

Teen participants saw LGBTQ youth in their schools placed, socially and perhaps physically, into heterotopic spaces as a result of being publicly homosexual. While they simultaneously emphasized that LGBTQ students in their schools were no different from anyone else, students repeatedly returned to the idea that being gay both places one socially in a space apart, in which one may be judged solely based on sexuality, and that there are rules of sexuality and gender performance that come with being out. The heterotopic spaces in schools as spaces that have rules governing access to them exclude those who they claim to serve by applying the rules very literally, so that the student who dresses as a girl but has the body of a boy must be searched by male guards. On the other hand, heterotopias can be too inclusive, and can implicate those who resist an identity. Gay–Straight Alliances have been criticized for serving as spaces in schools that serve to identify students who do not claim an LGBTQ identity, and where a student who is being harassed about sexuality might be sent, for her safety, regardless of her sexual desires (Rasmussen, 2006). This GSA might not be attended at one school because most students would not want to be identified so publicly as LGBTQ (Michael, interview 5/12/06). Heterotopic spaces can include spaces where non-LGBTQ students become uncomfortable because they do not conform to the norms of queer performance and do not understand the significations of the LGBTQ students, as in the girls' locker room when the basketball team arrives, in which a "vibe" (Veronica, interview, 5/19/06) makes a straight girl feel uncomfortable.

As with queer theory's criticisms of identity politics, student participants in this research expressed impatience with the behavioral imperatives of claiming queerness. They felt that by publicly proclaiming LGBTQ status, students often felt compelled to dress, talk, act, think, and be queer. In contrast, in their own experiences they knew queer people who did not fit the stereotypes, and who were "like how any other teenage[r. . .] would be." The respondents exhibited a complex understanding of identity in which their peers could be both members of their community, be that a racial, ethnic, language, or nationality community, and also queer. They voiced a common critique of lesbian and gay identity activism which advocates for tolerance using the same politics in every community. Students explained that tactics for acceptance and tolerance may be different for their friends, that they may be "not really in your face about [their sexuality]" (Vanessa, interview 6/09/06). Nonetheless, the participants are not less accepting of their friends, family members', or their own queerness, and they understand it as part of the person's identity, intersectionally intertwined with their race, class, and culture (Collins, 2003; Loutzenheiser and MacIntosh, 2004). The LGBTQ peers of the participants in this study are claiming sexuality that meets their sexual and emotional needs and their bodies' desires in ways that do not require them to seek community outside of their racial and ethnic groups. Their "queerness" allows them to maintain ties with their friends, families, and communities. This queering of queerness may express a new way of blending the normative expectations of families, sexual and gender positions that defy categories and embrace fluidity and of creating community across difference.

Heteronormativity Contested: Students are Out

Every student in the interviews said that peers in their school were publicly "out," especially the girls. As reported above, most of them knew several girls who identify as lesbian or bisexual, but only one or two boys who identify as gay or bisexual. Some of them knew of teachers in their schools who are out, such as Angela who said about her teacher, "He's definitely gay. He says it to everyone. Yeah, he has piercings and everything" (interview 5/12/06). The reason that these students give for knowing there are gay students in their schools is that the LGBTQ students are willing to claim an identity and share it with classmates. Annabelle states, "They come out and say it. They come out to your face and say, you know, 'I'm gay. I'm lesbian.' Whatever. We don't have any trans at our school" (interview 5/19/06). Many LGBTQ students embrace the symbols of the gay movement and "wear colors, the gay pride colors, everything, representing" (Emma, interview 6/15/06). The participants are most willing to claim an LGBTQ identity for someone else if the student has told them that he or she identifies as queer, or wears obvious symbols of a queer identity.

They are less willing to make this claim about those whom they have not heard proclaim their "outness," and question how a person could know, just looking at someone, that he or she is LGBTQ. Both Vanessa and Annabelle in their journals record an incident in the mall, where they saw two girls walking together, one "dress-down (tee, jeans, very loose fit), but I usually call that a laundry day" (Vanessa, journal 5/19/06). Vanessa sees "nothing outlandish . . . that would make me assume that they were lesbians, but only their [rainbow] flag made me aware of it" (ibid.). She then asks herself questions about the existence of a "gay way of dressing" and whether or not "being gay makes you a different person, or is it society?" (Vanessa, journal 5/19/06). Omar also notes the inability to tell if a person is gay by the way he is dressed, recording in his journal, "[At the subway station] I see two gay men making out on the Mezzanine level. They appeared to be dressed to fit in and I would never have thought them to be gay if I had not seen them kissing" (journal 5/23/06). In these instances, the participants claim queerness for others where they feel the person has declared himself or herself, with symbols representing gay pride or with gay sexual behavior, such as kissing another person of the same sex. Even though Omar (interview 5/19/06) claims in the focus group that behavior does not define a person as gay, in the subway station he sees the men's behavior as a declaration to the waiting passengers that they are gay, despite the fact that they don't fit a stereotypical picture of what gay men are supposed to look like.

There are different levels of being out and of declaration, however, where the suspicion of queerness has been raised about someone but is unverified. Philip says, "I've never heard him say that he's out. But I've heard other people say that he's gay, but I'm not sure, so I can't really say" (interview 5/12/06). Michael, a gay boy who is out at school, knows "there's other people . . . because they told me, but they're not out yet" (interview 5/12/06). And Vanessa reports from her school that there are students who are "not really in your face about it, but to a certain extent you know who is" (interview 6/9/06).

These students report a demarcation line between those who have declared themselves LGBTQ and those who have not declared themselves, regardless of their gender behavior, their sexual behavior or their self-knowledge of "being gay." Declaring oneself as belonging to a category, regardless of the fluidity of that category or of the sexual behavior in which one engages, is seen as important. Participants see this declaration as important in order to understand who their friends are, and as important to the health and happiness of the person. Those who are not forthcoming about their suspected sexuality are considered to be "kind of like denying themselves" (Cynthia, 6/2/06). Although LGBTQ students are not expected to be too "in your face" about their sexuality, they are expected to be honest with themselves about their desires. This honesty is important even though, as discussed in the last section, the participants also declare that sexuality is only a part of one's identity.

As my discussion of queer theory noted, its proponents challenge mainstream views of biological heteronormativity as a set of hegemonic social norms that assume everyone is heterosexual and heterosexuality is superior, with homosexuality becoming a shameful, deviant state. Students in this study have felt the force of heteronormativity. They report the expectations that they will get married and have children, and that this is the goal of relationships. They worry that if everyone continues experimenting and becoming lesbian or gay, that humanity will not be able to reproduce itself (Veronica, interview 5/19/06). They do not have, as some queer educators propose (Rofes, 2000), a queered idea about sexuality that is separate from a notion of procreation and lifelong partnering. At the same time, they acknowledge the lesbian and gay and bisexual relationships that their friends or they themselves may be engaging in as a challenge to heteronormativity. They acknowledge that these relationships provide important pleasures and satisfactions to their friends that other relationships could or would not provide. In this sense, they understand their friends' or their own same-sex relationships as not inferior, shameful, pathological, or problematic. Student participants see the need for their peers to claim their sexuality as equally important and pleasing as heterosexual students' sexuality is for them.

These teens are working with discourses at play in the United States at this time: that gender is socially created *or* biologically given, that sexuality is genetically determined *or* freely chosen, that desire is voluntary *or* innate. All of these binary frames can be heard in their comments and they reason with each one, raising questions about the validity of the perspectives of their peers and challenging notions that they know are oppressive. They are quick to defend the humanity and right to respect of others who are different, even if they cannot themselves understand the reasons for the person's behavior or actions. They are willing to have a discussion about other ways of living and to challenge the beliefs that they see their parents, school administrators, some teachers, and some of their peers expressing. Their activist training has fostered some of these attitudes, and given them practice in deciding on the ethics of a situation by understanding it from the point of view of those who are being persecuted. They believe in social justice and are willing to question the beliefs they have been raised with and decide for themselves what is right, outside of the institutional truths about sexuality and gender such as those that come from religion, psychology, education, or medicine.

Conclusion

The teens participating in this study reported on their own attitudes and those of other students in their high schools. In some cases, they are using ideas expressed by queer theory to discuss their own and their peers' ideas about sexuality and gender, and identity politics, although sometimes they use essentialist notions of sexuality and gender, as well as uncritical notions of equality and tolerance of difference—which do not disrupt the superiority or naturalness of heterosexuality and binary gender—to discuss the kinds of rights they think LGBTQ students should be entitled to in schools. On the whole, these students express a complicated view of sexuality and gender—a view informed by the various media and discourses that they encounter in their daily lives, no doubt including television, political debates and news reporting, school lessons, music, and the ideas of their peers. Some of them are also active in communities on the internet, sharing ideas and stories with teens who do not necessarily live in their city or even their country. These ideas, perhaps contradictory and sometimes hard to reconcile with the ideas of their families, nonetheless have seeped into the ways that they are trying to make ethical choices about their interactions with their peers and the social justice causes for which they wish to advocate. They see the place of LGBTQ students in schools and in society as changing, difficult, and sometimes subject to injustice; and they universally advocate for recognition of the humanity of the person who is different.

They accept sexual fluidity in their friends. They accept that teens, both boys and girls, are sexual subjects (Fine and McClelland, 2006; Rasmussen, 2004, 2006) who choose different relationship configurations for different reasons, to meet their sexual and emotional needs. These needs are seen as real and valid, and the relationships are valorized for their ability to meet the needs of these teens. *As such, participants in this study are questioning the traditional binary construction that posits heterosexuality as normal and homosexuality as deviant.* These teens see their friends and peers not as the deviant Other, but as agentic sexual subjects with emotional and bodily desires expressed in a non-heterosexual relationship. This fluidity allows young people to try on different sexualities and gender expressions without committing to a lifelong sexuality or gender category, without taking on the assumption that they are biologically or genetically different. Students are not required to claim a natural basis for their desires and pleasures that makes them fundamentally different from their peers. This frees them to experiment.

Most of these students declare themselves political allies for LGBTQ students in their schools, and feel that political alliances can be made across identity categories. They affirm that each person should be able to pick the identity label for him/herself, and should not be limited by that label or boxed in to a "culture" by it. Several students voiced the idea that requirements for belonging to a group, whether a religion, subculture, or gender, are sometimes so rigid that they transform or mask the person in favor of the attitudes, dress, actions, ideas, activities that the group condones. This is similar to the anti-conformist attitude that Judith Butler (Butler and Salih, 2004) advances, in which she claims, "to install myself within the terms of an identity category would be to turn against the sexuality that the category purports to describe; and this might be true for any identity category which seeks to control the very eroticism that it claims to describe and authorize, much less 'liberate'" (121). The anti-essentializing moves of queer theory ring true to the teen participants in this study, who understand that society often "puts that status over your head" (Annabelle, interview 5/19/06) when it ascribes stereotypical attributes to a person who is perceived to be a part of a racial, ethnic, class, or sexuality group. The students subscribe to a politics based on affinity (Birden, 2005) rather than identity, an ethical approach that would entail working for changes in the schools' policies and practices for the greater integration of LGBTQ students on the basis of their citizenship within the school community and their rights as students.

Queer theory, because of its objections against essential queerness and identity organizing, is perceived to not allow for a very strong political action. Without the potential to engage activists based on their own identity interests, it is presumed that energy for a struggle will soon wane. Participants in this research argued against this conclusion. They engaged with a politics of justice on the basis of sexual and gender self-actualization. They promoted an ethics based on the freedom to pursue sexual and gender desires, rather than on a morality imposed by institutional powers. Also because of the many ways that young people are engaging with both modern and postmodern ideas of self and subjectivity, their peers sometimes imagine that LGBTQ youth have agency to choose sexuality and gender unimpeded. Students often did perceive that the situation was not too bad for LGBTQ students in their schools. They may not see much need to protest for changes in their schools if LGBTQ students are seen to get along easily and not be too disturbed by the verbal insults that they may hear in the halls or classes. As Michael says, "They may look like they don't care, but they do" (interview 5/12/06). The perceived ease with which students are coming out and declaring non-normative sexuality may mitigate the impetus to political action. Creating political action would require finding a specific problem around which to organize and creating a feeling of injustice that other students could relate to, rather than relying on sexuality as a unifying force.

Queer theory allows researchers to categorize the language that students are using—to draw a line between modernist conceptions of self and postmodern conceptions. But it also allows for other lines to be drawn, diagonally, through the discourses that are used in schools to relegate LGBTQ youth to certain spaces, certain behaviors, certain bodies. These discourses attempt to create for school districts, educators, and the public an epistemological ordering of bodies and desires that can be regulated by schools. If this means that schools have to become "tolerant" of LGBTQ youth, they are willing to do that as long as LGBTQ youth conform to certain behaviors and spaces. Queer theory demonstrates how youth are subverting these categories, and drawing from various discourses to produce their selfhood and sexual subjectivities and embrace their bodies and pleasures.

Notes

1   These strategies were formulated with the help of Dr. Michelle Fine, of the Social Psychology Department of the Graduate Center, CUNY.
2   All names are pseudonyms.

References

Aleman, G. (2004). Constructing Gay Performances: Regulating Gay Youth in a "Gay Friendly" High School. In B. K. Alexander, G. L. Anderson, and B. P. Gallegos, editors, *Performance Theories in Education: Power, Pedagogy, and the Politics of Identity*. Mahwah, NJ: Lawrence Erlbaum Associates, 149–171.

Birden, S. (2005). *Rethinking Sexual Identity in Education*. Lanham, MD: Rowman & Littlefield.

Blackburn, M. V. (2002). Disrupting the (Hetero)normative: Exploring Literacy Performances and Identity Work With Queer Youth. *Journal of Adolescent & Adult Literacy*, 46: 4, 312–324.

Butler, J. (1990). *Gender Trouble: Feminism and the Subversion of Identity*. New York: Routledge.

Butler, J. (1993). *Bodies that Matter: On the Discursive Limits of "Sex"*. New York: Routledge.

Butler, J. (2004). *Undoing Gender*. New York: Routledge.

Butler, J., and Salih, S. (2004). *The Judith Butler Reader*. Malden, MA: Blackwell.

Chesir-Teran, D. (2003). Conceptualizing and Assessing Heterosexism in High Schools: A Setting-level Approach. *American Journal of Community Psychology*, 31: 3/4, 267–279.

Cloud, J. (2005). The Battle Over Gay Teens. *Time*, 166: 15.

Collins, P. H. (2003). Some Group Matters: Intersectionality, Situated Standpoints, and Black Feminist Thought. In T. L. Lott and J. P. Pittman, editors, *Blackwell Companion to African American Philosophy*. Oxford: Blackwell, 205–229.

Dilley, P. (1999). Queer Theory: Under Construction. *Qualitative Studies in Education*, 12: 5, 457–472.

Dimitriadis, G., and Kamberlis, G. (2006). *Theory for Education*. New York: Taylor & Francis.

Epstein, D., O'Flynn, S., and Telford, D. (2000–2001). "Othering" Education: Sexualities, Silences, and Schooling. *Review of Research in Education*, 25, 127–179.

Fausto-Sterling, A. (2000). *Sexing the Body: Gender Politics and the Construction of Sexuality*. New York: Basic Books.

Fine, M., and McClelland, S. I. (2006). Sexuality Education and Desire: Still Missing After All These Years. *Harvard Educational Review*, 76: 3, 297–338.

Foucault, M. (1973a). *The Birth of the Clinic: An Archaeology of Medical Perception*. New York: Pantheon Books.

Foucault, M. (1973b). *The Order of Things: An Archaeology of the Human Sciences*. New York: Vintage Books.

Foucault, M. (1977). *Discipline and Punish: The Birth of the Prison*. New York: Pantheon Books.

Foucault, M. (1978). *The History of Sexuality: An Introduction*. New York: Random House.

Foucault, M., and Miskowiec, J. (1986). Of Other Spaces. *Diacritics*, 16: 1, 22–27.

Gamson, J. (2000). Sexualities, Queer Theory, and Qualitative Research. In N. K. Denzin and

Y. S. Lincoln, editors, *Handbook of Qualitative Research.* Thousand Oaks, CA: Sage Publications, 347–365.

Gay, Lesbian and Straight Education Network. (2005). *From Teasing to Torment: School Climate in America.* New York: GLSEN.

Human Rights Watch. (2001). *Hatred in the Hallways: Violence and Discrimination against Lesbian, Gay, Bisexual, and Transgender Students in U.S. Schools.* New York: Human Rights Watch.

Kumashiro, K. (2000). Theory of Anti-oppressive Education. *Review of Educational Research,* 70: 1, 25–53.

Kumashiro, K. (2001). "Posts" Perspectives on Anti-oppressive Education in Social Studies, English, Mathematics, and Science Classrooms. *Educational Researcher,* 30: 3, 3–12.

Landry, D. J., Darroch, J. E., Singh, S., and Higgins, J. (2003). Factors Associated with the Content of Sex Education in U.S. Public Secondary Schools. *Perspectives on Sexual and Reproductive Health,* 35: 6, 261–269.

Leck, G. M. (2000). Heterosexual or Homosexual? Reconsidering Binary Narratives on Sexual Identities in Urban Schools. *Education and Urban Society,* 32: 3, 324–348.

Letts, W. J., and Sears, J. T. (1999). *Queering Elementary Education: Advancing the Dialogue about Sexualities and Schooling.* Lanham, MD: Rowman and Littlefield.

Loutzenheiser, L. W., and MacIntosh, L. B. (2004). Citizenships, Sexualities, and Education. *Theory Into Practice,* 43: 2, 151–158.

Quinlivan, K., and Town, S. (1999). Queer Pedagogy, Educational Practice and Lesbian and Gay Youth. *Qualitative Studies in Education,* 12: 5, 509–524.

Rasmussen, M. L. (2004). "That's so Gay!" A Study of the Deployment of Signifiers of Sexual and Gender Identity in Secondary School Settings in Australia and the United States. *Social Semiotics,* 14: 3, 289–308.

Rasmussen, M. L. (2006). *Becoming Subjects: Sexualities and Secondary Schooling.* New York: Routledge.

Rofes, E. (2000). Bound and Gagged: Sexual Silences, Gender Conformity and the Gay Male Teacher. *Sexualities,* 3: 4, 439–462.

Savin-Williams, R. C. (2005). *The New Gay Teenager.* Cambridge, MA: Harvard University Press.

Sedgwick, E. K. (1990). *Epistemology of the Closet.* Berkeley: University of California Press.

Sen, R., and Fellner, K. (2005). *Learning Curves: Expanding the Constituency for Comprehensive Sexuality Education:* Applied Research Center.

Szalacha, L. A. (2004). Educating Teachers on LGBTQ Issues: A Review of Research and Program Evaluations. *Journal of Gay & Lesbian Issues in Education,* 1: 4, 67–79.

Young, I. M. (2000). *Inclusion and Democracy.* Oxford: Oxford University Press.

Personal Reflection

Queer Teens and Queer Theory

I have loved theory, or my ideas of theory, since I first took political science and philosophy classes as an undergraduate at a small Jesuit university in the Midwest. Arguing about ideas, imagining the ethical, economic, and political outcomes of different arrangements of societal priorities and legal structures felt very important to me, and even as I struggled to understand the theorists I was reading I was excited to know that such a conversation existed and to imagine that as a reader and a student I could be part of it. I sought out friends who also liked to debate Marxism, American pragmatism, and theories of justice. I studied revolutions, ethics, and epistemology and, like many undergraduates, began to understand the interconnected nature of fields of knowledge and the ways that it gets constructed in different disciplines. I was not sure, however, what place this theoretical conversation would have in my work life.

After graduation I pursued very practical fields, working in social services, youth development, and libraries. I studied for my Master's in library science, also taking classes toward a women's studies certificate. Authors like Linda Nicholson, Donna Haraway, Iris Marion Young, Gayatri Spivak, Susan Bordo, bell hooks, Teresa de Lauretis, Gloria Anzaldua, Eve Sedgwick, Biddy Martin, Nancy Fraser, Judith Butler, and Patricia Hill Collins challenged and liberated me, making space in my thoughts to examine notions of my identity, my commitments, my agency. These women, the conversations between them, and the contestations within feminism about racism, essentialism, power, and sexuality destabilized the certainty I had felt about these topics. By challenging a binary view of relationships and sexuality, these feminist and queer theorists complicated my world. I began to feel the complexities and challenges of lesbian identification.

Yet the media and scientific portrayal of queer people—especially high school students—as victims of violence was ubiquitous. In some cases, I knew, scientific research documenting this victimization did leverage force needed to create policy changes that might make schools safer for non-heterosexual youth. But these studies portrayed lesbian, gay, and, more recently, bisexual, queer, and questioning teens as suffering from psychological problems violence because they were not able to hide their sexuality or gender identity. The literature influenced the public discourse about LGBTQ youth, and informed public sentiment about them, eliciting both sympathy and loathing. Although I knew this research was important, and did not dispute some of its conclusions, I hoped that there was more to the experience of being adolescent and queer or transgender, that there was some *joy*, some *rebellion*, some *freedom* in claiming such identities and practices.

As a young lesbian librarian in the late 1990s in New York City, I became aware of the conversations and negotiations young people were engaging in concerning sexuality and gender. I was visibly queer with short, sometimes shaved hair and typically wore clothing that was not feminine. I inspired questions from students who came to me at the reference desk. "Are you GI Jane?" "Why do you wear your hair so short?" "Are you gay?" These were not hostile questions. The youth who approached me were looking for information and resources about queerness. Something about my queer visibility made me approachable, made me look safe.

This contact with queer youth convinced me that research showing teens simply as psychologically scared and victims of violence because of their sexuality did not tell the whole story. The teens I was talking to were active agents in the struggle to understand their desires. They were searching for narratives that told a variety of stories about gay teen experiences. While they were certainly strategic in whom they revealed themselves to, they were not hiding their sexuality. They were in the process of making spaces safe for themselves, while demanding the opportunity to do desire the way they wanted. I felt there was something more complex than victimization occurring with these young people in their negotiations with their world and sexuality.

I wanted to bring the theory that had so energized and excited me during my years at university into conversation with my work in the library and the young people I encountered on a daily basis. I now felt comfortable engaging with the ideas in feminist and queer theory, but I was worried about engaging in empirical research. I was plagued with questions: How does a researcher begin studying the role of agency and subjectivity in the sexuality and gender performances of teen lives? How do I begin to understand what teens are thinking, feeling, saying, doing, wanting, and needing in terms of sexuality and gender policy and justice, in schools and in other aspects of their lives? How do I understand teens as both victims of violence or oppression based on their sexuality *and* as political and social agents working for the relations and possibilities that they want to see in their lives? To whom does it matter what queer kids, transgender kids, or straight kids think about sexuality and gender? And how would theory—queer theory in particular—help me to understand the many layers of sexuality and gender subjectivity in young people?

I began my forays into empirical research before beginning my doctoral work. I wanted to know how LGBTQ teens were using the library as a source of information in their sexual identity process—if and how they used both fiction and non-fiction materials, and what they felt was missing in the library collections. I conducted two focus groups with high school students in after-school settings and collected surveys at a youth-led conference on sexuality for queer and transgender youth. I made some valuable findings in terms of library collections and what teens wanted and needed, but I did not have the skills to interpret their responses to interview questions and focus group discussions in a more sophisticated way. I could count the "yes's" and the "no's", but was not able to explain any further. I felt dissatisfied with my abilities, and longed to be able to integrate the theory I felt explained so much about myself with young peoples' voices concerning their desires and needs. I longed to dispute the punitive and limiting conceptions that seemed prevalent about young people's negotiations with their sexuality and gender.

The theory I encountered in doctoral studies gave me the language to articulate a more complicated vision. I wanted to use this new language to talk about the mismatch I perceived between the generalized assumptions about queer youth and the being and living they experienced.

My current research is demonstrating that teens are finding spaces between and on the edges of hegemonic discourses of gender in which to fashion themselves as sexual subjects. They are actively engaging with their formation, performing gender in the ways that best meet their needs. The theoretical ideas that I have encountered in Butler and Foucault support these developments and challenge me to think about gender and sexuality as culturally constructed, historically specific, and interpersonally negotiated. These theorists allow me to identify in young people's words and actions attitudes more creative and joyful than media and psychological assessments provide. My chapter in this volume represents only the beginning of a conversation I will facilitate, between the words of young people about sexuality and gender and the words of queer theorists.

Epilogue

MICHELLE FINE

It is an honor and delight to write an epilogue to this volume, produced just six years after Jean arrived at the Graduate Center, CUNY. The volume is indeed a tribute to Jean's deep theorizing, careful mentoring, and critical educational vision. And her very good taste in students.

Now you have consumed and undoubtedly admired the intelligence and craft of the six theoretically inspired, politically engaged, and empirically evocative projects that occupy the centerfold of the book. These writers have carefully excavated both *material injustices* and *assaults on dignity* that people living in poverty, youth of color, immigrant and queer youth endure daily as they perform the seemingly innocuous task of going to school. And these researchers have documented *protest* embodied, written, voiced, and acted upon. In this epilogue I want to interrogate *how* these scholars use theory, design, and method to argue for the justice claims they so eloquently assert; justice claims embedded within—and then across—these chapters. But first, allow me to situate the work historically, geographically, and politically.

Five of the six projects were conceived and pursued in neoliberal New York City, early twenty-first century, with Michael J. Dumas's chapter on Seattle as the exception. The city's economy, housing stock, and government were well into the seduction of the new elite, aggressively turning their backs (further) on the poor and working class. Just post 9/11, the "war on terror" was in high gear. The Bloomberg–Klein regime at the Department of Education was already committed to radical recentralization, high-stakes testing and management by MBAs and lawyers. Most high schools were begrudgingly preparing students and faculties for the five high-stakes exit examinations (Regents) and beginning to show signs of rising discharge rates, especially among immigrant youth. The Department of Education was marketing and funding a mad rush of "small schools." Very young bodies were showing up in GED programs as lawsuits were brought and threatened for illegally discharging or not accepting "marginal" students. Previously large schools, even when "broken down" into small ones, suffered from substantial overcrowding managed with more security personnel and police. The *New York Times* writer Samuel Freedman ran an exposé on the Bloomberg–Klein administration's unprecedented shifting of dollars and management to private contractors (2006), claiming they have "reinvented [the] school system [with] many more private components than ever before, which come under very little outside scrutiny."

In this historic moment, poor bodies of color were no longer needed by the US economy but were being aggressively recruited by the military and the prisons. This was, and remains, a nation where "imprisonment now rivals or overshadows the frequency of military service and college graduation of recent cohorts of African American men. For Black men in their mid thirties at the end of the 1990s, prison records were nearly twice as common as bachelor's degrees" (Pettit and Western, 2004, 164). At the same time that parents were told "86 percent of high schools are undesirable," DOE administrators also informed them that now they have "choice." The LGBTQ rights movement was in full swing, as was the virulent backlash against it.

In this political, cultural and economic context, these six research projects were crafted. Grounded in cities of complex racial and class struggles, reflecting national growth in racialized wealth gaps, the essays in this volume paint scenes of educational contention: highly intricate local stories in which low income youth, their educators, parents, administrators, community members and/or security guards tangle in struggle; sometimes in solidarity. With social theory as lens, these essays model exquisitely how critical researchers can analyze local ethnographic moments using what Madeline Pérez, borrowing from Bourdieu, calls "structural anecdotes"—data revealing intimate traces of political economy, state policy, dominant cultural ideologies, and institutional dynamics. At the same time, these writers search for, produce, and expose the hidden and explicit, quiet and loud, individual and collective tactics of protest enacted by youth, parents, and educators. By grafting fine-tuned attention to shouts and whispers of resistance onto a wide-angle landscape that links political and cultural economies to everyday life in school and community, the essays make a significant contribution to critical scholarship on educational policy and practice.

Theorizing Educational Policy, Politics and Practice: How and Why

Well educated by Jean and well informed by their own intellectual, educational and activist biographies, the writers in this volume have refused to design projects that would collude in or legitimate what Fanon described as a closed society: "[a] society that ossifies itself in determined form . . . a closed society [is one] where it is not good to be alive, where the air is rotten, where ideas and people are corrupt" (Fanon, 1967, 182, 224–225). Instead, as if in conversation with Antonio Gramsci, they have designed projects that disarticulate what is and rearticulate what could be, recognizing that: "the objective of ideological struggle is not to reject the system and all its elements but to rearticulate it, to break it down to its basic elements and then to sift through past conceptions to see which ones, with some changes of content, can serve to express the new situation" (Gramsci interpreted by Mouffe, 1979, 192).

These writers rely on the stretch of theory to connect the messy local to larger political, economic, and cultural formations; to deconstruct and reimagine. They trace data buried in bodies, whispers, poetry and hidden transcripts as refractions of broader political, economic, and cultural arrangements. They seek, construct, and chronicle individual and collective acts and movements of protest lodged in the face, behind the backs and/or under the radar of sustained injustice. They engage lively and provocative conversation about the dialectics of theory, empirical material and action. Together, they pull theory across body and psyche, from story to structure, from critical theory to collective protest (see Farmer, 2004; Katz, 2004; Weis, 2004 for other strong examples of social theory that tie fine-grained, local ethnographic evidence to political economy).

The combination of Jean Anyon's opening chapter and the brief "journeys through theory" help readers understand *how* critical social theory has shaped, and been refashioned by, these empirical projects. I want to pause for a moment to consider the varied braids of theory, method, and epistemology that lace up this volume. That is, I try to identify, briefly, how these writers use theory to advance their work *conceptually*, *methodologically*, and *epistemologically*: what they know, how they learn it, and how they shape the very questions they address. In the final section of this epilogue I will dig a little deeper, to elaborate the varied ways in which these writers deliberate *between* theory and their empirical material.

Conceptual Use of Theory

In the most direct use of theory, Kathleen Nolan and Michael J. Dumas explicitly rely upon social theorists to help them interpret their ethnographic sites or sights, navigating how they might look at their evidence. Nolan turns to David Garland's writings to frame how discipline, control, and what he calls "penal management" saturate public education. She then extends and modifies his analysis, arguing that youth do not actually have to be arrested to be disciplined; that the threat and performance of almost-arrest invade the bodies and consciousness of students and educators in ways that simultaneously disrupt schooling and, for some, create calm; stiffen schools into compliance, provoke them into chaos and still satisfy desires for peace in the hallways.

Michael J. Dumas imports Nancy Fraser's understanding of the politics of redistribution and recognition into the varied struggles engaged historically by the African American community against, with or despite the public schools in Seattle. With the help of Fraser, Dumas explicates the distinct and shared justice claims of movements that may seem at odds, including for example the fight for fiscal equity, racial integration and then more recently resegregation. Drawing here on the words of activist Don Alexander from the Save Our Southend Schools, Dumas has written on the *Black educational imagination*, articulated over time and space, as a form of what Michael Omi and Howard Winant (1994) call a "strategy of *war of position* . . . predicated on political struggle—on the existence of diverse institutional and cultural terrains upon which oppositional political projects can be mounted and upon which the racial state can be confronted" (81).

In conversation with Garland and Fraser, Nolan and Dumas use theory to *complicate* their questions about the school to prison pipeline, the Black racial imagination and politics on the ground; to *wrestle with the dialectics of contradictory evidence* (e.g., the calming and chaotic influences of police in schools; the tension between pro-integrationists and pro-segregationists both in the Black community); and to *generalize theoretically* from their very particular contexts to craft sophisticated arguments for use by other researchers, policy-makers, activists, and/or practitioners dealing with over-policed schools in a time of heightened carceral consciousness and racialized education struggles in the "post Civil Rights era."

Theory Informs Method

Jen Weiss and Madeline Pérez draw on theory in another way. Working with the writings of James Scott, Pierre Bourdieu, and Michel de Certeau, Weiss and Pérez seek less assistance with interpretation, but more theoretical wisdom about *method*. They turn toward these theorists to help them determine *where* to look for evidence—in hidden transcripts; in "plain view"; in the forms of cultural capital and "funds of knowledge" practiced by immigrant communities.

Both Weiss and Pérez are interested in hidden transcripts and buried knowledges. Each, therefore, had to invent socio-culturally meaningful research practices that could tap these knowledges and produce new forms of evidence. With Scott, de Certeau, and Bourdieu in their backpacks, they also drew from their experiences as organizers and writers. Jen Weiss is a nationally recognized activist in the worlds of youth spoken word who wove her rich knowledge of youth into her research design, constructing writing projects as the platform for documenting youth desire, protest and demands. Madeline Pérez is also a well-recognized organizer, on the west coast and east coast, within parent organizing movements. Pérez created spaces for Latina mothers to gather together with educators, unearth their cultural and gendered funds of knowledge, and resurrect their silenced expertise. Together they read, wrote, remembered their educational biographies, visited and critiqued schools and re-emerged as authors of a politically and practically significant volume for and by parents concerned with the politics and the parenting of high school "choice" in New York City. With theory folded into design, Weiss and Pérez carried their theorists into new neighborhoods, strengthened by their own "funds of knowledge" and strong commitments to writing and organizing.

Theory as Grounds for Epistemological Reversals
And then there is the third space or third way for engaging with theory. Eve Tuck and Darla Linville draw on Linda Tuhiwai Smith and Judith Butler, Indigenous and queer theorists respectively, as theoretical "elders" who have incited *epistemological reversals* of the question—Where is the problem? Refracting the gaze off of Native, pushed-out, queer or over-researched bodies and onto violent histories of genocide, homophobia, systematic miseducation, and push-out practices, Tuck and Linville designed projects with strong political, theoretical, and epistemological commitments to dispute existent categories, challenge dominant perspectives and "out" normalized institutional practices. Perched to speak back to theory and policy, these activist research projects refuse the binaries, problematize the "victim" designation, deflect the hegemonic shame, and refashion critical analyses to be told not about "marginal peoples" but about historically oppressive ideologies and institutions and defiant peoples. As Eve Tuck argues, in these projects theory has been deployed "to destabilize and decenter conventional thinking that speaks against our experience; to refuse to sit still and be researched; to rehistoricize our relationships to the colonizer and domination; to escape a 'logic' that runs counter to our own knowing."

Separately each essay articulates significant theory driven empirical work. As a collective, I want to argue, they constitute what Cindi Katz calls a *countertopography*, when she writes:

> [A]ny effective politics challenging a capital inspired globalization must have similar global sensitivities, even as its grounds are

necessarily local. This is different from a place based politics . . . Built
on the critical triangulation of local topographies, counter-
topographies provide exactly these kinds of abstractions interwoven
with local specificities and the impulse for insurgent change.

(Katz, 2001, 1225)

In her book *Growing up Global* and her essay "On the grounds of
globalization: A topography for feminist political engagement," Cindi Katz
traces the long arm of globalization as it shapes growing up in the Sudan and
in Harlem, New York (2001, 2004). With a fine ethnographic eye that
penetrates deeply within each site, Katz calls for social analyses that trace
globally, and dig locally, through a "spatialized understanding of problems."
Across the chapters in this volume we read a countertopography of *educational dispossession* and *defiance*.

Theorizing Dispossession

Accumulation by dispossession is about dispossessing somebody of
their assets or their rights . . . we're talking about the taking away of
universal rights and the privatization of them so it [becomes] your
particular responsibility, rather than the responsibility of the state.

(Harvey, 2004, 2 of 6)

David Harvey writes on the *geographical dynamics of capital accumulation*
and *uneven geographical development*. He tracks the flow of capital, ideas,
cultures, and bodies across and within national borders (2004), dis-
tinguishing *capital accumulation by expanded reproduction* from capital
accumulation by dispossession whereby common goods are taken from
people. Harvey's writings help us trace the systematic dispossession of
public education from low-income students, youth of color, immigrant and
queer youth. As public educational funds are handed over to private
management firms, testing companies, publishing houses, private security
and policing organizations, the very conditions of public teaching and
learning degenerate. Schools as spaces for educational inquiry and curiosity,
for youth development and community self-determination, fall under siege,
are threatened with extinction, and end up fighting for their lives (see Cook
and Tashlik, 2005; Cordero, 2005; Fine, 2005; Stovall, 2005). With these
strategic policy moves of dispossession by privatization, state responsibility
for the provision of *adequate* education falls off the hook as contractors'
profits swell (Freedman, 2006). Police-in-school and military recruitment
budgets grow and youth of color slowly disappear. While none of these
dynamics of dispossession is new to public education, the racialized and

classed consequences—economic, educational, health, civic and criminal justice—are quite dramatic. The chapters in this volume reveal *how* the ideological and material blades of dispossession cut through schools, communities, and bodies, locally and nationally, and at what cost.

As we can see throughout this text, dispossession is carved precisely, with a very sharp edge, around the contours of race, ethnicity, class, and sexuality. Flowing through serrated *circuits of dispossession*, ideological assaults pierce the skin; racist and homophobic assumptions populate the "common sense," and political and economic opportunities float overseas or way up the class ladder. Domestically, the urban poor are in receipt of a brutal and aggressive form of state-sponsored abuse and neglect, whereby the bodies of too many low-income young people are being prepared for disposability (Anyon, 2005). And yet military recruiters—like the old, homophobic cartoonish images of child molesters—can be found waiting just outside the building, behind a tree, with free video games of war, if you just step into my van.

There is perhaps no more vivid illustration of *accumulation by dispossession* than contemporary policies that systematically alienate, discourage, discharge, and push out youth from public high schools as Eve Tuck has explicated in her chapter: practices that saturate public schools with police and criminal-justice surveillance but not dictionaries, as Kathleen Nolan, Jen Weiss, and Michael J. Dumas reveal; schools that deny fundamental recognition to Latino/a (Pérez) and African American youth, their families, and advocates (see Dumas) and queer youth (see Linville); schools that ideologically slide accountability and blame onto the backs of mothers (see Pérez). These chapters bear witness to the praxis of dispossession from ethnographic evidence gathered in and around schools, community-based organizations, juvenile facilities, and GED programs. They articulate the racialized, classed, and sexualized capillaries and also consequences of this new imperialism at home (Harvey, 2006).

The evidence amassed here, however, does not only lay bare the micropractices by which political, economic, and cultural institutions are dismantling public investments in low-income communities. These ethnographers click on their ethnographic high beams to expose systematically *how* the public sphere—for poor youth in particular—is being realigned and re*framed*. With "disorderly conduct" provoked, monitored, and punished, neoliberalism marks not a hollowing of the public sphere but a realignment and colonization of public spaces: disciplining, threatening, and exiling so many youth, parents, and educators.

In Kathleen Nolan's ethnography of "penal management" as enacted within schools, we listen to Jermaine who is defending his humanity and we see adults "on the edge," warned by the arrest that they dare not dissent. Most adult bodies, painfully narrated by Dean Henry, can't or won't get involved because "I know those teachers who got arrested." In Nolan's piece we witness the contagion of surveillance and terror, and we hear her brilliant insight— that social institutions are being integrated into a carceral-industrial complex, even as individuals are being exiled from civil society. In conversation with Garland and Foucault, Nolan reveals the micro-practices by which dominant ideologies about the necessity and inevitability of overpolicing are produced despite counter-evidence. Although the rate of violent incidents dropped, the rate of in-school ticketing and arrests continued to rise. The new carceral consciousness was laminated; untroubled by contradictory data.

Producing dispossession is, of course, expensive. Indeed massive infusions of public funds are being redistributed into low-income schools and communities, toward the containment of families, youth, and educators in low-income schools and communities. These redistributions penetrate, *although never fully saturate*, teenaged bodies, curdling dreams and overdetermining destinies of (il)legitimacy. As Arjun Appaduri argues, perhaps one of the most unjust distributions among youth is the belief in a tomorrow—their aspirational capacity. Years ago, Frantz Fanon called it the experience of "crushing objecthood"—that is the realization that despite the desire to learn, grow, be recognized and "attain the source of the world," people who have been systematically oppressed discover that they are "an object in the midst of other objects" (Fanon, 1967, 109). Miseducation commits both symbolic and structural violence across generations (Bourdieu, 1998; Woodson, 1933/1990).

But another electrifying circuit travels across these pages, carrying substantial evidence of *resistance* and *defiance*, scribbled in young people's writings and performed in their spoken words, narrated by their mothers and voiced by some of their teachers (Anyon, 2005; Fabricant, forthcoming; Heavens, personal communication; Stovall, 2005). Urban youth living in poverty, breathing the fumes of racism and homophobia, witnessing fiscal abandonment, have few illusions about school or the labor market. They, their families and many of their educators, nevertheless embody *thick desires* to be educated or to educate, to work in ways that are meaningful, to engage with politics, to be treated with respect, and to speak with voices that will be heard (see Fine and McClelland for theoretical treatment of thick desire, 2006).

The young people represented in this volume are at once due, denied, and desiring a broad range of opportunities for meaningful intellectual, political, and social engagement, the possibility of financial independence, sexual and reproductive freedom, protection from racialized and sexualized violence, and a way to imagine living in the future tense (Appadurai, 2004; Nussbaum, 2003). A theoretical framework of *thick desire* (Fine and

McClelland, 2006) situates these youth within a human rights framework, recognizing that youth of color, living in poverty, who are immigrant and/or queer, are growing up within political, economic, cultural, and sexual *contexts and movements* that enable but, more often, disable them. The chapters in this volume offer up evidence in the micro-processes of everyday life, excavating *how* laws, public policies, ideologies, and institutional formations intervene on young women's and men's sense of economic, social, and sexual possibility. And how youth and their families speak back.

Circuits of Dispossession/Circuit Breakers

Writing on *circuits of dispossession* in urban education, Jessica Ruglis and I have been tracing the strategic moves of capital, policy, and ideology that function to exile poor and working-class youth of color, immigrant youth, queer youth from public institutions of development and shuttle them toward institutions of carceral containment, the streets, low-wage labor, inadequate education, and poor health outcomes (forthcoming). We have relied upon the writings of David Harvey, Frantz Fanon, and Linda Tihuwai Smith, with Gloria Anzaldúa, W. E. B. DuBois, Angela Davis, Pauline Lipman, Stanley Aronowitz, and Jean Anyon to articulate the ways in which conservative corporate interests have gentrified the public sphere, creating a new "common sense" about those youth of color considered pollutants or contaminants, in the language of Mary Douglas (1966/1984), undeserving or a threat to security in more contemporary discourses of expulsion.

We can all recite the differential, and worsening, gaps in educational, criminal justice, and health outcomes by race and class. And we know too well that these outcomes are represented in popular culture as if due to bad, private choices by youth or their families. As a set, the critical accounts in these six chapters boldly refuse this line of analysis. Without occluding the agency of youth, their families or their educators, the scholars in this volume lay these inequitable outcomes at the feet of deliberate public policy decisions and normalized institutional practices.

The essays in this volume stimulate our analysis in two significant ways. First, the chapters encourage us to attend deliberately to the troubling ways that *ideological degradation* enables *structural disenfranchisement*. Across essays, we hear how representations of "damage" lay the groundwork for structural violations of human rights. Criminal representations of low-income urban youth of color, splashed on the covers of newspapers, flashed in the photos and running commentary on the lower frame of FOX News, displayed and reproduced in film and video are, in the language of Bourdieu, "drip fed" into public consciousness (1998). Once these young people have been demonized in the media and popular culture, it is *understandable if not imperative*, for policy-makers to move troops of police officers and surveillance machinery into school buildings. Kathleen Nolan argues this point well "Indeed I would argue that it would be nearly impossible to justify the criminalization of misbehavior if the youngsters subjected to the disciplinary practices were not already demonized."

So too, once low-income mothers are portrayed as without resources, unconcerned about education, or interested but too burdened or incompetent to "choose wisely" (see Pérez), it matters little whether or not they are given "quality options" for their children's education. Once queer youth, or LGBTQ students, are represented as troubled, "at risk" of alcoholism and suicide, vulnerable and/or deviant, it makes no sense to challenge homophobia institutionally and create affirming schools but it does obligate, perhaps, schools to offer psychological services in the queer ghetto (Linville).

If students (or parents or educators) are entrapped by economic, political, cultural, sexual and educational conditions that provoke "disorderly conduct," as seen in these texts, then it is easy for the state to argue a duty to hold them accountable—that is, remove them—through push-out, alienation, unchallenged harassment, boredom, or the carceral archipelago, in order to "save" the good ones. (See Nolan, Weiss, and Tuck.) As Michael J. Dumas argues: "I would contend that the system—the institutional processes of dominance and (dis)advantage—serves as a mechanism through which inequitable relationships are formed and produced. *Maldistribution* and *misrecognition* are, in this sense, instantiations of the system left unchecked."

From these intimate qualitative accounts, we see then, that the first move in dispossession is to *dis*; render these youth dis-posable; humiliated in public as Jermaine was; petrify (in both senses of the word) their teachers as Dean Henry was—scared so they can't move; shatter their subjectivities so that they [mostly] can't or won't resist *in plain view*; convince them, perhaps, that it would be best to exit as if their leaving were of *their own free will*. The ideological and material disenfranchisement of youth in poverty, of color, immigrant and queer youth are twinned moves of power that render disenfranchisement natural.

But these writers do not stop here. These essays "strike back" by documenting subterranean and public enactments of protest and dissent. They remind us through spoken word and walkouts (Weiss), pleas for dignity (Nolan), relentless community advocacy for racial justice (Dumas), Indigenous theorizing back (Tuck), organizing parents (Pérez) and deconstructions of gender or sexuality hierarchies by queer *and* straight youth (Linville), that the subjectivities of those targeted by oppression are never fully flattened. Flickers of desire, protest and resistance can be found if you know where to look. Jen Weiss writes in her chapter, "Trying to distance themselves from the power of surveillance to discipline and control, profile and patrol, . . . students desire to resist its invasiveness, . . . [and] to protect themselves from its sting. As the student poems show, writing about the realities associated with school policies may be one of the most effective ways of maintaining some distance from the pain of policy effects."

Madeline Pérez carved a space for and with Latina mothers in the Bronx to challenge the "ugly racial steering in the New York City schools" and expose the illusion of "choice" in a city where "86 percent of high schools have been deemed undesirable by the Department of Education." Pérez translates Bourdieu and invites him into this space to help mothers re-view what she calls "structural anecdotes" of pain and resistance in their biographies. Creating spaces for parents with educational researchers and teachers, the knowledge of these women was honored and the unjust distribution of material resources, opportunities and dignity were contested. Borrowing from Bourdieu, they gathered together to unpack "how institutional and organizational forces converge around what on the surface may appear to be an individual, personal, or idiosyncratic matter."

With a rhizomic sprout that Deleuze and Guattari would admire, resistance and protest leap off these pages. Eve Tuck quotes Deleuze and Guattari: "Nothing is more beautiful or loving or political aside from underground stems and aerial roots, subterranean stems—a rhizome ceaselessly establishing connections in semiotic chains . . ." Protest seeps under and over ground. Outrage can be heard at community meetings and in students' poetry. Desperation spiked with outrage can be read at the student walkout and parents' shocking visits to more privileged schools. Defiance is narrated by Latina mothers who discover their "funds of knowledge," in demands for queer "inclusion, [that is] more than a day, a week or a chapter in the curriculum," and in the writings of Indigenous theorists who refuse to "stand still" and be researched. As Eve Tuck reminds readers, "Theorizing back requires us to reprove and reclaim theories that have been used against us . . . that have fed our own self abnegation . . . Researching back and theorizing back are refusals to speak against ourselves, shifting the scrutiny off our own bodies and rightly placing it upon the institutions that naturalize racism, misogyny, gross disparities of wealth, homophobia and neglect."

These persons, movements and moments are the *circuit breakers*: the individuals and collectives who refuse to allow the moves of dispossession to expel their babies; destroy their dreams; colonize their schools. These are the mothers, community advocates, the youth and the educators who insist that all children deserve; who contest the very categories designed to contain them. Darla Linville marks this commitment most dramatically when she quotes Judith Butler as saying, "to install myself within the terms of an identity category would be to turn against the sexuality—the very eroticism it claims to authorize, much less 'liberate.'"

Bearing witness and creating poetry of protest, dreaming Black and theorizing back, queering schools and creating retreats for mothers so they will never retreat again . . . these are strategic moves of power by and for communities that take seriously theory, critique, desire, and action. In this volume, these desires for material justice and dignity shimmy from New York City to Seattle, across schools and parent organizing, from spoken word in the Bronx to Gay–Straight alliances. Like synchronized lights on Second Avenue, these are mobilized moves of disorderly conduct, engaged by youth, parents, community and educators, insisting on a public sphere of justice within and around schools, prisons, and the economy. Not to be trivialized, these "hidden transcripts might be denigrated by some as unimportant [but] they are in fact the building blocks without which more elaborate institutionalized political action could not exist" (Scott, cited by Weiss this volume).

On the Deliberate Use of Theory

To conclude, I want to review the elegant and clever moves of theory undertaken by these young scholars as they have labored at the dense intersection of theory, empirical material, and commitments to action. I want to lift up for consideration how these writers have creatively engaged the *deliberate use of theory*. I borrow from Habermas's notion of *deliberative democracy* to signify a process of working, in this case between theory and research, that is deeply social, moral, open to reflection, and committed to interrogating contradiction, difference, and dissent.

As the post-chapter reflections attest, this deliberative process can be hard work, often frustrating, confusing, and lonely. Each has waded through social theory and wrestled their data in rigorous conversation with social theorists and then produced a conceptually rich and methodologically sophisticated project. Many of the reflections speak of piles of books, (not) finding time to read, resisting the writers, worrying about betrayal of informants. And then falling in love with theory and inventing creative ways to deliberate between theory and research. It is the nature of this deliberation that I want to amplify—for these are the gifts of these essays.

Although encouraged to use theory, these writers don't simply "begin" their chapters with famous men and women and then wander into their own analyses. They don't glibly "authorize" their findings by locating them alongside a critical theorist in parentheses. They do not superficially "fit" their data into a pre-existing theoretical frame. To the contrary, these writers knead theory, research, and action. They engage with ideas, writers, and politics from far and near, in order to prepare conceptually the grounds in which to plant their work. Let us consider the lessons they offer, on how to engage deliberately with theory and research.

Reading these chapters we can feel the profound influence of Michel Foucault, Michel de Certeau, Saskia Sasken, Judith Butler, Linda Tuhiwai Smith, Pierre Bourdieu and others in the full historic and political contexts in which these ethnographic accounts have been placed. Social theory, in varied forms, implicates a *full accounting of the political forces, institutions and persons* at the heart of educational policy and practice. Theory warrants that history, political and structural forces be documented, as the rich contexts within which ethnographic dramas unravel (for an excellent example see Farmer, 2004).

Thus, for instance, Kathleen Nolan, Michael J. Dumas and Darla Linville move in closely to capture what Geertz (1973) would call thick description and they carefully zoom out with wide-angle theoretical lens, revealing how researchers can peel back the layers of politics, economics, culture, sexuality, and ideology in order to understand schools as a contentious stage on which large and small, remote and local, macro and micro battles are being waged and performed.

A second way in which these writers deliberate between theory and research involves their empirical reconstitution of social theory: what Michael Buroway calls *reconstructing social theory*. Michael J. Dumas, Kathleen Nolan, and Darla Linville initially rely upon and then empirically complicate reproduction theory in their projects. While social class stratifications are unequivocally reproduced by dominant public institutions, Nolan tracks the simultaneous reproduction of the "criminal" class; Michael J. Dumas implores reproduction theorists to consider the dialectical relations of economic, cultural, and racialized reproduction; and Darla Linville reminds us of the subtle and dramatic practices by which compulsory heterosexuality saturates and is implicated through and across economic classes, in the curriculum and culture of public schooling. (see also Weis, 2004, on the circuits of White working-class reproduction over time; Zaal *et al.*, 2007, on Islamophobia as it is reproduced in schools).

Writers in this volume not only reconstruct reproduction theory, they also significantly elaborate and challenge some of the long-held assumptions of resistance theory. With fine attention paid to underground forms of protest and resistance, Eve Tuck, Madeline Pérez, and Jen Weiss interrogate what lay beneath behaviors that seem filled with despair or alienation. They reframe, theoretically, performances that may appear "compliant and quotidian [as . . .] actually . . . tactical and significant" (Weiss, this volume). In this collection, social theories of reproduction and resistance have been reconstructed significantly, on the ground "up" so to speak, from empirically driven projects.

A third use of theory practiced in this volume involves *theory mobilized to inform research design and methods*. Madeline Pérez, Jen Weiss, and Eve Tuck needed to create designs that could produce, provoke or incite evidence of the social capital Bourdieu elaborates, the subterranean critique that Scott seeks and the indigenous knowledges Smith documents. They crafted theoretically enriched research activities or methods through which the mothers could unearth and re-view their own forms of knowledges; poetry workshops in which youth could begin to put words to the emotions of "like being stalked" (Weiss), and activities in which young people could collectively sketch Problem Trees (Tuck) to facilitate the narration of folk theories, trunks and limbs about the (in)justice of educational opportunities and outcomes. Each of these writers drew from social theory to activate a *theory of method* that would enable youth and their mothers to produce hidden, buried, and long-silenced knowledge.

A fourth and related use of theory involves radically *reconceptualizing traditionally disparaged outcomes*: moving from signifiers of shame to dynamics of social criticism. Perhaps most vivid in the work of Eve Tuck and CREDD, key notions drawn from Indigenous theory recast existentially, historically, and politically "outcomes" that have been assumed shameful, bad, and deficient. Thus, we learn in this chapter that the GED, to those who pass the test, may feel not like a disparaged credential but like a lifeline out of oppressive schools; a capillary of hope; a vehicle to pursue education even as these young people critique schooling. Jen Weiss makes explicit that her choice of theory enabled her to reconceptualize behaviors that may have seemed to be simply alienated (e.g. "choosing" invisibility; hiding under a hoodie) but are filled with dignified refusal to engage. So too Darla Linville repositions students who don't come out, or even those who narrate homophobic comments, as young people who may not be experiencing internalized homophobia but instead be testing the moral waters of their schools, that is, reading the homophobic thermometers of vulnerability that characterize unsafe schools. Thus, with the assistance of social theory, these writers reconsider outcomes traditionally viewed as "unhealthy" to be potentially resilient responses to toxic institutions.

A fifth use of theory that these chapters model involves relatively *straightforward conversations between researcher participants and social theory*. An ethical problem raised in a number of these chapters, and by other writers, involves the troubling use of theory-as-voiceover. Researchers worry about imposing theory onto the words of participants; ventriloquating or editing participants to speak the theory; or occluding the complicated, sometimes contradictory narrations of participants in order to fit with well-ironed theory (see Linda Alcoff, 1991–1992; Ruthellen Josselson, 2004, for significant analytic treatment of this concern). In this volume, a number of the writers subverted this problem by intentionally creating conversations between participants or co-researchers and social theory—in text or in person. Jen Weiss references "theorizing with participants, not just about" them, drawing on Stephen Ball's definition of theory as "sets of possibilities for thinking through." Weiss explains how helpful it was to "juxtapose theory with the thoughts and perceptions of youth to 'unstick us.'" Like the mothers who worked with Pérez and the youth who were pushed out now studying meritocracy, in these participatory action research projects, a conversation ensued between theory and researchers. They read together; deconstructed theory; tried it on and modified it, and then crafted their own analytic insights.

By so doing, theory was also a tool that researchers used to *interrupt the common sense by interrogating taken-for-granted assumptions.* Whether we turn to Kathleen Nolan's observation that security guards continued to write summonses even though the high school violence rates dipped; or to Michael J. Dumas's desire to understand why there are no dictionaries at Cleveland; or to Eve Tuck's radical challenge of the GED as a get-away rather than a dead end, we can appreciate how theoretically driven empirical work gives researchers the license to contest fiercely hegemonic discourses that naturalize and laminate injustice. If these researchers just asked people about the state of affairs of disciplinary tickets, dictionaries, or the GED, in all likelihood they would have heard legitimation discourses rather than critical analyses. Herein lies the strength of a critical theoretical lens which authorizes a different kind of questioning; a broader base of persons questioned; an analytic strategy for lifting up both hegemonic and hidden transcripts.

For writers like Eve Tuck and Darla Linville, theory was further instrumental as a warrant to *shift the unit of analysis.* That is, theory was a strong guide for authorizing the shift of the research gaze, particularly from the "group" to the policies, ideologies, and practices of institutions. When CREDD decided to turn its gaze from the "pitiful dropout" to the defiant push-out, and to analyze critically the alienating schools fled and the lies of meritocracy challenged, theory, method and politics of the "graduation and dropout rate debates" were fundamentally transformed. When Darla Linville and her co-researchers decided not to study the terrified queer adolescent but to interview straight and LGBTQ youth in order to interrogate the institutional policies and dynamics that cement compulsory heterosexuality into the curricular and cultural walls of schools, they were leaning on theory—Butler in particular—to authorize a reversal of the gaze.

These writers, however, not only engage theory to shift the unit of analysis but they rely on theory to track what Tuck calls the *rhizomic connections and linkages*: the "unseen roots" and branches connecting relationships and change. The rhizome, as a theoretical tool, enables Tuck to conjoin economics, education, health, alienation and pride in the wavy study of the GED. Theory is the glue of legitimation that allows Tuck to move between Indigenous knowledges and push-out practices; meritocracy and desire; humiliation and get-aways. Neither qualitative nor quantitative methods alone will shed light on these deeply rooted, historic, and twisting relationships. These connections are not likely to be named explicitly in individual interviews, focus groups, or even ethnography, and not in quantitative regression analyses. And yet with the help of theory these very rhizomic linkages allow readers to see how global and national policies mark the bodies and aspirations of urban youth.

Finally, and perhaps most powerfully, across these essays theory helps us *reimagine the relation of the academy to organizing, community-based politics, and policy work.* Madeline Pérez admits that it wasn't until she read that Bourdieu had engaged in radical struggles from the academy, that she was willing to take the power of his theory into her activist work. Indeed across these chapters we see some projects connected firmly and explicitly to community-based organizing. Others are designed to chronicle the "radical possibilities" (Anyon, 2005) of community-based mobilizations for educational justice. And some projects are committed to the politics of radical ideas: fundamentally changing the theoretical terms of the debate is appreciated here as significant political work. It is perhaps most fitting to close with the words of Michael J. Dumas on this point: "Ethnographic and other qualitative researchers focus on how community organizations and teacher activists understand the gap between their educational dreams and what they understand as the current educational reality. This is the scholarship we all need: research rooted in a critical understanding of injustice and imbued with a sense of hope that transformation is indeed possible ... activist researchers, working with community, might more clearly articulate the complex reasons for the lack of dictionaries at Cleveland and envision a more empowering and empowered politics with which to respond."

This volume, as individual essays and as a rich collection gathered with strong mentoring from Jean Anyon, signifies the vibrancy of the next generation of critical educational studies in which theory, research, and action are joined. Dedicated to resuscitating a contentious public sphere where dissent can ride on the wings of hope to create a very different tomorrow, these writers are both eloquent and analytically sophisticated about their ethnographic sites. As significant, however, these six scholars have been extremely generous in teaching us how to deliberately engage with theory, in our research, for change. Filled with urgency and intelligence, these essays are the material evidence of critical scholarship linked to social movements, within and across local spaces, fortified with social theory and rich evidence. While most days I find little reason for hope in the academy, these young scholars restore a critical sense of what is possible, what is necessary, and what is next.

Note

Thanks to Jean Anyon, Michael J. Dumas, Darla Linville, Kathleen Nolan, Madeline Pérez, Jessica Ruglis, Eve Tuck, and Jen Weiss for their comments.

References

Alcoff, L. (1991–1992). The Problem of Speaking for Others. *Cultural Critique*, 92, 5–32.
Anyon, J. (2005). *Radical Possibilities: Public Policy, Urban Education and a New Social Movement.* New York: Routledge.
Appadurai, A. (2004). Capacity to Aspire: Culture and the Terms of Recognition. In R. Vijayendra and M. Walton, editors, *Culture and public action.* Stanford: Stanford University Press.
Bourdieu, P. (1998) *Acts of Resistance.* New York: Polity Press.
Cook, A., and Tashlik, P. (2005). Standardizing Small. *Rethinking Schools,* 19, 4. www.rethinking schools.org.
Cordero, H. (2005) When Small is Beautiful. *Rethinking Schools,* 19, 4. www.rethinkingschools.org.
Douglas, M. (1966/1984). *Purity and Danger: An Analysis of Concepts of Pollution and Taboo.* New York: Routledge.
Fabricant, M. (Forthcoming). *Organizing Hope to Revive Public Schools: CC9's Parent-led Campaign for Educational Justice in the South Bronx.*
Fanon, F. (1967). *Black Skin, White Masks.* New York: Grove Press.
Farmer, P. (2004). *Pathologies of Power: Health, Human Rights, and the New War on the Poor.* Berkeley, CA: University of California Press.
Fine, M. (2005). Not in Our Name. *Rethinking Schools,* 19, 4.
Fine, M. (2007). Expanding the Methodological Imagination. *The Counseling Psychologist,* 35: 5, 459–473.
Fine, M., and McClelland, S. (2006). Sexuality Education and the Discourse of Desire: Still Missing After All These Years. *Harvard Educational Review,* 3, 297–338.
Fine, M. and Ruglis, J. (Forthcoming). Circuits of Dispossession: The Racialized and Classed Realignment of the Public Sphere for Youth in the U.S. *Transforming Anthropology.*
Fine, M., and Sirin, S. (2007). Theorizing Hyphenated Selves: Researching Youth Development in and Across Contentious Political Contexts. *Social and Personality Psychology Compass,* 1: 1, 16–38.
Freedman, S. (2006, September 13) The Not-so-public Part of the Public Schools: Lack of Accountability. *New York Times,* B16.
Geertz, C. (1973). Thick Description: Toward an Interpretive Theory of Culture. In *The Interpretation of Cultures: Selected Essays.* New York: Basic Books, 3–30.
Gramsci, A. (1971). *Selections from the Prison Notebooks.* New York: International.
Harvey, D. (2004). A Geographer's Perspective on the New Imperialism. http://globetrotter.berkeley. edu/people4/Harvey/harvey-con4.html. Accessed December 15, 2007.
Harvey, D. (2005). *A Brief History of Neo-liberalism.* New York: Oxford University Press.
Harvey, D. (2006). *Spaces of Global Capitalism: A Theory of Ueven Geographic Development.* New York: Verso.
Josselson, R. E. (2004). The Hermeneutics of Faith and the Hermeneutics of Suspicion. *Narrative Inquiry,* 14: 1, 1–28.
Katz, C. (2001). On the Grounds of Globalization: A Topography for Feminist Political Engagement. *Signs,* 26: 4, 1213–1234.
Katz, C. (2004). *Growing Up Global: Economic Restructuring and Children's Everyday Lives.* Minneapolis: University of Minnesota Press.

Mouffe, C. (ed.) (1979). *Gramsci and Marxist Theory*. London: Routledge.

Nussbaum, M. C. (2000). *Women and Human Development*. Cambridge: Cambridge University Press.

Omi, M., and Winant, H. (1994). *Racial Formation in the United States: From the 1960s to the 1990s* (2nd ed.). New York: Routledge.

Pettit, B., and Western, B. (2004). Mass Imprisonment and the Life Course: Race and Class Inequality in U.S. Incarceration. *American Sociological Review*, 69, 151–169.

Stovall, D. (2005). Community Struggle to Make Small Serve All. *Rethinking Schools*, 19, 4. www.rethinkingschools.org.

Weis, L. (2004). *Class Reunion*. New York: Routledge.

Woodson, C. (1933/1990). *The Mis-education of the Negro*. New York: Africa World Press.

Zaal, M., Salah, T., and Fine, M. (2007). The Weight of the Hyphen: Freedom, Fusion and Responsibility Embodied by Young Muslim-American Women During a Time of Surveillance. *Applied Developmental Sciences*, 11: 3, 164–177.

Author Biographies

Jean Anyon is the author of *Radical Possibilities: Public Policy, Urban Education, and a New Social Movement* and *Ghetto Schooling: A Political Economy of Urban Education*. Her articles on social class, race, and the political economy of schooling have been reprinted in almost fifty edited collections, and translated into four languages. She is Professor of Social and Educational Policy in the Urban Education Doctoral Program at the Graduate Center of the City University of New York.

Michael J. Dumas is Assistant Professor of Social and Multicultural Foundations in the College of Education at California State University, Long Beach. A graduate of the Urban Education Doctoral Program at the City University of New York, he has published (with Jean Anyon as second author), a chapter in *New Directions in Education Policy Implementation: Confronting Complexity*. He is currently working on a theoretical essay on Stuart Hall and Black education politics.

Michelle Fine is Distinguished Professor of Social Psychology, Women's Studies and Urban Education at the Graduate Center, City University of New York. Among her books are *Framing Dropouts, Beyond Silenced Voices* (with Lois Weis), *Off White, Working Method* (with Lois Weis), and most recently *Revolutionizing Education: Youth Participatory Action Research in Motion* (with Julio Cammarota).

Darla Linville is a doctoral candidate in the Urban Education Doctoral Program at the City University of New York. As a former young adult librarian, she is interested in literacy and teen literature. Her publications include an article in *Race, Gender & Class*, a chapter in the forthcoming *Social Justice, Peace, and Eco-Justice Standards*, and a forthcoming article on Foucault's care of the self in adolescent constructions of sexuality and gender.

Kathleen Nolan is Assistant Professor of Education at Mercy College. She received her doctorate in 2007 from the Urban Education Doctoral Program at the City University of New York. She has taught high school in the Bronx, NY. Her publications include the chapter, "Learning to do time: Willis's model of cultural reproduction in an era of post-industrialism, globalization, and mass incarceration", with Jean Anyon as second author, in *Learning to Labor in New Times*.

Madeline Pérez is completing her Ph.D. in the Urban Education Doctoral Program at the City University of New York. Her dissertation studies the experiences of middle school children and parents who are navigating school choice policies in New York City. Madeline has worked as a community/parent organizer in New York and California, and has taught courses in school counseling and family–school relations. She is the co-author (with a team of Latina parents) of *The Family-to-Family Guide to Small High Schools in the Bronx*.

Eve Tuck is a doctoral candidate in Urban Education Doctoral Program at the City University of New York. Her research interests are urban and Indigenous school non-completion, the consequences of education policy, and youth perspectives on schooling. Recent publications include chapters in Denzin and Giardina's *Ethical Futures in Qualitative Research: Decolonizing the Politics of Knowledge*, and (with her youth co-researchers) Cammarota and Fine's *Revolutionizing Education: Youth Participatory Action Research in Motion*.

Jen Weiss is a doctoral candidate in the Urban Education Doctoral Program at the City University of New York. She is founder and former director of Urban Word NYC, an after-school program providing uncensored writing and performance opportunities to youth since 1999. She is co-author of *Brave New Voices: Youth Speaks Guide to Teaching Spoken Word Poetry*, and author of several forthcoming publications on urban high school surveillance policy and youth resistance.

Index

Lightning Source UK Ltd.
Milton Keynes UK
UKHW020743020719
345405UK00018B/269/P